CONTENTS

CULTURESHOCK!
A Survival Guide to Customs and Etiquette

HONG KONG

Betty Wei
Elizabeth Li

GRAPHIC ARTS
BOOKS

Marshall Cavendish
Editions

Photo Credits:
All photos by and from Betty Wei Liu except pages 11, 25 (Builders Federal (HK) Limited; page 38 (Hong Kong Government); pages vii, 12, 54, 64, 68, 123, 152, 153, 161, 163, 166, 187 (Hong Kong Tourism Association, Singapore); pages 7, 58–59, 114 (AFP); pages 99, 107, 125, 127, 136, 145 (both), 151 (both), 165, 171 (Corel Stock Photo Library); pages 109, 202–203 (Lonely Planet Images). ▪ Cover photo: Lonely Planet Images.

All illustrations by TRIGG

First Published in 1995
Copyright © 2005 Marshall Cavendish International (Asia) Private Limited

This edition published in 2005 by:

Marshall Cavendish Editions
An imprint of Marshall Cavendish International (Asia) Pte Ltd
1 New Industrial Road, Singapore 536196
Tel: (65) 6213 9300, fax: (65) 6285 4871.
Email: te@sg.marshallcavendish.com
Online bookstore: www.marshallcavendish.com/genref

and

Graphic Arts Center Publishing Company
P.O. Box 10306, Portland, Oregon 97296-0306
United States of America
Tel: (503) 226 2402
Website: www.gacpc.com

Please contact Graphic Arts Center Publishing Company for the Library of Congress catalogue number

ISBN 981-261-123-1 (Asia & Rest of World)
ISBN 1-55868-931-1 (USA & Canada)
ISBN 0-462-00807-X (Europe)

Printed in Singapore by Times Graphics Pte Ltd

Cultu...
anyor...
from c...
and re...
expatria...
culture s...

Writter...
experience...
information...
of disorienta...
style that is e...
arm readers v...
lives as norma...

Each book i...
with the first im...
country. To under...
people—where th...
traditions they live...
This is covered in th...

Then on with the...
the greatest of ease. A...
accommodation, get t...
and running, enrol the...
of health. But that's not...
way, venture out and try...
and travel to other areas....
of the country before dis...
side of things.

To round off, snippets c...
before readers are 'tested' c...
country. Useful words and ph...
guide and list of books for fur...
for easy reference.

FOREWORD

Hong Kong is full of surprises, paradoxes and contradictions. Some are so obvious, so much a matter of routine or usually so well hidden that no one notices them.

THE BELLS OF NINE QUEEN'S ROAD, CENTRAL

Twelve one-metre high figures of civilians and warriors in classical Chinese dress, each carrying a traditional Chinese Zodiac animal, ride on a carousel in a Western-style clock tower at Nine Queen's Road, above the bustling business district in Central. These figures, rotating on individual axles, come out of their nest several times a day to parade in formation forwards, backwards, and outwards. They move their arms, nod their heads, and bow to the pedestrian and vehicular traffice, in time to the computer-operated music of twenty-five bells.

Whereas the appearance of the figurines is undoubtedly Chinese, the clock tower is derived from the western tradition, as is the carillon of bronze bells with its span of two octaves. They were cast in the Netherlands, at the Royal Bellfoundry Petit en Fritsen, which has been producing bells since the middle of the seventeenth century. This quaint performance, so unexpected in twenty-first century Hong Kong, is all but drowned by city noises and is totally ignored by most passers-by. Nevertheless, it is appreciated by discerning individuals who stop to look and listen. At least one pedestrian is tempted to risk her reputation for sanity, by returning the salute whenever she happens to be near when the bells chime.

The figurines and carillon in the clock tower illustrate how whimsically Hong Kong has adopted the traditions of China and the West. Not all aspects of this multi-cultural mix in Hong Kong blend so smoothly, however; nor is the blend always so palatable.

Do not expect Hong Kong to be totally changed since 1997 just because it is no longer under British rule. Now that almost a decade has passed, the Hong Kong people have returned to the business of making money. Nor should you worry about the future of Hong Kong lest it be swallowed by the giant monolith of which it has become one. With the eyes of the world on Hong Kong, China will not be able to compromise

CULTURESHOCK!

A Survival Guide to Customs and Etiquette

HONG KONG

Betty Wei
Elizabeth Li

GRAPHIC ARTS
BOOKS

mc **Marshall Cavendish**
Editions

Photo Credits:
All photos by and from Betty Wei Liu except pages 11, 25 (Builders Federal
(HK) Limited; page 38 (Hong Kong Government); pages vii, 12, 54, 64,
68, 123, 152, 153, 161, 163, 166, 187 (Hong Kong Tourism Association,
Singapore); pages 7, 58–59, 114 (AFP); pages 99, 107, 125, 127, 136,
145 (both), 151 (both), 165, 171 (Corel Stock Photo Library); pages 109,
202–203 (Lonely Planet Images). ▪ Cover photo: Lonely Planet Images.

All illustrations by TRIGG

First Published in 1995
Copyright © 2005 Marshall Cavendish International (Asia) Private Limited

This edition published in 2005 by:

Marshall Cavendish Editions
An imprint of Marshall Cavendish International (Asia) Pte Ltd
1 New Industrial Road, Singapore 536196
Tel: (65) 6213 9300, fax: (65) 6285 4871.
Email: te@sg.marshallcavendish.com
Online bookstore: www.marshallcavendish.com/genref

and

Graphic Arts Center Publishing Company
P.O. Box 10306, Portland, Oregon 97296-0306
United States of America
Tel: (503) 226 2402
Website: www.gacpc.com

Please contact Graphic Arts Center Publishing Company for the Library of
Congress catalogue number

ISBN 981-261-123-1 (Asia & Rest of World)
ISBN 1-55868-931-1 (USA & Canada)
ISBN 0-462-00807-X (Europe)

Printed in Singapore by Times Graphics Pte Ltd

FOREWORD

Hong Kong is full of surprises, paradoxes and contradictions. Some are so obvious, so much a matter of routine or usually so well hidden that no one notices them.

THE BELLS OF NINE QUEEN'S ROAD, CENTRAL

Twelve one-metre high figures of civilians and warriors in classical Chinese dress, each carrying a traditional Chinese Zodiac animal, ride on a carousel in a Western-style clock tower at Nine Queen's Road, above the bustling business district in Central. These figures, rotating on individual axles, come out of their nest several times a day to parade in formation forwards, backwards, and outwards. They move their arms, nod their heads, and bow to the pedestrian and vehicular traffice, in time to the computer-operated music of twenty-five bells.

Whereas the appearance of the figurines is undoubtedly Chinese, the clock tower is derived from the western tradition, as is the carillon of bronze bells with its span of two octaves. They were cast in the Netherlands, at the Royal Bellfoundry Petit en Fritsen, which has been producing bells since the middle of the seventeenth century. This quaint performance, so unexpected in twenty-first century Hong Kong, is all but drowned by city noises and is totally ignored by most passers-by. Nevertheless, it is appreciated by discerning individuals who stop to look and listen. At least one pedestrian is tempted to risk her reputation for sanity, by returning the salute whenever she happens to be near when the bells chime.

The figurines and carillon in the clock tower illustrate how whimsically Hong Kong has adopted the traditions of China and the West. Not all aspects of this multi-cultural mix in Hong Kong blend so smoothly, however; noris the blend always so palatable.

Do not expect Hong Kong to be totally changed since 1997 just because it is no longer under British rule. Now that almost a decade has passed, the Hong Kong people have returned to the business of making money. Nor should you worry about the future of Hong Kong lest it be swallowed by the giant monolith of which it has become one. With the eyes of the world on Hong Kong, China will not be able to compromise

Chapter 6
Food & Entertaining 133

Chapter 7
Leisure Activities 148

Chapter 8
Learning the Language 192

Chapter 9
Working in the Country 199

Chapter 10
Fast Facts 212

ABOUT THE SERIES

Culture shock is a state of disorientation that can come over anyone who has been thrust into unknown surroundings, away from one's comfort zone. *CultureShock!* is a series of trusted and reputed guides which has, for decades, been helping expatriates and long-term visitors to cushion the impact of culture shock whenever they move to a new country.

Written by people who have lived in the country and experienced culture shock themselves, the authors share all the information necessary for anyone to cope with these feelings of disorientation more effectively. The guides are written in a style that is easy to read and covers a range of topics that will arm readers with enough advice, hints and tips to make their lives as normal as possible again.

Each book is structured in the same manner. It begins with the first impressions that visitors will have of that city or country. To understand a culture, one must first understand the people—where they came from, who they are, the values and traditions they live by, as well as their customs and etiquette. This is covered in the first half of the book

Then on with the practical aspects—how to settle in with the greatest of ease. Authors walk readers through how to find accommodation, get the utilities and telecommunications up and running, enrol the children in school and keep in the pink of health. But that's not all. Once the essentials are out of the way, venture out and try the food, enjoy more of the culture and travel to other areas. Then be immersed in the language of the country before discovering more about the business side of things.

To round off, snippets of basic information are offered before readers are 'tested' on customs and etiquette of the country. Useful words and phrases, a comprehensive resource guide and list of books for further research are also included for easy reference.

CONTENTS

The carrion at Nine Queen's Road.

its pledge on Hong Kong: one country, two systems—until the year 2047, at least.

EVER-CHANGING HONG KONG

Do not let street and shop signs in Roman letters delude you into believing that everything is 'just like home'. However well prepared you are on arrival, cultural misunderstandings lie in wait for you. As a newcomer to the community, it is you who will have to adjust to the native culture, and the culture in Hong Kong is complex indeed. Be ready to see Hong Kong perpetually in motion. Appearances, as well as substance, can change every day. It is very important to keep an open mind and a cool head as you approach life in this city. Once acclimatized, you will enjoy the wonderful opportunities and life-styles Hong Kong has to offer.

THIS BOOK IS WRITTEN FOR YOU

This book is written for you, an English-language reader newly arrived or expected in Hong Kong, to take up a job and make a home for yourself—and for your spouse, if you have one. It is also for short-term visitors who want a deeper understanding of what makes Hong Kong tick than can generally be gleaned from tourist literature. Besides giving factual information, an attempt is made to explain some of the prevailing attitudes and states of mind. It is our hope that, by gaining an appreciation of some of Hong Kong's complex and varied cultural traditions and institutions, you will reduce the frustrations of transition from your native culture to that of Hong Kong. Facts and background are not skimped, but our emphasis is on showing how you can adjust with greater ease; and, as a result, enjoy your Hong Kong experience more fully.

ACKNOWLEDGEMENTS

We would like to thank the friends and organisations listed here for allowing us the use of their materials and publications for the very first edition of this book. We have been using the materials since. Heep Hong Society for Handicapped Children: Great Chefs; Hong Kong Land and Constance Ching; Government of Hong Kong (now HKSAR) Government Information Service; the Departments of Transportation and Immigration; Hong Kong Housing Authority; Hong Kong Tourist Association; St. John's Cathedral Counselling Service and the Reverend Karol Misso; United States Consulate General; Hong Kong Academy for Performing Arts and Susanna Chan; and Kowloon Dairy and Eric Li; Frank Welsh's *A History of Hong Kong*, with its timely publication, has proved invaluable.

We are grateful to the many friends who have had their patience taxed by being forced to listen to the content of the book infinitum. We are particularly grateful to my daughter, Frances Katharine Liu, who has expended many hours in updating the content of this edition.

The courtesy and consideration, care and ingenuity of the editors of Marshall Cavendish International (Asia) Private Limited are much appreciated.

Betty Wei
August 2005

MAP OF HONG KONG

CHINA

HONG KONG

SOUTH CHINA SEA

FIRST IMPRESSIONS

CHAPTER 1

There must be endeavours,
but let there be no anxious expectation.
—Mencius (c. 372–289 BC)

You can sense immediately the pulse of Hong Kong as your plane touches the Chek Lap Kok airport runway on the edge of the blue waters of the South China Sea amidst shrub covered mountains. Meanwhile, you hear a flight attendant telling you not to unbuckle your seat-belts and not to retrieve your belongings from the overhead bins before the plane comes to a complete halt. You personally consider this counsel utterly superfluous while at the same time becoming aware of an excitement generated by your fellow passengers as they take exactly the action the flight attendant was warning against, by piling themselves and their belongings into the aisles in order to push their way off the plane before anybody else.

THE NEED TO RUSH

When you are more accustomed to the local ways you will realise that this trying to get ahead of everybody else in every endeavour one undertakes is a Hong Kong characteristic. It is not only that people feel it essential to arrive at their destinations in a hurry, they actually need to get there ahead of everybody else. This is called one-upmanship; Western terminology, perhaps, but a Hong Kong trait. At times, this quality is a positive and necessary one; it is what leads Hong Kong to try harder, in order to gain a competitive advantage over the rest of the world. It is only during the last score years that ordinary people have had the opportunity to share in a prospering economy—where power and wealth had been held by a small privileged minority. This one-upmanship serves to describe the urgency felt by the Hong Kong people, and in time perhaps you as well, in their race to achieve the often very demanding goals they set to accomplish.

> You will live in Hong Kong under more pressure than at home if you hope to succeed here. Before you realise what is happening, whether or not you notice it yourself, you will be pushing and shoving too.

This urgency to rush out of the aircraft is a harbinger of things to come. What your antennae should be telling you is that, despite the Hong Kong Tourist Association's logo of a cute abstract dragon signalling a leisurely way of life, Hong Kong is not a sleepy fishing village of the Third World.

Since almost everybody you encounter personally in Hong Kong will be speaking English, or at least something that resembles English, and since the street and shop signs are bi-lingual—in Chinese script and Roman letters—it is difficult to imagine that anybody, especially you, would experience any cultural shock in Hong Kong. You see a fashionably clad and well-groomed populace, for instance, and instruments of instant communication: a computer with email in every home and office, and the latest technological hand held communication device in every hand. Local English-language dailies are more than readable, and world-wide newspapers (*The Asian Wall Street Journal*, the *Financial Times* and *International Herald Tribune*) can be delivered to your desk before nine. English-language broadcasts are available on radio and television. American-style fast food is on hand at strategic street corners; bread, cold cuts and cheeses are found in delicatessens. Even bagels are freshly baked each day. So, how can you be wrong when you perceive Hong Kong as a Westernised modern community?

Below the veneer, however, there exists a society where traditional values and prejudices hold sway. Do not be misled by Hong Kong's superficial modernity; keep watch for deep-rooted traditions. No matter how seasoned you are as a traveller or as a resident in foreign lands, you will feel some degree of cultural shock. As a new arrival, you must be prepared—indeed, well prepared—to overcome this, if you are to make the most of the unique experience of living in Hong Kong.

A PLACE OF DIVERSITY, WHICH IS NOT CHINA

Unlike many Asian cities, where there is a native culture that can be defined because it is based on a single tradition, Hong Kong is a place of immense superficial diversity and contrast—and greater underlying complexity. Situated on the edge of a once-Communist monolith that is also the homeland of the ancient Chinese civilisation, the polity of Hong Kong is essentially a British creation. While the population is predominantly Chinese, the administration and laws are still in the British tradition. It is a teeming city, with expensive boutiques vaunting the world's most celebrated names; yet the marketplace is still full of the cunning of the developing Third World. Hong Kong is an important centre of international commerce and finance, but the majority of Hong Kong's business undertakings are small and family owned. From the beginning, people of cultures other than Chinese and British have lived and worked in Hong Kong. Tradesmen from around the world have brought with them their own ways of conducting business and personal relationships, in accordance with their own cultures.

Circumstances of post-Second World War political and economic development in Asia facilitated the territory's growth into the modern metropolis of today; but old traditions, some long discarded in China and by Chinese communities elsewhere, still persist in Hong Kong. Eastern and Western cultures, not just Chinese and British, are found side by side. Without a command of Cantonese you will miss a lot of colour, but you still can get around Hong Kong.

Newly arrived, and overwhelmed by unfamiliar surroundings, you may not immediately appreciate the existence of the variety of cultures. Your senses are so bombarded, visually, aurally, and in every other respect, that it is difficult to react to the place with your intellect. You may choose to perceive Hong Kong as another

Chinatown, very much like the one at home, only bigger and noisier—if you had such a neighbourhood at home. In which case, just as when touring your home Chinatown, you will note only the exotic features, or what you understand to be Chinese characteristics, without perceiving the Western modifications.

This deduction is difficult to fault, because ninety-five per cent of the population of Hong Kong are ethnic Chinese, and are indeed Chinese in appearance. In addition to almost seven million ethnic Chinese residents and visitors, other Asians reside in or visit Hong Kong. Among the largest numbers of Asian residents are nationals of the Philippines, Malaysia, Japan, Thailand, Korea, Indonesia and Singapore. Many of these visitors are of Chinese descent. To the non-Asian eye, Hong Kong looks Chinese. However, just as not all Asian tourists in Europe and America are Japanese, the Asians in Hong Kong are not all Chinese. And you will not be the only one unable to tell the difference.

Mistaken Identity

A Cantonese banker we were acquainted with was walking down Chater Road in Central one bright Sunday morning, carrying in his right hand a heavy briefcase. He was wearing a pair of white trousers, an unfortunate choice as red hundred-dollar bills were rather prominently visible through his back pocket. This acquaintance also wears glasses and sports a crew cut. As he neared the corner across from what is now the Ritz Carlton Hotel, three youths accosted him. Our acquaintance felt a hand on his back while two men jostled him from right and left. Without thinking, and showing instant reflexes left over from his training as a private in the United States Army, he knocked down the man on his right with his briefcase, and held the man on his left in a half nelson. Meanwhile, as he spied the third youth with a fistful of his red bills, he swore at them in the exquisite street Cantonese he had picked up as a young student in Stanley. Taken aback, the youths returned his money and apologized: "We are sorry. We did not mean to harm you. We thought that you were Japanese!"

If you have never been to China, perhaps you will assume instantly that Hong Kong is another Chinese city. Under no circumstance should you commit the *faux pas* made by the Lebanese wife of an Omani businessman who proudly announced that they had been to China and visited four Chinese cities: Taipei, Singapore, Bangkok and Hong Kong. Please remember that, although under Chinese rule, Hong Kong is not a traditional Chinese city, and Hong Kong culture is distinct from that across the border. Even if you ignore the difference in clothing and grooming styles, Hong Kong people display a distinct countenance that bespeaks daring and self-assurance.

Or, if you do not look at the people at all, but notice only the Western-style architecture and the glamorous shops featuring merchandise from Europe, you will get a completely different impression. Once, a Chinese American woman from Honolulu, who is married to a local Chinese, was asked by a tourist to point out the direction of Chinatown.

So there is a shot-silk effect. Depending on the orientation of your eye, Hong Kong is modern-Western but with underlying Chineseness, or it is Chinese with a surface of English-speaking internationalism. No one sees it as half and half.

BEAUTIFUL MOUNTAINS AND WATER

Hong Kong is on the coast of the Asian mainland. The Special Administrative Region—comprising Hong Kong Island, Kowloon, New Kowloon, the New Territories, and 235 islands in the South China Sea—has a land area of 1,100 square kilometres, or 424.7 square miles. Geologically it is a part of one of the mountain chains of South China where it runs into the sea, with the peaks remaining above the water as islands. The topography is dominated by steep granite and volcanic hills covered with shrubs and grass. A large number of the outlying islands have no fresh water and therefore are not inhabitable. With new landfill and disturbance of the environment, the harbour no longer seems so clear; pollution has become a serious problem.

Your first impression of Hong Kong can easily be one of a concentration of tall skyscrapers amidst beautiful mountains. Carl Crow, a traveller of an earlier era when visitors came to Hong Kong by sea, noted in the 1933 edition of his *Guide to China* that 'there are grander sights to be seen in the world, but few more picturesque and graceful than that of Hong

Aerial view of the Tsing Ma Bridge.

Kong—[especially] the entrance to the harbour and the panoramic view from the mountain.' These same mountains and harbour greet today's visitors still, whether they arrive by sea or air. Although the tall buildings that came into being during the intervening years have dramatically changed the silhouette of Hong Kong, the excitement of the mountains and water has not abated. The vista is still magnificent, although huge land reclamation projects have created more real estate by cutting down the sides of mountains. Regardless of how you fare in Hong Kong, its mountains and waters will remain a thrilling image in your mind for the rest of your days.

A PLACE OF EXTREMES

As befits an arena of worldwide competition, certain extremes in the lifestyle are worth noting. Hong Kong boasts the world's highest per capita use of cellular phones and radio pagers. While these means of communication make it possible for individuals to keep in constant touch with their homes and offices, thus gaining an edge over those without, they are annoying to others around them. As a result, cellular phones are banned from many places, including private clubs.

Hong Kong has taken pride in enjoying a high consumption of protein, including a great variety of shell-fish. The claimed link between the traditional South China diet of salt fish and nose cancer may have no more basis than the purported connection between nose cancer and the penchant of the Hong Kong population for picking their noses. However, with worsening water pollution, hepatitis has become increasingly common. Media attention has been focused on unhealthy minerals in local seafood. Another study established further ill consequences of the high protein diet. The cholesterol count of rich-blooded Hong Kong residents has surpassed the United States equivalent. Heart disease and obesity among the population are of increasing concern.

The old adage that you do not get fat by eating Chinese food is bunk, as you will find if you eat like a native. But still, life expectancy is 84.3 years for women and 78.6 years for men. There are over 30,000 restaurants, including one with floor space of 14,000 square metres that can accommodate 6,000 patrons at a time. Since the 1980s, there has been a proliferation of restaurants, serving everything from Moroccan food to pizza.

Hong Kong has the distinction of being the home of the world's first billion US dollar edifice, the headquarters of the Hongkong and Shanghai Banking Corporation. The desire to drive the biggest and costliest car available means Hong Kong leads the world with the largest per capita ownership of Rolls Royces, as well as with the highest number of Mercedes Benz outside Germany. In fact, the world's longest public parade of Rolls Royce cars, 114 of them, took place in Hong Kong. In 2004, another parade of Rolls Royce cars to Guilin started in Hong Kong.

The world's first Braille edition of a daily newspaper, *South China Morning Post*, was published in English in Hong Kong. Hong Kong is Asia's most popular travel destination. In the year 2002, travellers made 16.56 million trips entering and leaving Hong Kong. In 2003, the number of travellers was 15.53 million.

Rural Hong Kong

Much of Hong Kong is urban, yet in spite of extensive construction of multi-storeyed new towns in recent years, almost seventy per cent of the territory has remained rural. There are still traditional villages, unfrequented woods, and wildernesses with wild animals. Country parks occupy almost forty per cent of the total land area. But as there is little flat land for the fast growing population, rural Hong Kong is giving way to urbanisation.

The Hong Kong Government has constructed new towns —from villages and new land reclaimed from the sea. At the beginning of the 1990s, the rural areas often displayed evidence of abandonment and neglect; but many of the village houses now show signs of wealth. Common sights in Kam Tin, a village of the Tang clan, are large television sets in air-conditioned rooms, and luxury motor cars parked outside.

Urban Splendour

The curtain-walled skyscrapers during the day and the glittering neon lights at night make Hong Kong one of the most striking cities on earth. The Central District of Hong Kong Island boasts some of the world's most magnificent buildings.

An early twentieth century geodetic survey showed that Hong Kong and New York, alone among leading deep-water port cities, stood on rock foundations that could withstand buildings of any height. With property prices quoted by the square foot, it is understandable that Hong Kong has developed upwards.

For almost twenty years, the tallest building in Hong Kong was the 52-storey Connaught Centre, completed in 1973 and renamed Jardine House in 1989. Today, it is dwarfed by the many tall buildings of Central, Western and Wanchai, as the huge buildings have been dwarfed by the tall hills behind them. Until the International Finance Centre opened in 2003, the tallest building was the Central Plaza in Wanchai. Dotted among the skyscrapers can be found large sculptures by Henry Moore.

ARCHITECTS AND ARCHITECTURE

Building design reflects the local competitive spirit of free enterprise. Financial and commercial establishments vie with each other in their choice of prestigious architects and modern materials, with no expense spared.

The Hong Kong office of the Bank of China, designed by the American architect I M Pei, scion of a noted banking family from Shanghai, dominates the ground from which the ascent begins from Central to St. John's Anglican Cathedral and goes on to Government House. The bank also kept the original building at the junction of Queen's Road and Des Voeux Road, an imposing edifice of pre-1949 vintage.

The Hongkong and Shanghai Banking Corporation is a formidable power in Asian finance—an issuing agent for Hong Kong's currency and the principal depository of the Hong Kong Jockey Club's receipts. A neighbour of the Bank of China on Queen's Road, it is housed in

The Hong Kong headquarters of the Bank of China was designed by American architect I M Pei.

Twin pillars of the colonial era as joint issuers of Hong Kong's currency, the Standard Chartered Bank and the Hongkong and Shanghai Banking Corporation.

a wondrous combination of modern architecture and civil engineering. The new structure was designed by Sir Norman Foster, a prestigious British architect. With a desire never to be outranked or out-addressed, the Hongkong and Shanghai Bank has assumed the address One Queen's Road, Central.

As a result of energetic campaigns by concerned residents after the demolition of the charming Hong Kong Club in the early 1980s, several buildings of the era before World War II have been spared from the developer's hammer. The clock tower on the waterfront across from Central is the only remaining segment of the old terminus of the Canton and Kowloon Railway, but the domed Supreme Court building, now the home of the Legislative Council, is still standing. Above the hill from Queen's Road, the French Mission of red-brick, built during the nineteenth century, has been renovated and is now the Court of Final Appeal. The Cathedral of St John remains a graceful white church with a blue ceiling.

CROWDS

The crowds in Hong Kong are immediately noticeable. During lunch time from noon to around two-thirty on week days, there truly is no space for the faint-hearted or weak-limbed on the city's pavements. Jay-walking is a game people play all over the world, but where else do pedestrians need to queue eight deep for traffic lights to change, in order to cross the street? It is still possible to cross the street without loss of life or limb, since traffic in Hong Kong generally does obey regulations. However, in 1997 a driver carelessly lost control of his vehicle in Central, killing one person and injuring several others on the street, so pedestrians still need to pay close attention to the traffic. And public bus drivers recently threatened to go on strike when the Government considered raising the penalty for running a red-light, claiming that it would add to their stress-levels.

Getting into an elevator (or lift) in an office is a serious challenge. First of all, no matter what time you find yourself in front of this vehicle, there will be a crowd assembling. The button, of course, will have been pushed already. Still, everybody—perhaps not you, but everybody else—will be pushing the already lit button, not once, but tapping it several times, like a barometer whose reading refuses to come down. When the thing arrives, the people inside will be pushing their way out, and your companions will be pushing their way in. Do not be horrified at this display of bad manners: there is so little space in Hong Kong, and so many people, that, if you do not rush ahead and take up the space, you will lose it to somebody else. And since the concept of private space is alien to Hong Kong, no one minds being crowded. Just do not lose your cool when everyone in your elevator crowd pushes the button at least a dozen times.

MOVING OPULENCE

Traffic is indeed impressive—not only for its sheer volume. In contrast to many Asian cities, it does move smoothly—albeit erratically at times when Hong Kong drivers are behaving true to form, trying to get ahead of everybody else. The roads are filled with luxury automobiles, vital symbols of their owners' status. Makers of Rolls Royce, Jaguar, Mercedes, BMW, Toyota Crown and Lexus are enchanted with their sales in Hong Kong. One car in six is a Mercedes Benz; and one in every sixty, a Jaguar.

It was no surprise when the Rolls Royce Company chose Hong Kong as the site of the longest-ever parade of its products in September 1996. With the Peninsula Hotel alone operating a fleet of ten Rolls Royces, the Mandarin Oriental Hotel and the Inter-continental Hotel operating two each, (Inter-continental also has a fleet of 18 Daimlers)—and a certain private individual said to own more than ten 'Rollers', 1 per cent of the company's production resides in Hong Kong. Glimpses (or, rather, sounds) of other high-powered cars—Porsche, Ferrari and Maserati, for instance—are also a part of the daily Hong Kong experience. If Cadillacs and other luxurious products of Detroit do not seem so prevalent here, it is because Americans insist upon driving on the right side of the road whereas Hong Kong traffic keeps to the traditional British left. Altogether, there were 524 thousand registered motor vehicles in the territory during the calendar year 2003.

SMELL

As soon as you get off the plane, your nose will tell you that you are in Hong Kong, though what you notice is far less pungent now that the airport has been moved away from urban congestion. Various parts of Hong Kong have special smells. In Western, for instance, the atmosphere is permeated with the smell of creatures that once lived in the sea. For those who occasionally venture into the abyss of this district, the smell may be exotic. To the residents it is, understandably, offensive. The Urban Council tried in 1981 to license the local industry of shark's fin processing, in order to establish a certain standard of hygiene. Less than a dozen establishments had come forward to be counted, by the deadline.

Hong Kong residents put hygiene requirements and the smell well behind their fears that, with more stringent standards, the processors might have to raise the price of the delicacy. This is known as the Hong Kong value system. The Government, however, due to various pandemics of recent years, such as SARS in 2003, has had to enforce exemplary hygiene standards.

Of course, throughout the territory one experiences all manner of exotic smells. During the rainy season, clothes Hong Kong people wear tend to smell like wet laundry. When people live in high rise estates without laundry dryers, their indoor-line-dried clothes give off a specific scent that is especially noticeable in closed spaces such as elevators. Hong Kong residents are not as obsessed with cosmetic deodorants as Americans; so, during the long, hot and humid summer, your nostrils will be working overtime without enjoyment.

NOISE

The predominant language in Hong Kong is Cantonese, a Chinese dialect known for its complicated tones and colourful expressions. To the uninitiated, the language seems loud and harsh, nasal and guttural, all at the same time. Cantonese women and children, influenced by television, whine at the top of their voices. Their menfolk do not take a back seat in this respect. They carry on conversations on public transport and in lifts, at the top of their lungs.

Traffic noises are deafening as well. Although Hong Kong drivers do not honk so incessantly as their counterparts across the border, our drivers play their car or mini van radios just as indiscreetly. When the air-conditioner is on, and the windows are shut, at least the noise is confined to the interior of the vehicles. When the weather is cooler, drivers leave their windows open, and create additional noise pollution. In any case, when you are in a taxi, the driver is never content with fewer than two noise emitters: his radio connecting him with his central dispatcher crackling away whether or not there is a message, and the car radio tuned to a talk-show rattling away in Cantonese—or making a variety of sounds known euphemistically as Cantopop.

If Chinese restaurants anywhere in the world ever considered sound proofing, this novel approach to gracious dining has not occurred to owners of restaurants in Hong Kong. Despite sometimes luxurious decor, the decibels in restaurants are extremely high. It is not only the conversation of the diners at the tops of their voices, but thunderous noises of music or televisions blasting, and announcements over loudspeakers: together they are deafening.

It is tempting to conclude that the noise bombarding Hong Kong is what makes the people of Hong Kong so grouchy all the time. However, before you decide to become a house-bound recluse during your entire stay, you should note that noise is associated by the Cantonese with happiness and togetherness; and that, to the ordinary Chinese in Hong Kong, silence signifies solitude and loneliness.

CONCLUSION

If your first impressions warn you that Hong Kong is a harsh place, please appreciate that it is also an exciting place full of wonderful opportunities. The people are industrious and they approach each day with anticipation. Once they get to know you or know who you are, they are also friendly and helpful. A few grumble about their rewards, but most are willing to work hard to achieve their goals. You must overcome your initial hesitations, if you have any, and become a part of the vibrant Hong Kong scene as soon as you can.

OVERVIEW OF LAND AND HISTORY

CHAPTER 2

History supplies little more than a list of people who
have helped themselves with the property of others.
—Voltaire (1697–1778)

EARLY HISTORY OF HONG KONG

It is generally known that Hong Kong owes its founding in 1841 to British merchants who wanted to expand their trade in China. From the very beginning a free port—in the sense that there was neither limitation on the articles of trade nor discrimination against any trader because of his nationality—Hong Kong soon became an important entrepôt between South China and the rest of the world.

After 160 years, it has evolved into a major centre of international finance and industry as well. In an address to a gathering of scholars in August 1993, the Chief Secretary of the Hong Kong Government averred that 'Hong Kong's business is business'—still. In this regard, he was reflecting the perspective of the Government as well as reiterating the prevailing ethos of the community.

At the end of June 1997, this freewheeling community was handed over to the People's Republic of China. The Joint Declaration of 1984 between the governments of Britain and China, and the Basic Law promulgated by the Chinese, have promised that the current economic and social system of Hong Kong is to continue for another fifty years, under the policy of *One Country—Two Systems*. So, until the year 2047 at least, *laissez faire* capitalism as practised in Hong Kong, with all its economic, political and social implications, is expected to continue.

THE CANTON SYSTEM AND THE OPIUM WAR

The Opium War (1840–1842) is so named because the immediate purpose of Britain in sending warships and troops against China was to further the opium trade. This war had a tremendous impact on China, opening it to Western influences as traditional Chinese institutions and values began to change after the war. To understand the commercial and materialist character of Hong Kong, it is helpful to be aware of the nature of foreign trade in China before 1842 and of the circumstances under which Hong Kong came into being.

From 1760 until the Opium War, all foreign trade in China, except Russian, was limited to the port of Canton. Known as the Canton System, this single-port policy confined foreign traders to their quarters on the waterfront of Canton. Their families and dependants had to remain in Portuguese Macau. At no time were the traders permitted direct access to Chinese retailers, since all buying and selling had to be conducted through merchants franchised by the Imperial Government to handle foreign trade. They were known as *hong* merchants, and their firms as *hongs*. Articles of trade were limited, with the Chinese importing almost nothing from Britain, so British traders had to pay for their purchases in China with specie. To offset this imbalance, the traders smuggled into China opium grown in India, a commodity that the Chinese paid for in cash.

As time passed, the illicit opium trade became the most controversial issue between the Chinese government and British traders at Canton. Import, growth, sale and use of opium had been forbidden by imperial decree; but the quantity imported increased, especially after 1826 when officials at Canton became a part of the smuggling network. Between 1828 and 1833, British traders took from China 29.6 million (Mexican) dollars in silver, and the Americans another 15.8 million. This outflow of specie turned the balance of trade against the Chinese, considerably alarming the court because the drain of silver led to stagnation in the Chinese economy. In addition, widespread opium addiction among the populace, especially the troops, had become a serious problem. Therefore, the Chinese government pulled out all stops in enforcing its anti-opium policy.

Since the end of the eighteenth century, the British had tried to persuade the Chinese government to relax all trade restrictions. The Chinese had seen no need to respond. As the monopoly of the East India Company ended in 1834, and as the Industrial Revolution demanded an ever wider international market for British manufactured goods, individual British traders in India and China more than ever wanted to end the Canton System. They lobbied Parliament, and eventually succeeded in securing their government's support through the deployment of forces to China. It was these traders who eventually set the tone for Hong Kong.

When Commissioner Lin Zexu (1785–1850) destroyed 21,306 chests of opium confiscated from British traders in May 1839, an excuse was provided for Britain to send warships to China. The British victory was swift, and several agreements were made, culminating in the signing of the Treaty of Nanking in August 1842. The treaty opened five Chinese coastal ports to British trade, and ceded Hong Kong Island to Britain.

THE CHOICE OF HONG KONG

The British Government had wanted consular presence at the Chinese ports, but it had not been London's original intention to establish a British colony in China. If the creation of a British administered community on Chinese territory had been contemplated at all by British officials on the scene during the war, their first choice would have been Chusan, an island at the mouth of the Yangzi which had been a bustling port in coastal and maritime trade. Lord Palmerston, British Foreign Secretary at that time, could not understand why the British Crown or Government needed the aggravation of 'a barren island with nary a house upon it'.

Traders in Canton, on the other hand, had come to appreciate the deep and sheltered harbour of Hong Kong as early as 1836, and had envisaged it as the site of a British colony. A correspondent had written in the 25 April issue of the *Canton Register* that 'if the British lion's paw (were) to be put down on any part of the south side of China, let it be Hong Kong', and 'let the lion declare Hong Kong to be under his guarantee, a free port, and in ten years it will be the most considerable mart east of the Cape'.

Captain Charles Elliot (1801–1875), Superintendent of Trade in Canton since 1835 and later British Plenipotentiary to China, was the first official to recognize the strategic advantages of Hong Kong. Elliot was the son of a Governor of Madras and a cousin of Admiral George Elliot of Elgin Marbles fame. He noted that the geographical location alone would make Hong Kong an ideal site for entrepôt trade between China and Southeast Asia—and with the rest of the world. The climate was favourable; at least its hot and humid summer was no worse than that of Canton, reasoned Elliot. Fresh water was also plentiful. The island was relatively free of residents, which was also an advantage.

Despite London's disapproval, Elliot directed British warships to take possession of Hong Kong in January 1841. British and international traders followed. A land auction was held in June that year, and the creation of Hong Kong was on its way. Colonel Henry Pottinger (1789–1856), later Elliot's successor, who had spent one day in Hong Kong in August 1841 before sailing up the coast to carry the war to the Yangzi, also found Elliot's choice attractive. When Elliot was recalled by London for disregarding Palmerston's instructions 'as if they were waste paper', British possession of Hong Kong had already been assured. Pottinger returned in early 1842; declaring it a free port, he stayed on as the first Governor of Hong Kong.

Opium, and Additions of Territory

Despite the significant role played by opium traders in starting the war, there was no mention of opium in the Treaty of Nanking. The opium destroyed by Commissioner Lin had been collected by Elliot from individual traders, among whom were some of the most celebrated names in Hong Kong. William Jardine yielded 7,000 chests personally and 2,000 from his firm, Jardine Matheson and Company.

An early issue of the *Hong Kong Gazette*, showing the cargo and ballast of each vessel in port, recorded that one out of every four ships bringing goods to Hong Kong carried opium. The commodity was usually transferred to smaller receiving ships, however, rather than being stored on shore.

Dent and Company gave up the next largest number of chests, followed by the Parsee trading house Heerjeebhoy Rustomjee, and the American firm Russell and Company. These firms were among the first to set up operations in Hong Kong. Hence, shortly after the arrival of the British, Hong Kong became a centre of the opium trade. At first the traders were tolerated as smugglers by the British administration, but they eventually gained respectability when their businesses became successful—and more so when they no longer handled opium.

These firms also provided trade-related services in shipping, insurance and banking: for themselves and sometimes for other firms as well. As the volume of trade grew, a need arose for a bank in Hong Kong to handle foreign exchange, remittances and trade financing. Attempts were made by several London banks to begin business in Hong Kong and China, but they were not successful because they did not have local interests as their topmost priority. The Hongkong and Shanghai Banking Corporation, established in 1864 in Hong Kong, with its Shanghai operation starting a year later, was to enjoy a virtual monopoly over the financing of foreign trade with China. It became the premier bank in Hong Kong. The Hong Kong Jockey Club, the Hongkong and Shanghai Bank, and the Hong Kong Government have remained the most powerful institutions in the colony.

Soon after 1843, British traders yearned to expand trade in China beyond the coastal ports, and the British government negotiated to have a resident minister in Peking, but the Chinese were not responsive. The same wishes were also harboured by the French. When Chinese authorities, in search of suspected pirates, boarded the *Arrow*, a lorcha owned by a Hong Kong Chinese trader but flying the British ensign, the British had an excuse to start hostilities in China once more. This war was known in history as the Arrow War or the Second Opium War (1856–1858). British and French troops landed in Tientsin and marched to Peking, destroying the imperial summer retreat at Yuanmingyuan and driving the court into exile. The Treaty of Tientsin of 1858 granted diplomatic representation in Peking to the British and legalized the opium trade. In addition, closer to Hong Kong, the peninsula of Kowloon and Stonecutters Island in the harbour were ceded to Britain. The border between British Hong Kong and China became known later as Boundary Street, in Kowloon.

Towards the end of the nineteenth century, while Japan gained strength as an international power, China was losing control over its own territory. Rivalry between the imperialists intensified. In 1895, under the terms of the particular treaty that ended the First Sino-Japanese War, Japan garnered concessions similar to those of other 'treaty' powers in China. Before long, China was to be divided into different spheres of influence by the powers. To protect Hong Kong against all other imperial aspirations, Britain leased from China in 1898 the rest of Kowloon and an area north of Kowloon all the way to the Sham Chun (Shenzhen) River for ninety-nine years. Included in the same agreement were 235 islands in the South China Sea between Hong Kong and the Chinese coast. It is the 99-year lease for this area, comprising New Kowloon, the New Territories and the outlying islands, that came to its predetermined end on 30 June 1997.

HONG KONG IN THE 19TH CENTURY

At first, Hong Kong was the name of the colony, and Victoria was the principal settlement in Hong Kong. Queen's Road, the colony's main thoroughfare, also named after Queen Victoria, was the shoreline above high watermark at that time. Trading houses were built along the shore in Wanchai with business premises on the front and residences to their rear. The Chinese village at Wongneichong had been a thriving settlement and remained so for some time; but the newer Chinese businesses and residences were away from the shore in their own bazaars separate from the international business community, such as Canton Bazaar near where Pacific Place is located today, and in stalls where

Central Plaza is now. It was these bazaars that gave the Chinese *hongs* in Hong Kong their beginning.

Within a short time, the *taipans* (heads of the major companies)—or their wives—felt the need to separate themselves from the lower-echelon employees of their companies, according to Chan Wai Kwan in his book *The Making of Hong Kong Society*. They were also looking for a cooler location where the houses might take better advantage of the sea breezes. Therefore, residences were built on the Peak, 565 metres or 1,823 feet above sea level.

Carl Crow described these houses in 1933 as being 'in tiers … perched on narrow ledges quarried out of the sides of the hill and reached by precipitous flights of steps.' Despite fog, humidity, and an ascent so difficult that it was possible only on foot or in sedan chairs, the breezes on the mountainside had made Hong Kong summers at least tolerable. The Chinese did not begin to live on the Peak until after World War II. The non-Chinese middle-class, for the lack of a better term to describe middle-management employees of the trading companies, many of them Portuguese or Eurasian, concentrated their residences in Wanchai. Marriages between European men and Chinese women (as distinct from cohabitation) were carefully registered in order to protect the legal rights of the children.

Life was gracious for the Peak dwellers because servants, both indoor and outdoor, were plentiful. At first, furniture, luggage, alcoholic beverages, tinned food and all other comestibles deemed to be necessary for Western-style survival in an alien land, were brought to Hong Kong by ship. Gradually they began to be made here. There was little social mixing between Government officials and the *taipans* then, or between the *taipans* and the rest of the foreign community, and certainly even less between the foreign community and the Chinese.

Government House, where it now stands, was first built in 1855. The early governors and officials, unwilling to be identified with the traders who were definitely not of the gentry background, did not invite the business community to dine. This was the Victorian era, when class distinction

A house on the Peak, designed in the 1920s for gracious living. Saved from redevelopers by limited access inherited from sedan chair days.

was at its height. The more relaxed social atmosphere at Canton had not been transported to the new British colony. Forty-three persons in Hong Kong were considered to be socially acceptable at Government House in the mid-nineteenth century, but at the races it was another matter.

Horse racing had been held in Macau annually in February even before the Opium War so, after moving to Hong Kong, the horsy set of the international—especially the British—community duly attended the annual race meeting in Macau in the week of 20th to 25th of February 1843.

However, the ill-timed announcement issued in January 1844 by Governor Pottinger, also serving as British Pleni-potentiary in China, that the British Government considered the territory of Macau a part of the Chinese Empire, had so enraged Portuguese authorities that participation or even attendance by British nationals at the Macau Race meeting was impossible. As a result, the most suitable piece of flat land on Hong Kong Island was appropriated to serve as a race course. Since the area was filled with muddy rice-fields, and was a breeding ground for malaria-carrying mosquitoes, it was named Happy Valley to confer a more auspicious aura. The Chinese call this area, more fittingly, *Pao Ma Di* (literally Ground for Running Horses). Both names have survived.

The Hong Kong Jockey Club was organized that year. To put priorities in Hong Kong in proper perspective, you may wish to know that St John's Cathedral was constructed in 1849 and land was not granted to build schools until 1873, but the first official race meeting was held at Happy Valley in 1846. Although the Chinese immediately caught on to the joys of betting on racehorses, they did not become members of the Jockey Club until after a number of them had played a significant role in settling the General Strike in Hong Kong in 1925. As an expression of acknowledgement for saving Hong Kong, the Jockey Club began to admit Chinese members in 1926. The largest horse-owner in Hong Kong at that time was Eu Tong-sen, the noted herbal medicine man from Malaya who was a legend in Hong Kong as the builder and owner of several European-style castles. The castles are all gone now, but the herbal medicine shop he founded is still in business. At its height, his stable had twenty-three horses. Sir Paul Chater, chairman of the stewards for thirty-four years, could boast only eighteen horses in his heyday. The register of the Club, dating back to 1935, shows that the first Chinese steward of the Hong Kong Jockey Club, Chau Sik-nin, the original owner of Dairy Farm, was elected in November 1946.

The Chinese in Hong Kong in the 19th Century

Ever since the beginning, there had been Chinese in Hong Kong. The Treaty of the Bogue, concluded in October 1843, gave Chinese nationals free access to the new colony. This complete freedom of movement for the Chinese lasted until World War II. For the imperial Qing government in the 1840s, however, the transfer of sovereignty of territory to the British was a greater obstacle than consigning to alien rule a population of 3,650 residents scattered in twenty villages, and another 2,000 on fishing boats. After the formal cession of Hong Kong, Elliot announced that Chinese residents in Hong Kong were under British sovereignty, and were, consequently, British subjects. Except for the abolition of torture in criminal trials, the Chinese were to be governed in accordance with the 'laws, customs and usages of China'. This pronouncement had the effect of segregating the Chinese residents in Hong Kong from the rest of the population. In 1844, the Chinese Government formally acquiesced to British jurisdiction over the Chinese population in Hong Kong; and in time, all laws came to be applied equally to all residents.

Two Chinese community leaders, who had accrued a fortune by provisioning the British during the Opium War, secured land from the Government to construct the Man Mo Temple on high land above Central in 1847. The Temple Committee later assumed leadership in the Chinese community, until 1868 when the Tung Wah Hospital Committee was organised. This committee then became the forum for the business and community leaders of the Chinese population. The founding of the temple reflected the sense of community responsibility of early Chinese leaders in Hong Kong. It was a public spirited gesture, to provide religious facilities for the fast growing Chinese community which was then made up of settlers from Canton and its environs. The temple was a place of prayer, and a repository for coffins until the dead could be returned to their native districts. From the outset, the temple acquired property around it, and so in time became extremely wealthy.

Traditionally it was not the state, but the urban gentry and the clan elders in villages, who assumed leadership in settling disputes, succouring the poor, and shouldering the costs of religious festivals and theatrical performances. These responsibilities embraced religious patronage, which included temple construction. In 1851, shopkeepers of Sheungwan were allowed to participate in paying for successive renovations of the temple, and it was they who elected the members of the Man Mo Temple Committee. Later, the Temple Committee gained wider support from the Chinese community, by then expanded to embrace speakers of other dialects. The Man Mo Temple Committee was a major benefactor of the Tung Wah Hospital and the orphanage Po Leung Kuk, major charitable institutions whose committee members were also leaders of the Hong Kong Chinese community from the 1870s onwards. In 1895, the community had grown to 237,670 in a population of 248,498.

Christian missionaries, active in Hong Kong immediately after the British troops took possession, organised schools for Chinese boys to learn the English language and to acquire general knowledge. The Morrison Education Society moved to Hong Kong in 1842. It had been founded in Canton in 1835 by British merchants in memory of Robert Morrison, the first Protestant missionary in China, who had also served the foreign business community in Canton in other ways. Men trained in this institution later won renown in business, several serving as compradors for major *hongs* here and in Shanghai. This type of education did not equip them with the essential background in Chinese classics for the civil service examinations, thus depriving them of the traditional path to success as officials and scholars. But it did give them an opportunity to be of service to the then advanced-thinking officials in their attempts to modernise China. Jung Wing (1828–1912), for instance: he was a student at the Morrison Academy and the first Chinese to graduate from an American university—Yale College, the class of 1854. He proposed several projects to Li Hongzhang (1823–1901) and Zeng Guofan (1811–71). These proposals included the manufacture of steamships, modern weapons and cotton textiles in Shanghai.

Towards the end of the 1860s, the importance of the Chinese in Hong Kong was beginning to be recognised. In 1865, 121,497 out of the 125,504 residents of the colony were Chinese. In 1869, when the Duke of Edinburgh, the popular second son of Queen Victoria, visited Hong Kong, he spent one day attending receptions and performances organised by the Chinese residents.

By the 1880s, the bulk of Hong Kong's wealth was passing into Chinese hands. In 1888, among the eighteen corporate and personal ratepayers paying more than $1,000 annually, seventeen were Chinese, and only one (Jardine, Matheson and Company) was British in origin. The Chinese did not take part in law making until 1880, when election of members by functional constituencies was being discussed between the Governor and the Colonial Office; Ng Choy, the first Chinese barrister admitted to the Hong Kong bar in 1877, was later the first Chinese to be appointed to the Legislative Council.

20TH CENTURY HONG KONG

As the twentieth century opened and progressed Hong Kong became a sanctuary for Chinese revolutionaries and political activists. Sun Yat-sen (1866–1925), a native of Heungshan just north of Macau, and leader of the revolution that ended the Qing dynasty in 1911, was educated in Hong Kong at the College of Medicine for the Chinese. Sun had used a cottage near Tuen Mun in the western New Territories as his base of operations. The Qing government objected to this use of Hong Kong so the colony denied him permission to remain. He moved his base to Japan, where there were a great many Chinese students. A museum in his honour is about to come into being at the time this guide is going to press.

During the 1910s the international movement to abolish opium focused a great deal of attention on Hong Kong. By 1914, however, major interest in Europe and Great Britain went elsewhere: World War I started in August. Frank Welsh notes in *A History of Hong Kong* that 'German nationals were interned and German businesses closed down, and Hong Kong's Britons volunteered in great numbers, but the prosperity of the colony waxed, in part due to that old stand-by opium.' Whatever the cause, the business community continued to thrive. The Kowloon-Canton Railway, linking Hong Kong to the Chinese hinterland of Hankow, was begun during the tenure of Governor Sir Matthew Nathan in 1905.

After the founding of the Chinese Communist Party in 1921, the cadres organised labour unions in the major port cities of China, notably Canton and Shanghai; and also in Hong Kong. China was under the control of the warlords after the death of Yuan Shikai. Sun Yat-sen had established a government in Canton, where he was advised by an agent of the Comintern, the international Communist movement. After the 30 May 1925 'Shanghai Incident', when students and labourers were killed by Chinese and Sikh policemen under the command of two British officers, general strikes started in Canton and Shanghai, and spread to the colony of Hong Kong.

Labour unrest first took place in Hong Kong with the seamen's strike in 1921, and subsequently against foreign shippers at the dockyard where Taikooshing now stands. The general strike in 1925 was widespread and more serious. There was a boycott of all British imports, and a prohibition on all ships using Hong Kong as an entrepôt. Hong Kong's economy was devastated. It was the colony's Chinese leaders who ended this spate of labour unrest in Hong Kong, as the political coalition between Sun Yat-sen's heirs and the Chinese Communist Party ended.

From that time forward, Chinese leaders were recognized as a formidable force in Hong Kong. As late as 1930, however, left-wing unionism was still present in Hong Kong. In that year, the Vietnamese revolutionary, Ho Chi Minh, was active in Hong Kong in the service of the Comintern; but when the Nationalists under Chiang Kai-shek took control of China and worked with Shanghai's financiers and capitalists, Hong Kong was able to breathe a sigh of relief.

Administration of Colonial Hong Kong

Following the administrative pattern for a British colony, the Government of Hong Kong from the outset has been headed by a Governor, first appointed by Queen Victoria by Letters Patent. Members of the Executive Council and the Legislative Council were senior civil servants and, until February 1993, the commander of the British Armed Forces in Hong Kong was an *ex-officio* member of the Executive Council. The first non-official members, Thomas Paul Chater, an independent broker, and James Jardine of Jardine, Matheson and Company, were appointed to the Executive Council in 1896. Subsequent non-official members included *taipans* of the leading British *hongs*.

Until 1984, higher level officials were all brought from Britain, while middle and lower level civil servants were hired locally. Many of the local civil servants were educated at the University of Hong Kong after it was established in 1911.

With the signing of the Joint Declaration in 1984, however, a policy of *localisation* began to prepare for the administration of Hong Kong after the departure of the British. The sole language of government and the courts was English until 1973, when Chinese also was made an official language. Local officials, who are fluent in English and Cantonese, as distinct from expatriate officials most of whom have no command of Cantonese, began to be appointed to top Government jobs as late as 1992; at the end of 1996 directorate-level expatriate officials was 28 per cent. Local civil servants, no longer grumbling behind the scenes, organised into unions and became increasingly vociferous in making demands with full press and media coverage. What we have today in Hong Kong is a new phenomenon: local Chinese in various fields receiving what they consider to be their just rewards—which until a decade ago had been reserved to a privileged, mostly expatriate, minority.

Besides the Governor, the most powerful officials were the Chief Secretary and the Financial Secretary. The Chief

Secretary was head of the civil service, and was also the Deputy Governor. In setting the budget, the Financial Secretary was responsible for the fiscal, economic and monetary policies of the government.

World War II in Hong Kong

The Japanese invaded China in July 1937. By 1938, much of China was occupied by Japanese forces, including the province of Guangdong immediately north of Hong Kong. An influx of refugees escaping from Japanese occupied areas brought the population of Hong Kong to more than one and a half million in 1939. After the Japanese attacked Pearl Harbor in December 1941, Great Britain, as an ally of the United States, was officially at war with Japan.

Japanese forces marched across the border from Guangdong, and on Christmas Day, despite valiant efforts by the Hong Kong Volunteers, Governor Sir Mark Young surrendered to the Japanese army in a candlelit room at the Peninsula Hotel. Until August 1945, Hong Kong was under Japanese rule. Buildings and factories were stripped, and materials were sent to Japan. Even libraries were raided and some rare items were taken from the University of Hong Kong to the Toyo Bunko. These books were returned after the war. The Japanese attempted to assimilate Hong Kong into their Empire, and proceeded to change the names of streets and buildings. The Peninsula Hotel, for instance, was renamed *Toa* (Great Eastern). During the war jobs were few and the economy of Hong Kong came to a virtual halt. There was a tremendous shortage of food.

There were individual heroes, however. British and Allied civilians were interned in Stanley on Hong Kong Island; military personnel in Shamshuipo in Kowloon. Sir Lindsay Ride, an Australian professor of medicine and later Vice-Chancellor of the University of Hong Kong, organised an intelligence network—BAAG (British Army Aid Group)—to sabotage the Japanese war effort. Sir Lindsay escaped from internment by simply walking out of the camp. He eventually found his way to Chongqing, China's wartime capital, and won the protection and support of Madame Chiang Kai-shek. Although he did not succeed in getting the American Air Force to fly him back to Kaitak, he was present in Hong Kong when the Japanese officially surrendered at Government House on 16 September 1945.

Hong Kong After 1945

The return of Governor Sir Mark Young to Government House was followed by a period of uncertainty because Hong Kong was expected to be reclaimed by China since all 'unequal' treaties at the expense of the Chinese had ended in 1943. The civil war left the Communists ruling China, but diplomatically isolated. As a result, British rule in Hong Kong was not disturbed. Also as a result of the civil war, many refugees fled to Hong Kong. In 1931 the Hong Kong population who were British subjects totalled 73,866, comprising 61,640 Chinese, 6,636 Europeans, 3,331 Indians, 1,089 Portuguese, 717 Eurasians and 453 others—less than a tenth of the total population at that time. After the Japanese surrender in 1945, the Hong Kong population numbered about six hundred thousand. By the spring of 1950 it had risen to 2,360,000.

The postwar immigrants were of a different calibre. They were refugees, not small traders who wanted to come to Hong Kong to make a fortune, nor peasant labourers from Guangdong crossing the border to earn a subsistence. Many of them, especially those from Shanghai and Ningbo, had been bankers, entrepreneurs, financiers or industrialists; more than a few had come with their capital largely intact. Those without capital understood the value of financing and, working with the banks (sometimes hat in hand), they provided leadership in developing industry—textiles, garments, shipping, and electronics—and the transformation of Hong Kong into an international arena of finance and industry. It was partly due to the efforts of these entrepreneurs, observed Welsh, that 'during the 1960s... Hong Kong acquired what have become its typical modern attitudes; that single-minded dedication to money-making which powered the engine of expansion'.

The professionals—lawyers and physicians—especially those without English, could not transfer their skills into the Hong Kong marketplace. On the other hand, Hong Kong gave able and forthright women from Shanghai an opportunity to come into their own. Baroness Lydia Dunn, born in Shanghai, became a Director of Swire's—and an active politician who spearheaded the efforts of the Hong Kong Development Council and served as Senior Executive Councillor. Anson Chan, the first local Chief Secretary of Hong Kong, was born to a family from the Shanghai area.

The District Boards

In 1967, the City District Office scheme was introduced; there is no direct relationship with the Legislative Council. Members of 18 district boards were elected in 1994, with 346 elected and 27 *ex-officio* members who were rural committee chairmen. The principal function of the boards is to advise the government on local concerns as well as general Hong Kong issues, such as environment improvement and various projects which would take place in the districts. The district offices located throughout the territory serve as direct links between the government and individual residents.

Growth of the Legislative Council

The Legislative Council owes its origin to British colonial practice. The first non-official members were appointed to the Legislative Council in 1850. The Chamber of Commerce elected its first non-official member to the Legislative Council in 1884, thus starting the tradition of functional constituency representation in Hong Kong. Understandably, all legislation proposed by the Government was passed, with very little acrimonious debate, until 1991—by which time the representation of functional constituencies was wider and more varied, and the council had acquired its first eighteen directly elected members.

Today, members of the Legislative Council are elected both by functional and geographical constituencies. The last election in 2004 returned two of Hong Kong's most colourful characters to the Legislative Council. Albert Cheng, a controversial radio host who had been assaulted in his office and fired from his job for his considered by some to be outrageous utterances; and "Long Hair" Leung, noted for his leadership in anti-establishment demonstrations, his Che Guevara t-shirts in all colours, and of course, for his unkempt hair.

RETURN OF HONG KONG TO CHINESE RULE
One Country, Two Systems
On 30 June 1997, when the 99-year lease of the New Territories came to an end, Hong Kong was handed over to China. When Prince Charles, representing the United Kingdom, and the last British Governor wrote the final sentence of this chapter of British imperial history by stepping onto the yacht *Britannia* and sailing away from this colony into the wild blue yonder, the 156 years of British colonial rule of Hong Kong came to an end. Hong Kong became a Special Administrative Region of China.

Background of the Exercise
In 1981, the British Parliament passed the British Nationality Act, giving the right of abode in Britain to the people of the Falkland Islands and the people of Gibraltar, but excluded the much more numerous people of Hong Kong. The following September, the then Prime Minister Margaret Thatcher, aglow from victory in the Falkland Islands, went to Beijing to discuss what would happen to Hong Kong when the lease for the New Territories expired. Conversations between the British and Chinese officials were not productive; nor did the atmosphere appear to be cordial. As a result, Hong Kong went into a siege mode as supermarket shelves were emptied of rice, oil and toilet paper.

The Sino-British Joint Declaration
Two years later, Prime Minister Thatcher again went to Beijing. This time, there were more concrete results, in the shape of the Sino-British Joint Declaration of 26 September 1984. The two parties agreed that China would 'resume

exercise of sovereignty' over Hong Kong in July 1997. The capitalist economic and social systems, the Hong Kong laws, and the judicial and educational structures would all remain substantially unchanged for not less than fifty years, or at least until the year 2047, hence the slogan: *one country, two systems.*

Annex I of the Joint Declaration provided that the HKSAR would have its own form of government—with its institutions intact, including a governor. There was to be a high degree of autonomy from the Chinese Government in Beijing. The HKSAR would keep the right to levy taxes, and the taxes would be retained in Hong Kong. It would determine its own financial and monetary policies, and issue its own convertible currency. All rights and freedoms guaranteed by current laws would be respected. Chinese armed forces would be stationed in Hong Kong, but would not interfere in the internal affairs of the HKSAR.

The Basic Law and the Joint Liaison Group

The Joint Declaration also stipulated that the National People's Congress of the People's Republic of China was to proclaim a constitution for the HKSAR as soon as it was feasible. This constitution—the Basic Law—was promulgated in April 1990 by China. It declared that all Hong Kong laws then in force were to be maintained, except where the laws contravened the Basic Law.

Meanwhile, representatives of the Chinese and British governments—the Joint Liaison Group—met at scheduled times to discuss the transitional process. It was a bilateral group; Hong Kong did not form a third party. The Group held its meetings in Beijing, Hong Kong and London. Problems over the speed of democratization and the financing of the new airport produced angry words from time to time, but eventually compromise solutions were found to enable a generally smooth transition.

Issues of Democratic Development

At the time of the Basic Law, all members of the Legislative Council were appointed. In 1991, Hong Kong held its first direct elections—for eighteen of the Legco sixty seats. Twenty-one of the rest of the seats were to be elected by functional constituencies—namely business and professional bodies. The others remained ex-official or appointed by the Governor.

In July 1992, Christopher Francis Patten, a recent cabinet minister who had just lost a parliamentary election, arrived as Governor of Hong Kong. The appointment of a politician, rather than a China expert from the foreign service, should have given Beijing a premonition that there were going to be changes during the five years before the Handover. Whatever the Chinese leadership had in mind, they kept their thoughts to themselves.

Governor Patten soon announced his proposed political reforms, notably the enlargement of the franchise for the Legislative Council elections due in 1995. The voting age would be lowered to eighteen, and the number of elected seats would go up. This proposal fell far short of the 'one man, one vote' concept of democracy understood by the general public, but, even so, Beijing's reactions were not favourable. With the deadlock in the Joint Liaison Group, Patten considered referring his enlargement of the franchise proposals to the Legislative Council, while Beijing growled. In 1995 a new Legislative Council was elected in Hong Kong and passed a series of laws which the Chinese found objectionable, charging that Patten was moving the goal posts from where they were at the time of the Sino-British agreement. The changes in electoral laws were vacated by the Provisional Legislative Council after 1 July 1997.

The Process of Transferring Power

The Preparatory Committee, comprising ninety-four members from Hong Kong and fifty-six from China, was established in 1996 to prepare for the transition to the new order. The Committee created a new Provisional Legislative Council, and also a Selection Committee to nominate a candidate to be the Chief Executive of the HKSAR. Note the change in nomenclature: the top administrative officer was to be called Chief Executive, not Governor, to rid Hong Kong further of its colonial image.

While the press and the people in Hong Kong speculated on various notables, quiet words were circulating on the streets of Beijing and the barber shops in Hong Kong that the choice was Tung Chee-hwa, a world-renowned shipping executive, who is fluent in Cantonese, Putonghua and the Shanghai dialect as well as English. It was accepted by the interest groups as well as the public that this was a wise choice. Tung's personal stature put Hong Kong on the global map, into such areas from palaces to broadrooms.

The Day of Transition—or Reunification with the Mother Land

By mid-June 1997, Hong Kong was turning into a media circus. Every major network and all the local television crews congregated near the Convention Centre, where the ceremonies and the festivities were to take place. The

The flag of the Hong Kong Special Administrative Region, a white stylised Bauhinia flower on a red background.

ceremonies and festivities took place on three days—30 June belonged to the British, the first two days of July to the new SAR. Chinese people everywhere rejoiced, as the Handover hysteria spread worldwide. The skies opened and the rains poured down without stop. The People's Liberation forces marched across the border before dawn. The populace cheered and threw flowers. Tung was sworn in. There were classical and popular concerts—with specially written music including a symphony entitled *1997* by one of the most celebrated composers of China, played by the Asian Youth Orchestra, and a handover song by Betty Tung, wife of the Chief Executive and a karaoke aficionado. There were fireworks, and a two-day holiday.

The First of July 2003

Somehow, the wisdom or lack thereof, of the Hong Kong high officialdom deemed it necessary to protect the Hong Kong people by introducing a more stringent security measure embracing all sorts of do's and don'ts involving freedoms of religions and of assembly. Various people, individually and as groups, objected. One major problem lay in the fact that the Government did not wish to consult.

On 1 July 2003, the anniversary of Hong Kong the British colony becoming Hong Kong Special Administrative Region of the People's Republic of China, a hot and blistering day, half a million people marched form Victoria Park to the Central Government Offices. In addition to Article 23, there were other grievances, most of which articulated in one guise or another. It became clear that the people of Hong Kong were not pleased with the Government. They realised that a new attitude would need to be adopted. The Secretary of Security, the official in charge of the bill, resigned, and the Chief Executive announced the postponement of consideration of the bill.

End of the Tung Administration

Tung was re-elected to another five year term in 2002, but it was clear that he was having an increasingly difficult time with the governing of Hong Kong. Meanwhile, Chinese leadership was changed as the leaders who negotiated the retrocession of Hong Kong to Chinese sovereignty retired. In early 2004, the Chinese leadership told Tung that he was not performing his duties as well as the leaders in Macau in public, with the Press in tow.

Eventually, Tung resigned on 10 March 2005. Citing ill health and advancing age, Tung could no longer spend seven days a week, from seven to eleven, working for the good of Hong Kong.

Tung's resignation was accepted by the Central People's Government leadership on 12 March. According to Article 53 of the Basic Law, if the Chief Executive resigns, the Chief Secretary will assume the duty as acting Chief Executive for a maximum of six months. Following this article, Donald Tsang, the Chief Secretary for Administration under Tung, was appointed acting Chief Executive the same day.

A New Era

On 25 May 2005, Donald Tsang resigned as Chief Secretary for Administration to run for the post of Chief Executive of Hong Kong. Tsang was seen as the forerunner for the post as a result of his extensive experience and high apporval ratings. However, there was concern by some commentators that Tsang's close association with the past British colonial administration would lead Beijing to distrust him—Tsang was created a Knight Commander in the Order of the British Empire in 1997 for his long-time service to Hong Kong. Despite these misgivings, Tsang won the support of a wide spectrum of society ranging from pro-democracy groups to business tycoons.

When Tsang submitted his nomination form on 15 June 2005, it bore the signatures of 714 out of about 800 members of the Election Committee. As each member can only endorse one candidate, it meant that Tsang had the support of the majority of the Committee. Later that same evening, the returning officer declared Tsang as the only valid candidate qualified to be the new Chief Executive of Hong Kong.

On 21 June 2005, Donald Tsang was officially appointed Chief Executive of the HKSAR by the State Council of the

Central People's Government to complete the remainder of Tung's term, which ends on 30 June 2007.

At a State Council meeting held in Beijing to study the result of the Chief Executive Election 2005, Chinese Premier Wen Jiabao noted Tsang has been serving the Hong Kong Government for more than 30 years and has made great contributions to the successful implementation of 'One Country, Two System'.

Premier Wen also said that based on Tsang's strong executive skills and familiarity with the city's overall situation and the Government's operation, he was confident that Tsang and his team would be able to lead the territory in overcoming difficulties and promoting prosperity and stability.

PEOPLE

CHAPTER 3

People only see what they are prepared to see.
—Ralph Waldo Emerson

AT THE BEGINNING OF THE 21ST CENTURY, Hong Kong boasts a multi-ethnic population. Until the mid-1980s, broadly speaking, of course, there was a Chinese society in Hong Kong and an expatriate one—though this leaves out of account the Indian, Portuguese, Eurasian and Jewish communities. There were British *Taipans*, American businessmen, British civil servants, German manufacturers and Japanese salarymen—each more or less staying within their national/occupational group. Even among the Chinese, Cantonese kept to themselves, as did textile manufacturers from Shanghai, ship-owners from Ningpo and rice merchants from Chiuchow. There were people who crossed the lines easily and often, but such sophistication was practised only by a few. After all, conversations were conducted in the language or dialect of a group, so mingling was difficult.

As the twentieth century drew to a close, however, we saw changes within and between the two basic societies. When multi-national institutions in Hong Kong no longer felt a need to employ Britons as managers, and when increasing numbers of ethnic Chinese—who had been educated overseas and were used to living abroad—returned to fill senior management positions, the lines that had divided the societies were no longer so clear.

When English-speaking sons and daughters of the new breed of tycoons entered the family firm, the language of communication became English—and the style of conducting business less orthodox. Morever, social life is no longer confined within ethnic groups: a cause and a consequence of the increase in intercultural marriages. But all these doesn't mean that traditional Chinese family-style business management is a thing of the past.

THE HONG KONG IDENTITY

How are the people of Hong Kong labelled? The terms Hong Kongers and Hong Kongese are beginning to be bandied about in the media; but somehow they sound contrived. Unlike the people of Germany who are referred to as Germans, of New York City as New Yorkers, of Glasgow as Glaswegians—and so forth—there is no single term in English that comes instantly to the tongue for the people of Hong Kong. In Chinese, they are known simply, and clearly, as *Hong Kong persons*—the name of the place followed by the word for *person*; but then, in Chinese, other peoples are called *Germany persons*, *United States persons*, *New York persons*, etc. This lack of a universally recognisable term for the people of Hong Kong is perhaps symbolic of the fact that no short label can adequately characterise them.

The Chinese population are asserting their identity as Hong Kong Chinese, not least to stress their distinctiveness from the Chinese of China and the Chinese in Taiwan. Their insistence on continued use of Cantonese, instead of learning Putonghua—Mandarin—in the schools was a source of controversy during the early 1980s, as was the issue of the simplified written characters developed in the People's Republic; but for various reasons there is no current public debate on these topics.

Since 1997, the SAR Government has adopted a policy to stress mother-tongue learning. Secondary schools, unless approved by the Department of Education, must teach in Cantonese. This move has remained controversial since, despite a lack of teachers competent to teach in English, the schools have maintained the posture that English-language education is preferable. The Cantonese-language learning through the secondary years, on the other hand, will enhance further the feeling of independent identity for the Hong Kong populace.

Commercial and Urban From the Start

From the outset, Hong Kong has been primarily a commercial and urban community. Not all the early inhabitants were British but, because the colony was, British firms were dominant. Even the first act marking British presence was a multi-racial one, reflecting the pluralist nature of the British Empire at that time, and subsequently of its colony Hong Kong. When Elliot took Possession Point in 1841, the troops he brought included 2,700 Indian soldiers. From then onwards, Hong Kong has welcomed people from all over the world—Americans, British, Chinese, Danes, French, Germans, Portuguese; Jews from Baghdad and Bombay; Hindus, Muslims, Parsees, Sikhs from India; and, in time, home-grown Eurasians. They were the traders and their employees, auctioneers, bankers, chandlers, charlatans, civil servants, coolies, lawyers, missionaries, painters, policemen, prostitutes, seamen, ship-builders, shopkeepers, saloon keepers, soldiers, and the newspaper editors who gathered and provided information. Perhaps not the Europeans, but some of their descendants have continued to live here, and have learned to use English and Cantonese, without being wholly absorbed into the Hong Kong populace. They have had to adjust to the prevailing culture but have kept certain traditions of their own; hence we find a multi-racial and multi-cultural society in Hong Kong, even without the expatriate residents.

Tsuen Wan and the Hakka Tradition in Hong Kong

Tsuen Wan, the first 'new town' created by the Hong Kong Government, is easily accessible by road and the MTR. Boasting a Town Hall with respectable acoustics, Sam Tung Uk Museum, the Panda Hotel, and proximity to the Maipo Marshes, Chek Lap Kok, and son the Disney facilities, Tsuen Wan today is very much on the beaten track of metropolitan Hong Kong.

Until the 1970s, Tsuen Wan comprised mainly agricultural villages of Hakka settlers. There was also a cottage industry of silk-weaving and noodle-making. Until the advent of modern taps, villagers depended on wells and streams for water, and as a source of power as well. Climbers to Hong Kong's tallest peak, Tai Mo Shan, began their ascent from Tsuen Wan. On the way, there was a village consisting entirely of water mills pulverising aromatic woods to make joss sticks.

(continued on next page)

(continued from previous page)

When British administration began in 1898, 3,000 persons were dwelling in 26 villages in Tsuen Wan. Each village had a population of between a few score to a few hundred, including Cantonese and Hakka.

Until recent years when dialect lines became blurred, the Hakka were outsiders, disadvantaged in several ways. They moved into the Guangdong Province during the Ming dynasty, where the Cantonese speakers were already settled. They were called Hakka ('guests') by the Cantonese who achieved instant superiority by referring to themselves as 'indigenous people of the land'. The Hakka lacked the corporate lineage structure of the Cantonese so had to compete individually against established clans. Their most renowned foray into Chinese history was the Taiping Rebellion in the 1850s when its leader was able to provide an ideology and a cause to arouse his fellow Hakka peasants—and the general Chinese populace as well, into staging an armed uprising which nearly toppled the Qing dynasty.

After the Taiping Rebellion collapsed in 1864, Hakka refugees came to Hong Kong, but not to the villages of Tsuen Wan. They sought sanctuary among the missionaries of the Basel Missionary Society in Western, where a number of Hakka had been engaged in the building trade since the early days of the Colony, many becoming prosperous. One such refugee, a Lee Tsin-kau, who died in 1885, left an estate estimated to be worth 400 dollars, a considerable sum at that time. Both Li and his wife had been baptized. Christian Hakka congregations were founded in the New Territories, including one near Fanling in 1898, but not many converts, if any, were noted among the Hakka villagers in Tsuen Wan.

Anthropologists maintain that the difference between the Hakka and the Cantonese was social rather than ethnic, but the two dialects were not mutually comprehensible. Since moving into Guangdong, the Hakka had lived alongside the Cantonese, but there was little social intercourse. Marriage between the Hakka and the Cantonese was forbidden, but apparently such taboo had not been so strictly observed in Hong Kong. Older Hakka residents in Tsuen Wan can recll today instances of Hakka men purchasing Cantonese child brides.

As elsewhere in the New Territories, Hakka farmers in Tsuen Wan cultivated fields and set up walled villages—with homes, temples, study halls, libraries, and schools. Sam Tung Uk was typical of these Hakka villages. Residents of Sam Tung Uk were moved to make room for the new town, but the village was preserved and renovated as a museum to reflect Hong Kong's pre-colonial heritage.

Founded by the Chan clan some two centuries ago, Sam Tung Uk was a single-surnamed village, meaning that its residents shared the same lineage. Without an outer wall, it was more a compound

(continued on next page)

(continued from previous page)

of single-storied residences than a true walled-village of the New Territories. The houses were attached to each other to save space and to share the good fung shui. The villagers first grew rice, then turned to vegetable farming. No consideration was given to sanitation as villagers fertilised their crops with night soil, and allowed dogs and pigs to scavenge without restraint.

The houses had earthen floors and no windows. Furniture was sparse, consisting of mainly pine trestle tables, backless stools, bedsteads, and cupboards stained reddish brown. Kitchen utensils were basic. Water had to be carried from the outside. The presence of an ancestral altar and a temple shows that the forebear and the gods were not neglected. The only source of light were the doorways by day and oil lamps by night.

Perhaps this saying reflecting the harsh life-style in pre-modern Tsuen Wan is no longer true in the new industrial town today. "If you want to become rich, go to the Gold Mountain (America). If you want to die, go to Tsuen Wan."

THE NON-CHINESE POPULATION OF HONG KONG

The Portuguese had been trading with China by water since the days of Vasco da Gama (1517). They had established a foothold in Macau, but moved to Hong Kong in 1849 following the murder of Governor J M F Amaral. Except for the Portuguese from Macau, the European population in early Hong Kong was not large, and in this context the American traders were included among the Europeans. In 1845, only 634 of the Hong Kong population of 24,157 were European. They did not stay long because they came to make as much money as quickly as possible and return to their home countries. They suffered so badly from the ills of the sub-tropics—malaria, cholera, smallpox, dysentery, and the plague—that as early as 1844 British authorities actually considered abandoning Hong Kong. It had become known as the 'white men's graveyard', for many Europeans did not survive their tour of duty here. The Colonial Cemetery in Happy Valley, established in 1845, allotted separate sections for the civilian and military dead. Within a twenty-one month period, 257 men (the equivalent of an entire regiment) succumbed. The commander,

General D'Aguilar, predicted the possible loss of a regiment every three years from endemic diseases. Shann Davies, in *Hong Kong Cemetery: Foreign Field, Foreign Devils*, counted graves of the Ninety-fifth regiment in the Colonial Cemetery: nine sergeants, eight corporals, four drummers, sixty-seven privates, four women and four children died in 1849.

Jews and Parsees in Hong Kong

Asian merchants who were among the earliest settlers in Hong Kong included Sephardic Jews from Baghdad and Parsees from India. The Sephardic traders in Canton and Hong Kong came during the nineteenth century from the Middle East by way of India, under the aegis of the Sassoons. The Parsees, Zoroastrians originally from Persia but settled in Bombay, were a part of the network of opium trade from India to China.

Descendants of the first foreign traders in the metropolis became a part of the expanding international mercantile interests of that time. Their names included Belilios, Kadoorie, Moses and Gubbay; or Ruttonjee, Mody, and Rustomjee; some of which are still prominent in Hong Kong today. They enjoyed business and personal links with the close-knit Jewish and Parsee communities in Shanghai and Bombay. At first they traded in raw cotton and general goods, and then took over the opium trade. Eventually, in Hong Kong as well as Shanghai and Bombay, they branched out into real estate, banking, shipping, warehousing, insurance, hotels, utilities and other industries, gaining power and influence locally as well as in the arena of international commerce. The first person from Hong Kong to sit in the House of Lords in Westminster was Lord Kadoorie (Lawrence Kadoorie), a member of the Jewish community in Shanghai and Hong Kong.

Indians in Hong Kong

From the beginning, the Indian community has been a major force in Hong Kong. Trade between India and China by land was of ancient origin. It was by these trade routes that

Buddhism, Buddhist iconography and Buddhist institutions came to China. In modern times, trade surged during the 1920s, when Indian merchants formed an integral part of the network smuggling opium to Canton. These Indian traders, mostly Bohras from Bombay, first worked with private traders of the East India Company, and then set up business in Hong Kong for themselves. From handling opium and cotton, they expanded to general goods, and were joined by other Hindu and Muslim traders. For many of their descendants, loss of Indian or Pakistani nationality was not critical as long as Hong Kong remained a British colony. This group is now given the right to live in the United Kingdom.

Except for Sikhs who came as a part of the military or police force, the Indian community is primarily a society of traders. The Sikhs, who have arrived throughout Hong Kong's 160 years, form the largest segment of the local Indian community.

The first Sikhs came with the British forces; later they came to work for the Hong Kong police. Some married Chinese women, and their descendants have merged into the Hong Kong populace and are indistinguishable except for their surnames. Perhaps because the first Sikhs had worked in law enforcement, it is understood that they cannot be enticed by Hong Kong's organized crime syndicates to rob their employers. Or perhaps it is because the Sikhs are thought of as tall and strong: they are still hired to work as guards for jewellery shops and other establishments handling cash. Resplendent in turbans that match their colourful uniforms, Sikhs stand out as doormen at leading hotels. Business firms of South Asian origin are strongly represented in the Hong Kong General Chamber of Commerce.

The International Community

The international community consists of more than Eurasian families, although such families have been an important part of Hong Kong almost from the start. Among the colony's wealthiest have been the compradors of the major *hongs*, one of whom, Sir Robert Hotung, was an early prominent Eurasian. Other families, not all as affluent, are still active.

Socially, the Chinese community remained separate throughout the nineteenth century. It had been an acceptable practice for certain non-Chinese residents to have Chinese mistresses as long as men did not flaunt their women before other people's wives. Difficulties arose, however, when the men were legally married to Chinese wives. One such problem arose when Daniel Caldwell, the Registrar General, married a Chinese woman.

In recent years, sons and daughters of Hong Kong Chinese families have gone abroad and brought back their foreign wives or husbands, creating a new Eurasian community. There are other American-Asian or European-Asian families. Depending on the native language of the mothers and where their children were born and reared, many of these children speak two languages.

A Eurasian marriage has a better chance of survival when living in the culture of the wife, or in a neutral culture. In Hong Kong, there are some wonderfully successful marriages, where both partners are mature and accommodating. We know of one English wife who lived with two non-English speaking mothers-in-law and a father-in-law. She learned to speak Cantonese, and brought up her children to be competent in both languages. It is to her great credit that she has adapted totally to the Cantonese culture of Hong Kong, while maintaining her sanity and independence and earning the respect and affection of her in-laws.

Other Eurasian marriages make other compromises. One French wife shares her husband on Sundays with his mother. He goes to church and eats lunch with the wife and children, and takes his mother to the cinema in the afternoon by himself, making no demand that his wife accompany them. As long as the Chinese mother-in-law is not overbearing, and as long as the foreign daughter-in-law observes a certain amount of understanding and civility, cordial relationships can be maintained.

In fact, the Hong Kong culture should be an excellent place for Eurasian marriages and their children, especially if one of the partners is Cantonese. It provides opportunities to live in the cultures of both parents, and the children can acquire both languages. Except where a current wife is much younger than the husband or than a divorced wife who is still living, problems that may arise will be due not to the nature of Hong Kong but to universal difficulties such as money, or children from previous marriages.

THE HONG KONG CHINESE

Understandably, the dominant culture of Hong Kong is Chinese. Sixty per cent of the population were born here, but thirty-four per cent were born in China. Since the early immigrants had come from the province of Guangdong, bringing with them their dialect and their traditions, Hong Kong is predominantly Cantonese in character.

> The characters of the written language are the same, regardless of dialect, but the vocabulary and syntax can be different.

Cantonese is the dialect spoken in the city of Canton (Guangzhou) and its environs. Dialects spoken elsewhere in Guangdong, Hakka or Chiuchow for instance, are not comprehensible to Cantonese speakers.

Hong Kong's popular culture is Cantonese, as is its street language (though with many modifications and additions to the original Cantonese tongue) so that the dialect spoken in Hong Kong has a character of its own. English has remained the working language of the international business world here. Among the Hong Kong Chinese, business and social conversations are still conducted in Chinese. Putonghua is used with increasing frequency. All automated answering systems greet you in Cantonese, English, and Putonghua. Minority ethnic groups, such as established Hindus or Sikhs, retain their ancestral languages at religious ceremonies, but they read and write English and also speak Cantonese. As a generalization, it is safe to say that the population of Hong Kong speaks and thinks in Cantonese.

Have the Hong Kong Chinese become more westernized than their counterparts in China and Taiwan? If so, is it because they have been living under British influence for over 160 years? The daily lives of Hong Kong Chinese have long been made comfortable by Western/Japanese gadgetry not enjoyed by their counterparts in Taiwan and the mainland until recently. Besides television and karaoke, the people are blessed with indoor plumbing and contact lenses. In many respects, British Hong Kong has surpassed even the most advanced western countries in modernity, while retaining traditions abandoned on the mainland as China underwent successive political and modernization programmes twice during the twentieth century. In superficial appearance and social attitude, the Hong Kong Chinese may have changed beyond recognition since the days immediately after the Opium War; but, as they were indoctrinated by Confucius and their parents long before making the acquaintance of Adam Smith or Georgio Armani, their thinking has remained essentially Chinese.

THE MAIN RELIGIONS OF HONG KONG

Since Hong Kong's is a multi-cultural and heterogeneous society, it is understandable that almost all major and minor religions are present here.

Confucianism

Strictly speaking, Confucianism is not a religion because it is not concerned with a superhuman power personified by a God or gods who exact obedience and adoration. Nor is it an established system of faith and worship. Confucianism does not address the question of life after death or the issue of salvation. It is a humanist philosophy that explicates certain principles of behaviour. Confucius (born 551 BC) was venerated as a teacher, never as a deity. As a moral principle and a political philosophy, Confucianism has permeated Chinese thought and personal relationships as well as national regimes for more than two millennia.

Taoism and Buddhism in Hong Kong

Taoism, also, did not begin as a religion. Intellectually it is a philosophy of withdrawal, a return to the state of nature when individuals led a simpler life free from the structures and strictures of society. Its exponents were proposing an alternative to the incessant warfare of the time, and to the rigid political system propounded by adherents of the Confucian and Legalist schools. Popular Taoism did not come until later, when traditional deities and ancestors became amalgamated into what were thought to be Taoist practices; later a body of clergy evolved.

In its popular form, Taoism can be said to be a religion. Its clergy perform important rituals such as funerals, when they chant to exorcise the evil spirits that might be present to disturb the departed as well as their families. Certain historical figures known for their special achievements were added to the Taoist pantheon of immortals. The Eight Immortals, seven men and one woman, who had been endowed with mythical values and supernatural powers, are favourites among the Taoist pantheon. They are appealed to individually or as a group; as a group they make a favourite theme in Chinese art, and crafts.

Buddhism was the first all-embracing religion the Chinese had known, in the sense that the Buddha preached compassion for all living things and that Buddhism addressed the issue of salvation. It was Mahayana Buddhism, which did not demand total negation of worldly responsibilities here and now, that received popular acceptance as well as imperial patronage more than a thousand years ago. Since believers did not have to deny traditional deities or Chinese ancestors—and despite involvement by various Buddhist sects in political movements from time to time—the religion has survived, and it thrives in Hong Kong.

Chinese Vegetarianism

Being pragmatic people, Chinese Buddhists found a ready solution to the problem of vegetarianism as well. Monks, nuns and a large number of lay people were total vegetarians, but other adherents could become symbolic vegetarians.

Symbolic vegetarians do not eat meat on the fifteenth and the last days of the month, and they eat only vegetarian food on the first and last days of each year. Thus they satisfy themselves that, at the beginning and at the end of the cycle of the moon and throughout the lunar year, they have avoided the consumption of flesh. It is curious, however, that dishes made to avoid the consumption of flesh should be called 'vegetarian pork', 'vegetarian goose', 'vegetarian shark's fin', and so forth.

Buddhist and Taoist worshippers do not gather in large congregations at prescribed times on a given day. From time to time, monks and priests are called to lead recitations of the sutra but, as a rule, people commune with their deities individually. Worshippers kneel in front of the altar at home or in a temple, as they ask for their wishes to be granted; and may sit as they meditate or recite the sutra, holding their prayer beads in their hands. It does seem incongruous to see Western-clad individuals in modern Hong Kong in such traditional postures and, under the circumstances, it would be understandable if you did not take them seriously. Since you see individuals rather than a congregation at a service when you visit a temple, it is easy to forget that they are engaged in acts of worship and not putting on a theatrical performance. In any case, please remember that it is as inconsiderate to walk between Buddhist worshippers and their altars as it is to saunter between the pews or up and down the aisle during a Christian service.

A traditional Taoist ceremony held at the water's edge. The priest's gown is also embroidered with trigrams.

Taoist and Buddhist Temples in Hong Kong

When a temple in Hong Kong is identified as a *miao* or a *shi*, it is usually Buddhist. When it is called a *guan*, it is always Taoist. But you should not be surprised to find all manner of images crossing religious lines. Not counting street and private altars in shops and homes, there are almost four hundred Buddhist and Taoist temples in Hong Kong, including a number which are older than the colony.

Chinese temples are where spirits of the deities reside, although only their earthen or wooden images are visible. In Hong Kong, temples are also repositories of spiritual tablets, wooden plaques on which names of the ancestors whose spirits reside there were inscribed. In the native places, these plaques were placed in the ancestral halls, and there are still ancestral halls remaining in the New Territories.

Ching Chung Koon (Green Pine Temple) is a Taoist temple built in 1949 near Castle Peak in northwest New Territories. It is dedicated to *Lui Cho* (nicknamed Lü Dongbing), one of the Eight Immortals, and two of his followers of the eighth century. After successfully overcoming 10 temptations, he was taught certain skills by the first of the Eight Immortals—whose existence was probably mythical rather than historical.

> Temples in Hong Kong are rarely great monuments of architecture, and few contain valuable works of art. Though they welcome visitors, they are places of worship and pilgrimage, not solely tourist sites.

Lui was elevated to the status of an immortal after travelling throughout the empire slaying devils, for a period reported in some accounts to be as long as four centuries.

Taoist dating is similar to that of the *Old Testament,* sometimes difficult for human minds to fathom. From the twelfth century onwards, the Chinese populace began to construct temples in Lui's honour. The Hong Kong temple boasts a respectable library and a wonderful collection of *bonsai* trees, some with topiary work.

The Wong Tai Sin Temple in Kowloon, erected in 1973 on the site of an older Wong Tai Sin Temple built in 1921, stands as a reminder that religious fervour had not dwindled in Hong Kong despite modernisation and preoccupation with

A temple in a New Territories village. It takes more than one week for the coils of incense hanging from the rafters to burn from the outside coil to the centre. The red tag on each coil shows the name of the donor—an individual or organisation.

the amassing of money. Situated amidst the splendour and squalor of urban Kowloon, it is a large complex of buildings honouring a host of Buddhist and Taoist deities. The chief object of adoration here is the popular Taoist personage Wong Tai Sin. Wong lived in the coastal province of Zhejiang and developed an elixir of good health and eternal life. Given the *soubriquet* Tai Sin (Great Ethereal Spirit), Wong is venerated as a healer. Asking divine assistance for good health is like buying insurance, hence the popularity of the temple.

The outbuildings of the temple contain shops and includes stalls for fortune-tellers. Hong Kong people living abroad still send their relatives to the fortune-tellers at the Wong Tai Sin Temple for their services on major occasions, from naming a new baby to ascertaining the astrological compatibility of a couple intending to marry. To avoid confusion in case the intermediaries fail to pass on the exact message word for word, the fortune-tellers have adopted modern means of communication: the tape recorder or even VCD.

The Man Mo Temple in Hollywood Road, the first temple built on Hong Kong Island after the arrival of the British, was dedicated to *Man* (the God of Literature) and *Wu* (the God of War). Also within the temple was the Buddhist Bodhisattva *Guanyin*, popularly translated as the Goddess of Mercy, among whose attributes was the provision of male heirs.

Goddess of the Sea or Queen of Heaven

In a community dependent upon the water, the Goddess of the Sea and protector of those who sail on the waters enjoys an imposing edifice to house her image. This deity, called *Tin Hou* (Queen of Heaven) in Hong Kong, was venerated by the seafaring population all along the Chinese coast. You may find at least two dozen *Tin Hou* temples; some are small but most of them are splendid structures.

The most impressive *Tin Hou* temples are at Aberdeen, Repulse Bay, Yaumatei and Joss House Bay. They are not necessarily on the water's edge, though, as there has been massive land reclamation since their construction. Certain occasions, such as *Tin Hou*'s birthday, are still celebrated by the fisher folk and seafarers, with sounds and pageantry.

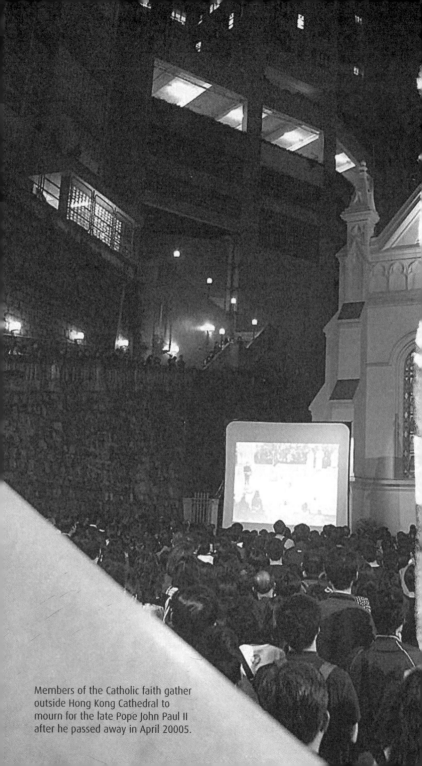

Members of the Catholic faith gather outside Hong Kong Cathedral to mourn for the late Pope John Paul II after he passed away in April 20005.

Christians in Hong Kong

It was difficult for a Chinese to be converted to Christianity: because of its monotheistic character and because early missionaries were bent on getting rid of the tradition which they termed 'ancestor worship', but which the Chinese had held to be important for several thousand years. Believing in pre-determination by fate, that one's destiny was prescribed from birth, the Chinese were not ready to accept the concepts of original sin and salvation through Jesus Christ. Early Jesuit missionaries were noted as purveyors of such Western technology as the calendar, astronomy and firearms to the Ming and Qing courts—but not for any large-scale successes in converting Chinese souls. After the Opium War, Roman Catholic and Protestant missionaries were active in proselytizing, as well as in modernising the Chinese curriculum, but the people did not flock to the religion.

The Roman Catholic Church

The first Roman Catholic mission in Hong Kong was founded in 1841. Today, the Roman Catholic Diocese, established in 1946, has fifty-nine parishes with more than 227,000 communicants, or about four per cent of the Hong Kong population.

Protestant missionaries were active in Canton and came to Hong Kong in 1841. They usurped the term *Christian* for their exclusive use, hence 'Christian church' in Hong Kong denotes a Protestant place of worship. Today, there are 1,200 Protestant congregations, with 260,000 members belonging to more than 50 denominations.

There is an Anglican cathedral, but the tremendous growth of Protestantism is due to the evangelical zeal of lay Chinese Christians. You may find a congenial church, because Hong Kong Christians are friendly and welcoming; but, if you do not understand Cantonese, your choice is limited. Not every denomination is represented here, but you will find a Christian Scientist and a small Quaker congregation. The larger congregations and parishes tend to be ecumenical. There are separate services in Mandarin and in Tagalog, a language of the Philippines. There are also Korean-language congregations.

OTHER RELIGIONS
The Bahai in Hong Kong

Among the early immigrants from South and West Asia were adherents of the Bahai faith. However, the greater number of Bahais in Hong Kong did not come and establish the religious institutions here until the middle of the twentieth century. Currently there are about 2,000 Bahais in Hong Kong. They can be found in all segments of the community.

Muslims in Hong Kong

There are 80,000 Muslims in Hong Kong. More than half are Chinese and believers from Southeast Asia or the Middle East. Others came, usually generations ago, from India, Pakistan, East Africa and West Asia. There are four mosques and two Muslim cemeteries in Hong Kong.

Hindus in Hong Kong

The Hindu Temple at Happy Valley has 12,000 members. Marriages are still arranged by parents, and are lavishly conducted. Once in a while, Indians make newspaper headlines, but most of the time they quietly follow their trades.

The best place to look for weekly religious information is in the Saturday *City* section of the *South China Morning Post*.

THE IMPORTANCE OF EDUCATION

Traditionally, in theory at least, China was a meritocracy, run by an officialdom of men who had passed the required series of civil service examinations—irrespective of their family background. To succeed in these examinations, a thorough grounding in the Classics was essential; hence the emphasis on education almost since time immemorial.

Although Hong Kong's traditions are material rather than intellectual, Hong Kong businessmen have always sent their children to the most prestigious schools and universities they could afford. Until recently, when other considerations began to intervene, family ambitions were for able sons and daughters to attend the University of Hong Kong in their undergraduate years, to build up a network of acquaintances useful in later life.

Gradually, they were sent to universities in the United Kingdom instead. As Hong Kong became more international, students headed for Australia, Canada and the United States. There is no indication whether this trend relates to aspirations for future residence. American degrees are increasingly popular with Hong Kong employers, especially when granted by institutions with snob appeal.

Records kept by the Institute of International Education in New York City show that during the early 1960s, fewer than 800 students from Hong Kong were studying in American colleges and universities; in the 1964–1965 academic year, 3,279 Hong Kong students were registered. The numbers increased steadily until there were 11,230 Hong Kong students overseas in academic year 1989–1990, 12,603 in 1990–1991 and 13,190 in 1991–1992. The 2001 government statistics give the number of Hong Kong students in the United States alone as 5,826. In the same year, there were 6,498 Hong Kong students in Australia, and 2,301 in Canada. (In 1996, there were 2,506 in the United Kingdom.) The numbers do not include students who enter these countries on immigrant visas.

Although Hong Kong now has seven universities and three other tertiary institutions that grant degrees and diplomas, including some which bestow professional and higher degrees, several factors may maintain the upward trend in foreign university study. First, the old instinct for higher education is coupled with the new competitive paper chase. Second, the expanding middle class includes graduate parents of school leavers. Third, Hong Kong may become a channel to Western universities for its non-HKSAR Chinese residents.

TRADITIONS AND SUPERSTITIONS

The first immigrants to Hong Kong brought traditions, superstitions, religious beliefs and practices from their own cultures with them. As years passed, the dominant traditions were those originated in South China.

Some of the festive celebrations, such as the Lunar New Year and Christmas, have become a part of the Hong Kong heritage and are observed as public holidays. Others, like the Hindu Festival of Lights and the Jewish Rosh Hashanah, are celebrated by the particular communities but have not become a part of the general culture of Hong Kong.

FUNGSHUI

In Hong Kong, *fungshui* is taken seriously. Literally meaning 'wind and water', *fungshui* is perhaps the single most important Chinese concept that is universally embraced in Hong Kong. The English equivalent of this term is geomancy, a system of divination by means of figures or lines, but the English term is almost never used in Hong Kong. Here, *fungshui* is a household word that is understood by everyone regardless of age, gender or national root.

Origins of Fungshui

As a metaphysical system of prophecy, *fungshui* had its origin in the *Classic of Changes*, one of the five influential texts of antiquity. The title of this work is sometimes also rendered in English as the *Book of Divination*. Its date of compilation is a matter of scholarly debate, but the work is believed to have been compiled in stages at different times. With stalks of the common yarrow plant, diviners developed a system using eight sets of three rows of whole or broken lines, as a replacement for reading cracks on bones and tortoise shells in the practice of their craft. Later the stalks were replaced by lines drawn on paper and arranged to constitute an octagon. The eight sets of trigrams, each comprising all possible arrangements of three rows of whole or broken lines, are often represented in Asian art and will no doubt be familiar to you before long.

Fungshui masters, as practitioners are called, examine all aspects of a structure—be it a building for the living or a grave for the dead. If it is a new structure, *fungshui* considerations

Fungshui masters usually use a board displaying the eight trigrams as a tool to help them in determining fungshui.

range from selection of the site, orientation of the building, alignment of the doors and windows, to the placing of furniture. If a building already stands, then the *fungshui* examination will consider the best way to readjust the forces in order to re-establish the natural balance and suit the demands of the owner. Good *fungshui* as an essential ingredient for any success is understood by the Hong Kong population. It is no less important in siting a grave because, in addition to ensuring peaceful rest for those buried there, it will enable them to negotiate with the powers that be to grant their progeny wealth, longevity and male heirs. Whether for topping out a building or digging a grave, auspicious dates are selected by *fungshui*.

The task for the *fungshui* master is, by interpreting the combinations of these trigrams, to choose the best *fungshui* for the specific circumstances under consideration. The *Classic of Changes* provides clues to such interpretations; so, in today's parlance, it can be called a diviner's handbook, albeit with a great deal of mystical power attached. The handbook has a number of appendices which further elaborate the metaphysical significance of these interpretations. The appendices were thought at one time to be the work of Confucius, perhaps by way of adding respectability to the book; but his authorship has been made more than doubtful by modern scholarship.

The *Classic of Changes* also contains a discourse on the *yin* and the *yang*, two fundamental forces which govern the creation and the working of the universe. *Yin* is the passive, negative, gentler or female principle of the universe. *Yang* is the active, positive, aggressive or male principle. Combined, the *yin* and the *yang* created the universe and made it work.

During the third century before Christ, intermingled in Taoist thinking with the *yin* and the *yang*, the system of *fungshui* began to be used more widely in the search for a balance between all elements of nature. Since that time *fungshui* has been concerned more with the working of the universe than with its creation. *Fungshui* masters must come from a well-educated background because, in addition to the *Classic of Changes* and the writings of the Taoist masters—Lao Zi (Lao Tzu) and Zhuang Zi (Chuang Tzu)—they need to be familiar with the Chinese systems of astrology and cosmology. In Hong Kong, fees for *fungshui* masters are calculated by the square foot—as the purchase price or rent for the premises will be when they appear on the market.

Actually, the practical considerations inherent in *fungshui* principles are comprehensible even to the uninitiated. In choosing the location and appointment of buildings, for instance, *fungshui* calls for the best way to make use of a given site, with fresh air and the safety of the inhabitants as top priorities. When the New Territories were added to Hong Kong in 1898, the tradition of *fungshui* was so firmly rooted among the villagers that the British administration had to heed it where possible. Chinese residents under the British administration have likewise been pragmatic. When ancestral graves gave way to modernization programmes of new towns and expressways, it was the villagers who made the compromise by making adjustments to the *fungshui*.

During the centuries since *fungshui* was first absorbed into Taoist thinking, a great deal of superstition has crept in. Today *fungshui* practices appear to encompass a lot of hocus-pocus. The land of Hong Kong is supposed to be filled with dragons—auspicious omens.

Kowloon (literally nine dragons), is so named because it is the land of eight hills. Each hill is said to be inhabited by a dragon, so there were eight dragons. The ninth dragon was added to honour the presence of an emperor who was visiting Kowloon at that time.

On the Hong Kong side, Garden Road is the spine of a sprawling dragon that faces the sea. When the new Bank of China building was under construction in Garden Road, the Hong Kong Chinese were said to be displeased because the structure was reputed to be sitting on the dragon's head. It is understood that adjustments had to be made in Government House in order to compensate for the loss of good *fungshui* to Hong Kong.

Even if you do not believe any of the *fungshui* principles and 'do not want to have anything to do with this nonsense', please remember that the people around you will be taking it extremely seriously.

In Hong Kong good luck means prosperity: arrangements must be made to ensure the best *fungshui* for home and office premises, so that a business and its owner can prosper. The best *fungshui* location faces the water with a mountain behind, an ideal not always possible in an urban community. Hence, water is brought into the premises in the form of a fish tank. Fish also deflect evil. 'Money corners' have to be found in every room through the planting of auspicious greenery and placing of lucky objects. In fact, plants are not such a bad idea since they are decorative and they bring warmth to any room, or balcony for that matter. Regardless of size, Hong Kong balconies are filled with green plants which make otherwise bleak and dirty buildings quite attractive. Mirrors are hung to deflect any ill luck that might be lurking. It can never be just any mirror placed at random. In order not to cause further deterioration in the *fungshui*, it must be a round mirror encased in an octagonal frame of eight trigrams with the correct configuration, placed under the direction of a knowledgeable *fungshui* master.

Evil spirits can be kept out of the premises by placing a screen at the entrance. While metal grid gates at the entrances of Chinese homes and offices may be a deterrent to thieves, screens just inside the doors are there to keep out intruders from the non-human world. Hong Kong's crematorium at

Cape Collinson, meanwhile, contains a columbarium of 20,000 niches each with capacity for two sets of ashes. The columbarium is built as an octagon, with windows resembling the eight trigrams.

LUCKY SYMBOLS AND NUMBERS

In the Chinese language, many characters, as Chinese words are called, have the same sound. There are 26 letters in the English alphabet, but 214 radicals with which to compose the Chinese characters. For instance, *two*, *to* and *too* sound alike but each word has a different meaning, completely unrelated to its homonyms; similarly lesson and lessen. But homonyms in the Chinese language are more numerous than in English. Sometimes more than a score of characters can have the same sound; different tones, maybe, but the same sound. No less a personage than Professor Lu Bisong, retired head of the Beijing Languages Institute and Chairman of International Chinese Language Teaching Association, reports that the largest number of homonymous characters in the language is 61.

In Hong Kong, words, and numbers also, take on special significance when they sound like something auspicious. Whether or not one approves of such superstitions, it is the practice to take as much luck as you can. The word meaning 'bat', for instance, is pronounced *fu*, which is a homonym for 'good luck'—as in *fu* of '*fu* (good luck), *lu* (good luck in the sense of a career) and *shou* (long life)', the three classically dressed porcelain figures you see in every restaurant and shop in Hong Kong. Hence you find bats painted on dishes, woven into scarves, and everywhere else as well.

Chang shou (long life) is used to greet a living person, wishing her or him many years on this planet. *Yong shou* (eternal life), on the other hand, is a term used only for the dead who are already enjoying life somewhere else for eternity.

Yu (fish) is a homonym for plenty. Especially at the last meal before the Lunar New Year, fish is always served but, in theory at least, never consumed. This is to symbolise the plenty that is left over from year to year. So, if you are a guest at a Lunar New Year's Eve dinner at a restaurant, do not touch the fish unless your host puts it on your plate. Even then, watch to see whether he eats his portion first.

There are many more examples showing how luck is important in Hong Kong. The colour red, for instance, symbolises happiness; therefore red is a lucky colour. White is the colour of mourning. That is why for auspicious occasions, such as birthdays, weddings, and certainly the Lunar New Year, cash gifts are encased in red envelopes, never white.

Butterflies symbolize marital bliss; and mandarin ducks, which always come in pairs, symbolize conjugal happiness and fidelity. Avoid wearing a green hat under all circumstances: it denotes a cuckold. Never give time-pieces as presents since 'clock' in Chinese sounds the same as 'end', translated as 'death' and 'demise'. Oranges are always good gifts because their colour symbolizes gold, and the large number of pits (seeds) inside symbolizes many sons.

Despite dressing in Western-style clothing, many Hong Kong Chinese still follow their traditional superstitions and will often consult a fortune-teller (right) when making important decisions such as changing jobs.

When visiting a sick Shanghainese-speaking friend, do not bring apples. 'Apple' is a homonym for 'death from illness' in the Shanghainese dialect. Do not ever give a book to anyone who has investments or enjoys betting, and this means almost everybody in Hong Kong, for shu in Cantonese sounds like losing.

Besides their penchant for certain words, the Hong Kong Chinese are partial to particular numbers. The number eight is *fa* in Cantonese, and hence is venerated because it sounds just like 'amassing'. What is being amassed? Money, of course, need you ask? Eight is a lucky number, so are 88, double luck, 888, triple luck, and 8888, multiple luck. But this not the whole story. Nine in Cantonese sounds like 'sufficient', so it is also desirable. Any combination of eight and nine will automatically mean amassing money until you are full to the brim. The Hong Kong Government, fully cognizant of this notion, auctions off car licence plates bearing such numbers each time a new series is issued. The world's highest price for a motor car number plate, five million Hong Kong dollars, was paid for licence number eight at an auction. The number three, which sounds like 'life', is popular as well. The number four, considered the most lucky number along the Yangzi, sounds like 'death' in Cantonese; so it is to be avoided wherever possible.

GETTING READY FOR LIFE IN HONG KONG

At this point you may think that you have made a major mistake in deciding to move here. The complexity of the Hong Kong environment cannot be overemphasized. A result of historical development, this complexity can be seen as a foundation of strong Chinese values under the authority of a British administration, topped with a veneer of cosmopolitianism which comes from being a major centre of international business. Here we offer descriptions and pointers to cushion and guide you through the maze. In Hong Kong more than anywhere, we believe newcomers need such informative insights as a Culture Shock! absorber.

Before we undertake an extensive discussion of the values embedded in the Hong Kong ethos, a few comments about adjustment as a process should be made. We shall describe three phrases, and five stages of adjustment. While these phases and stages are not mutually exclusive, we shall discuss them separately.

THREE PHASES OF CHANGE

When you leave one situation to enter another, you must go through these three phases of the adjustment process. The first phrase is the ending of what has been your life, the second is the 'space' between; and the third is the beginning of your new life.

Probably you are going to work abroad for the first time. As you hand over your responsibilities to your successor, there is a great deal of stress, and perhaps relief. There are the physical activities of moving out of one residence, perhaps selling a house which you have made into a family home and in which you have accumulated objects—part junk, part things you love and part both. Your children need your understanding and support as they take leave of their schools and friends. Then there are the social activities at which your colleagues, neighbours, friends and relatives say farewell. After all that, you arrive in Hong Kong and are looking forward to what promises to be an excitingly new life. If you have done your homework, you know what to expect,

It is interesting to recognize that while people undergo the experience, as you are doing, they expend time and energy thinking about the first and third phases of their move; but they often neglect the transitional phase, or take it so much for granted that its passage is hardly noticed. Perhaps this is because the phase is only transitory, in the sense that it does not last very long. A person changing jobs in the West may be expected to take only the two-day weekend between leaving the old job on Friday and starting the new one on Monday.

Here in Hong Kong no distances are involved, and we work on Saturday mornings; so the period of transition between two jobs may well be as brief as a day and a half. How long a person really needs, to move from the old situation to the new, depends on the individual. If the transitional phase is ignored, the shock he might experience later could be severe in inverse proportion to the time taken to adjust. The period of transition can be likened to the split second when a trapeze artist lets go of one swing, executes a fancy turn, and hopes that the opther swing is in place for him to grasp. With thorough preparation and precision timing, the danger of an accident can be minimized.

In the days when people changed hemispheres by sea, one became an expatriate imperceptibly as the ship glided round the globe. If a move to Hong Kong implied a big transition, then the voyage gave ample time for this middle phase. In making it physically to go from old desk to new over the weekend. Hong Kong style, the aeroplane has much to answer for psychologically.

FIVE STAGES OF ADJUSTMENT

It is useful to overlay the five stages of adjustment to the new situation on those three phases, as we examine them. The stages are: honeymoon; not like home; different, but how?; learn about the differences; and accept them. You might think that all the adjustment belongs to the third phase—that learning is on the job. But awareness of the changes comes a lot more quickly than your emotional adjustment; though the speed of your practical grasp hides the slowness of your mind and heart. To put it technically, a dysfunction may result from these different phases of adjustment—leading to an 'after shock', unpleasant in itself and likely to slow your progress through the three later stages.

The first stage of adjustment often resembles a honeymoon where everything is new and exciting. Time is usually filled with busy activities related to getting ready for the new environment. There is so much that demands attention that you will hardly fine time to miss what you have left behind. You need to unpack, first of all, and get to your office to start the new job. There are new people to meet and new routines to learn. Or, if you are the spouse, you will need to glean practical information on living in Hong Kong; for instance, where you will shop for groceries, or where you can find an electrician. You will also have to make sure that the children are adjusting to their new school and are making friends.

Once new daily routines have been established and superficial adjustments have been made, feelings of missing the old and familiar will surface. One may resent ways in which Hong Kong is not 'just like home'. At this, the second stage, you may behave untypically; but complaining, becoming easily irritable, lacking energy, experiencing difficulties in focusing on what you should be doing, and so forth. Instead of enjoying what is available, you concentrate on what us not. The duration of this stage depends on the original state and balance of one's mental health. Nevertheless, no matter how severely this stage has affected you, there is no need to make matters worse by worrying. You shall overcome; if not on your own, then with the help of professional people in Hong Kong trained to resolve such difficulties.

The movement from the second to the third stage is signalled by signs of awareness of the differences between the two cultures. One's reaction now is often to reject the strange culture in overt anger. These second and third stages are critical to move through; progress towards stage four is the beginning of recovery.

Stage four starts when you decide to invest time and energy in learning about Hong Kong—and perhaps begin also to analyze the differences between here and where you were. Increasingly self-confidence makes a more tranquil mind. At this point, support and reinforcement are needed as you adjust to new behaviour patterns. It is very useful now to have a mentor—what anthropologists call a 'cultural guide'—to serve as a sounding board and validate some of your assumptions. You may do well to take the role of 'participative observer' at this point, when your involvement in activities is just enough to experience the surroundings while leaving you sufficiently detached to analyze the experience.

What you achieve in stage four is fundamental to reaching your goal; acceptance of and participation in the fascinating culture of Hong Kong. That is stage five; and we hope you get there. For you will then be glad of your chance to enjoy the opportunities and pleasures provided by this unique patch of territory and by the people who give it its character.

HONG KONG VALUES AND BELIEFS

The values and beliefs operating within Hong Kong's culture are often deceptive, as you will appreciate after reading the earlier chapters of this book. The external modernity often misleads newcomers into believing "Oh, it is just like such and such a country' which they already know. Many expatriates voice the conviction that they will have no trouble in feeling at home in Hong Kong. After all, it is not like Beijing or Tokyo; English is in use here. However, as interactions with the Hong Kong culture increase, they begin to feel that something is not quite right, though they seem unable to put a finger on the problem. The Hong Kong Chinese may appear modern and indeed almost Western to the newcomer, because they do indeed speak English, and because they are dressed in the height of international fashion; but it will not be long before you discover that much is not what it seems. We must describe and analyze for you the fundamental values at work in Hong Kong society.

The Concept of Reciprocity

Hong Kong, like many Asian societies, places more emphasis on the interests of the collective whole than on those of its individuals. In behaviourial terms, taking initiatives, being too outspoken or expressing personal opinions strongly, can be perceived as disturbing the harmony of the whole.

The concept of *face*, and of the networked-self—*maijiang* and *guanxi*—solidify the web of relationships. Maijiang, literally meaning the *selling of credit*, is used when a person gives or is given face and when reciprocity is implicitly understood and expected. For instance, if a person has done something for you in some way, you are expected to do something for him in return. It does not mean that you have to pay him in cash, nor does the return favour have to take place immediately, but the account must be settled one way or another at one time or another. *Guanxi*, literally meaning the *interconnected system*, or in current English-language jargon, *networking*, is the base upon which a person can judge whether the relationship between the asker and the giver is such that the one can ask without the other having to lose face himself by saying no. Rather, the Chinese do not say no; they just do not say anything when they mean no. In this process, the individual belonging to a certain circle invests time, effort and favour—and so accumulates credit over a long span, occasionally extending through generations.

The Cantonese expressions *yau sum* (having lots of heart) and *sikdjo* (understanding what needs to be done) are often used by the recipient as a form of recognition that a favour has been performed on his behalf. Either term can also be interpreted as a form of thanks or as an indication that the news would be spread throughout the grapevine. Norms of behaviour in these groups are set through unspoken rules and built-in reinforcement mechanisms, The players automatically comply with the rule, whether it concerns lunch on a certain day of the week, exchange of certain information, the handling of birthday and other celebrations in a certain manner, or the monetary value of gifts,. Today, in some instances, especially in gift giving, he process has been simplified to speed and reduce 'accounting' activities. As older generations pass from the scene, such relaxations are easier.

This accounting process still involves exact registrations somewhere, in invisible mental ledgers. It is important to note the value of the present given to your son when he was married so that you can give back the equivalent when the giver's son marries. If reciprocity is broken, it could be interpreted either as the person who breaks the chain feeling that these activities are a waster of time, or as perceiving himself to be superior to this particular accounting system. Of course, if you are a *qweilo* (a foreigner) you do not have to comply; but if you are of the Chinese tradition, you are expected to know and act accordingly. In some instances, these activities can be registered under the category of *li* (ceremonial precepts), a prescribed way of conduct that has been passed down since ancient times. Special holidays are the time to pay back favours you still have outstanding,

and to visit in person the people who are important in your circle of influence.

This giving of gifts, or calling on people, is a form of acknowledgement; it is significant in certain social groups, but it can be carried to ridiculous extremes. For example, some individuals go as far as to measure themselves and their self-worth in terms of how many mooncakes they receive from certain people during the Mid-Autumn Festival. Importance is attached to the standing of the givers of these mooncakes. In the Western tradition, it is important for the boss to buy Christmas or Hanukkah presents for his employees. Under the traditional system of gift giving in Hong Kong, it is the other way round: it is the employer, or the father figure, who must not fail to receive; and the gifts are judged according to their value. Since compliance at an appropriate level is in effect mechanical, it is definitely not the thought that counts.

Chinese Social Relationships

A precise hierarchy implicit in the five-fold cardinal relationships described by Confucius, the *wu lun*, provides the strong foundation of the Chinese social order. These five relationships are those between sovereign and subject, father and son, elder brother and younger brother, husband and wife, and between friend and friend.

It is important to note that there are in Hong Kong certain old families whose position has been established in society for at least three generations–by virtue of wealth ancestrally established. Since their achievements were commercial rather than scholarly, their standards have been taken from what they perceived to be Confucian traditions rather than any real understanding of the philosophy. This has led to a great deal of uncomprehending inflexibility.

Filial Piety

In Hong Kong's familial relations, *xiao* (filial piety), the way the children must behave towards the parents is—to use modern terminilogy—embedded within the collective consciousness. It makes no difference whether a person uses the latest laptop computer or has studied nuclear physics, the *xiao* programme for relating to his family will appear on the screen of his subconscious—and everyone will act accordingly. Filial piety is more than showing respect for the parents, grandparents and all in the family who are one's seniors; it involves care, as well as catering to their wishes and whims. Care, that is, in the sense of affectionate regard; and ultimately therefore in the sense of the succour. Conflicts arise when the wishes and whims of the elders are not accepted by the younger generation or—worse—when members of the younger generation become pawns in the elder's game of power play.

There is another side to the *xiao* which is often confusing and contradictory in modern life. The concept of the extended family in feudal and agrarian societies worked well. As the workforce becomes more mobile, and economies become more complex, some Chinese traditions have to change or perish— such as the son entering the father's business, large and frequent gatherings, and offspring living with and caring for aged parents.

The hectic pace of Hong Kong life is placing high stress on many of the upholders of these traditions. Emigration amongst the professional population in the last ten years has left upheavals in its wake. Often ageing parents are not willing to leave Hong Kong, or are prevented from following the younger generation by a host country's immigration restrictions.

Demand in Hong Kong for nursing homes and homes for the olf is increasing—whereas ten years ago it was unthinkable that Chinese sons and daughters would be putting their parents into an institution instead of caring for them at home. The general trend is painful for families to accept, and they are paying a price for this change.

Loyalty

Nevertheless, family loyalty and solidarity provide members with tremendous comfort and support. Whether it is to attain business objectives or to soothe feelings of personal discontent, family members generally rally round, regardless of rights and wrongs. Within the Hong Kong family structure, the adage 'blood is thicker than water' is to the point. The saying, 'keep the irrigation water within your own farmland' also depicts the idea of keeping the benefit within your own family. This idea is most clearly seen in marriage alliances that solidify various business connections; though the modern concept of marriage for love makes it harder for families to dictate conditions to their offspring.

The principle of loyalty also applies also to the sovereign. In modern times, when there is no personal sovereign, it is represented by patriotism, or loyalty to the nation. This principle, *zhong*, is difficult to assess under present conditions in Hong Kong. Loyalty to the state is a recent concept. Twelve years ago, advocacy of rights and privileges for Hong Kong people as citizens was hardly thought of.

Loyalty to the employer, on the other hand, is of long standing. The old system of a son succeeding the father in a secure job, flourishing a generation ago, is rarely followed now. The general impression given by the Hong Kong workforce today is of mobility. Emigration of professional and technical staff led to widespread local recruitment and promotion of their successors, which broke the tradition of 'a job for life'. Competition to hire the best available professional has accelerated careers of young skilled specialists. This process created a strong and often haphazard flux if development, turning young and inexperience professionals into executives. The shift of political loyalty away from London and towards Beijing is apparent among those who clearly pledge loyalty one way or the other, though fence-sitting is much in evidence.

HIERARCHICAL NATURE OF PERSONAL RELATIONSHIPS

Professional and social relationships in Hong Kong, like personal relationships, are vertical in nature. The order of a hierarchy of rank and authority is clearly reflected in rituals and manners. Simple examples include precedence for seating at dinner tables, or even who walks through a door first. The submissiveness of the Hong Kong people to those above them is well known. Therefore, insubordination would never be overt. Generally, when an underling disagrees with people in authority he expresses his dissent through discreet sabotage; never in open argument. This seeming acquiescence combined with back-stabbing, a mix of passive and aggressive behaviour, comes about through ingrained lack of the courage to speak out against the general custom and against particular authoritarian decisions of a father, boss, teacher or husband.

The Qing dynasty epic, *Dream of the Red Chamber*, and the twentieth century modern novel *Family*, read by Chinese school children despite prohibition by parents, give plenty if examples of surreptitious flouting of authority. These lessons reinforce the tradition that achievement is by stealth. Indeed, the novels make it extremely clear why the Chinese are such great politicians and strategists.

On less of an epic scale, you can see something of this at work. An employee will seem to accept an 'inappropriate' task, and not carry it out. This is something most readers will remember having practiced, and having had practiced against them. But note that they remember because in each case the step was exceptional, not habitual.

Establish Your Guanxi Before Dealing

It is never quite de rigueur to confront any issue head on. Rather, it is important for you, the newcomer in the community, to invest time in finding out the *guanxi* between people. If you want to meet someone then find a third party, who has established guanxi, to sow some seeds first. Be patient and wait for the appropriate time. This process, although slow, will ensure that all parties are ready to discuss the topic in question. The process might be described in Western social science technology as 'managing expectations'. Use of third party mediation is common in Hong Kong. It is important to find the right party in terms of rank and status to represent your cause. Do not forget the invisible account, maijiang, when guanxi is used for giving or gaining face. There is no set formula. The procedure resembles an art that can only be perfected with practice; but before you begin to practise, you need awareness of your objectives and the route by which they might be achieved.

Trust

Next there is the issue of *xinyong*, trust. 'To earn your rights' is probably one of those concepts that the Hong Kong ethos takes for granted. The work ethic applies, no matter who you are or who your father is. Sometimes you hear that if you do not work hard in Hong Kong, there must be something wrong. There is so much work to be done in so little time, how can you be lazy? This type of programming starts in nursery school. Hardworking people are often perceived as trustworthy, but hard work alone is not enough. The concept of xinyong in the Hong Kong context is not easy to define. It is essentially tied into past performance in that invisible record of accounts, and intertwined with the concept of face and relationships. Therefore, credentials are diligently striven for; material symbols of wealth are often ostentatiously displayed; names of people are dropped, and one is seen: at the right places and with the right people. These all become parts of the show—and unspoken commodities for trading in the unseen market, the pragmatic co-operation system. Grapevine gossip is the unofficial policing of these networks, that keeps in motion the approved version of the information flow. Criticism is easily earned, Support from the community depends greatly on the image that has been created in one's circle of influence. These right circles provide Hong Kong's basic safety net.

Some local Chinese outsiders, though they understand the system, belong to no circle. They may go to great lengths to create an external image of belonging. Unfortunately, these images do not fool many pairs of eyes; and the hierarchical nature of society ruthlessly slots an imposter into his category of 'out' rather than 'in'.

The Inner Circle

Are you now ready to take the next flight out of Hong Kong? Well, don't. Obviously your experience will not be directed along such harsh lines. You will no doubt steer clear of entanglement with Triads and with family clans. You should just know that there are two impenetrable systems; one wholly evil, and the other with values independent of good and evil. Few if any of your Chinese contacts will be connected with organized crime. Most will be lightly or heavily involved with the family system, and all of them will always know better than you how it works. By no means all will be as calculating as we have suggested. It helps to have seen the worse nevertheless.

This is one reason for the suggestions we offer at the end of this chapter: the idea that a local colleague or client could be (or seem) more Western than Eastern or, in another dimension, more traditional than modern. If you know what to look for, and note his conversational responses, you may be able to approach him tactfully and to your mutual advantage. This, in turn, should ease your adjustment and help you to become engaged with rather than confused by Hong Kong.

WILLINGNESS TO TAKE RISKS

Hong Kong is full of people who live from day to day, with a penchant for taking risks. There is enormous interest and participation in Chance, and enormous profits are made through it—whether the medium is horse racing, cards, mahjong, the stock market, commodity trading, the big commercial deal or the thrill of leaving negotiation and bargaining and agreement to the last moment: 'pushing the envelope' as the Americans say. Some player's aim to create ultra-high-pressure as part of the fun, stimulating the adrenaline flow. For others, the pressure is a by-product, hazardous to health. In either case, it may become a viscous circle of addiction.

The networks and circles of influence are at times divided according to interest groups, rather like an inner ring at auctions, with different rules for different games. The price for newcomers of learning the hard way can be costly. and all the more so if a foreign newcomer chances his arm. One rule of thumb is, never enter into a big game unless you have the support of a big player. The strength of the informal structure makes it possible for those who grew up in the ethos to stay in the game and out-psych the competition. Ultimately, the one with the most staying power is the one who is best placed to predict and manipulate the outcome.

It may be news to some that fortune-telling is based on number combinations and statistics. But it is intuition that makes one sooth-sayer, one gambler or one entrepreneur more successful than another.

Do not be frustrated if you do not get a precise answer to your questions at times. Think in terms of 'it could be looked at from this angle or that angle". Accept 'it could be this… or it could be that…" as an interim answer.

The discrepancies between the formal and informal institutions will be the hardest elements of the culture for you to assess and negotiate. The more intangible aspects of a society, belonging to the realm of mental programming, manifest themselves through stories and folklore, heroes and superstars, rituals and ceremonies. As in many cultures, the grapevine reinforces versions of stories to mould the unspoken virtues. The well-loved activity of eating around the table for hours is, in fact, an indoctrinating channel. Such activities are crucial for the programming of young minds. The patriarchs of the family will emphasize the current gossip and elucidate virtues and consequences. It is also a time for pledging loyalty to the clan, as there are inevitably factions within the system, so that expressions and intentions are made clear.

The distribution of power and authority manifests itself in Hong Kong's invisible bureaucracy as person-centred. That is to say, the informal structure of the culture will allow some back-door diplomacy Obviously the British administration has created a strong formal bureaucratic system; however, in many of the more Chinese structures, the ultimate decisions are still made by the few in power. In terms of the variety of organizations—whether it is a marriage, a family or business—the concept of delegation of power or responsibility is difficult to implement. The 'expert' in charge of a seminar or workshop understands that participants find more comfort in an authoritarian style than in a democratic atmosphere. Resistance will be strong if too many decisions are left to the members.

What about the willingness to take risks as against the ability to live with uncertainties? The balance on the tightrope is the ability to make a split-second decision whether the person taking the risk will feel that he will have to shoulder the blame if things go wrong. There is much avoidance of decisions when a person lower down the hierarchy feels that the only reward would be punishment if things go wrong. Adopting 'A' shaped shoulders, which means pushing the blame onto someone else, known as *lai* in Cantonese, is a practice the children pick up early at school. Another process is what is neatly called *verbal taichi*, a form of slow motion discussion which gracefully avoids responsibility without overtly saying so. Mastery of these skills is difficult for those that did not grow up here. However, spotting these practices in action is at worst entertaining, and at best enlightening. The duality—of money risk and procedural caution—is a continuous balancing act that tests and exercises the life skills of those who thrive in Hong Kong, and keeps them on their toes.

A MASCULINE AND COMPETITIVE SOCIETY

Hong Kong is very much a masculine society. One might

say that no elaboration is necessary, because of its strong patrilineal-descent structure. Traditionally, female infants are not valued as highly as male. However, the concept of masculinity in Hong Kong can be expanded. It incorporates the meaning of 'big is beautiful' 'more is better', 'loud is louder' and perhaps 'flashy is sexier'. These values seem to be diametrically oppose yo some of the basic Chinese values of frugality, harmony within the group, respect for elders, and soon. Yet the competition that characterizes Hong Kong has mothers pushing their young children to strive to be Number One in the class, and the young executive to be promoted before his peers; the impetus thus acquired and sustained prompts each industrialist to surge ahead of his rivals. These tendencies are the strength and foundation upon which the success of Hong Kong is based. The myths and stories of heroic entrepreneurs reinforce them. Yet the dynamic interactions between the basic Chinese values and these masculine traits must be confusing to the newcomer, if not also, to the Hong Kong people themselves.

But neither those characteristics nor their combination is altogether strange. Consider football and other less artificial forms of tribal conflict. Participants know the rules. They are loyal to the captain or submissive to the chief, helpful to team-mates or members of the clan, They direct their risk-taking and aggression outwards. In Hong Kong, as on the field of play, they may seem to be little scope for neutral behaviour towards people who are neither family/firm nor rivals/opponents. 'We' are Montagues and everyone else must be a Capulet. Perhaps that overstatement is the right note on which to end this description of what is unusual—but by no means out-of-this-world—about the Chinese people of Hong Kong.

CONCLUSION

You must find your own nook in Hong Kong. It is not a bad place once you succeed in penetrating the veneer, and can build your own network of friends, shops, and colleagues. After all, this is an urban community rather than a small village. It is as impersonal as large cities elsewhere. Once settled, however, you will find yourself fitting in—perhaps not exactly as if the place had been made for you—but comfortably, in your own niche.

We have described the systems of thought and behaviour that are deeply traditional and intensely Chinese. These two characteristics do not always go together. When they do, and when they are at their finest, the combination may be called Confucian. Alas, the good name of the Sage is tarnished by people who are carelessly (or carefully) dignify anything of this kind as Confucian.

As mentioned, both the better and the worse aspects of the Chinese way of dealing are being weakened by education abroad and international practices in Hong Kong. We have also implied that, at their worst, these Eastern family networks resemble some of the local deceptions and disloyalties as an extended form of what makes fiction, and even life, in the West interesting and difficult. There is nothing wholly new under the Eastern sun.

So, what of the colleague or client with whom you are now lunching? Does he (or she) say rather little, from what seems to be a closed—not to say inscrutable—mind? Or is your friend being enthusiastically and convincingly more British than the English, or more American than the Yanks? Do not be deceived; but do not suppose that either of these acts is pure deception. The quiet luncher will understand you and your mental processes more than you his. The performance if the voluble chap is both a compliment to you and a piece of self-indulgence. However little the influence of tradition on him, though, he will still be more Chinese-minded than Western.

As he enjoys his roast lamb and roast potatoes, ask him what he eats asst home. Ask him (or her) about celebrating Christmas, and the Lunar New Year. Enquire how he spends his annual holidays, and with how many companions. You will do this as a combination of social chat and sympathetic interest in his variant of the Hong Kong way of life. It may help you to assess the extent to which he is equally 'at home' in his two cultures. He meanwhile will be taking a view of where you stand on the traditionalist-progressive (or conservative-liberal or formal-bohemian) spectrum. That is a game we can all play. Everyone inclines to one or other of those two sides. So don't forget to adjust your first assessment of him when you have decided whether he is more, or less, old fashioned than you are.

FITTING INTO SOCIETY

CHAPTER 4

People will forget what you said.
People will forget what you did.
But People will never forget.
How you made them feel!
—Maya Angelou (b.1928)

HOW DO THE CHINESE SEE THEMSELVES?

Ethnic Chinese, whether in China, Hong Kong or overseas, seldom think of fellow Chinese in terms of being just Chinese: Cantonese, Sichuanese, Shanghainese, yes, but never Chinese as a category. Strictly speaking, not everyone whose forebears had come from various counties of the Guangdong province—Taishan or Chiuchow, for example— should be lumped together into a single category as Cantonese; but when we speak in English the word Cantonese usually denotes people from the Guangdong province as a whole. The Cantonese-speaking public of Hong Kong, meanwhile, tends to describe all who do not command perfect Cantonese as Shanghainese or, on rare occasions, Shandongese. However, this practice is diminishing as more Chinese who speak northern dialects move into Hong Kong, and as local Cantonese-speakers begin to distinguish one non-Cantonese dialect from another. Also, with the influx of Mainland immigrants and tourists, Putonghua has become a third language in Hong Kong.

Some non-Chinese who have lived in Hong Kong for a long time also catch on to this way of thinking. A Cantonese-speaking senior government official from Britain informed the woman seated to his right at a dinner party some time during the early 1980s that he was puzzled in trying to categorise her. She was 'not a Hong Kong Chinese, not of the Shanghai textiles group, nor a Taiwanese intellectual'. While the woman would much rather have been acknowledged as a unique Chinese individual in Hong Kong who did not play *mahjong*, she appreciated the fact that he had managed to synthesise the Chinese propensity to categorise people geographically with the Hong Kong tendency to put people in their socio-economic groupings. Being an individual standing or falling on one's own merits is too alien a concept for nearly all Chinese, a concept this Briton had absorbed through his long association with the locals.

THE NORTHERN COUSINS WITH DEGREES FROM NORTH AMERICA AND EUROPE

Increasingly, citizens of the People's Republic of China are living and working legally in Hong Kong. Almost eighty per cent of shares traded on the Hong Kong Stock Exchange are those of companies owned by mainland Chinese interests. No longer the *nouveaux pauvres* of the world, Chinese businessmen populate some of Hong Kong's most prestigious clubs, wielding knives and forks as if to the manner born; which in a sense they must have been, in order to enjoy the privilege of being assigned to jobs in Hong Kong. However, this is perhaps not a fair assessment of the *Northern Cousins* in Hong Kong—as they are called somewhat condescendingly by the local Chinese, because of their lack of sophistication and their inability to communicate in Cantonese. Until recently they tended to congregate in certain areas, such as Wanchai, Western and North Point, where the rents were more affordable and where they had acquired property, causing the areas to be nicknamed the *Liberated Zones* of Hong Kong. However, since then PRC people have moved into prestigious neighbourhoods and integrated—at least outwardly—into the community.

We must correct this dated under-assessment in another context also. Many young men and women from China, educated overseas with professional degrees and a full command of English, are working in international companies in Hong Kong. Today, mainland students populate Hong Kong's tertiary institutions at both undergraduate and postgraduate levels.

G

are taking advantage of life in Asia.
skills they have always wanted. One
ed a doctorate from the University
are working on master's degrees or
father takes his infant daughter to
week, while his wife works—actively
ent of the child-care and household
ps under similar circumstances this
h had he stayed in his own culture,
all foreign families overcome their
actorily.

s tend to stick together with other
ndeed they manage to meet each
dren find it easier because they see
lren's school mates. It is difficult to
local Chinese, as a rule, even when
hinese origin. It is also difficult for
ick up relationships they had before
y find old relationships parochial or

plugged into the local expat network, you will
as you go about your daily chores. An expat
at a warehouse shop.

In addition to residents, short-term visitors from the Mainland flock into Hong Kong. The numbers have risen vastly since the introduction of individual as distinct from group visas.

According to figures reported by the accounting firm Deloitte, Touche, and Tohamatsu, of the 21.8 million tourists visiting Hong Kong in 2004, 56 per cent were from the Mainland. It is interesting that while Hong Kong shoppers go to Shenzhen and other cities of China in search of copies (mostly handbags and watches),

Mainland tourists come to Hong Kong to buy the genuine articles as they become increasingly brand conscious. A tourist was heard to remark in Putonghua at Pacific Place to her mates: "Why do you want to waste time in this store? I do not see anything with a recognisable brand name!" In order to raise the image of snob appeal, shopping malls such as Pacific Place no longer welcome tenants with middle class appeal. Mark and Spencer's had been told that its lease would not be renewed.

EXPATRIATES

The term 'expatriate', or 'expat' for short, defined in the *Oxford English Dictionary* as one who lives outside his own country by choice, may sound better than 'foreigner'. An expat is understood here as a resident of Hong Kong whose native culture is not that of a Hong Kong Chinese.

How will the locals view you? Regardless of your nationality, you will be a foreigner; but, if you are ethnic Chinese, you will also be a Chinese no matter how many generations of your ancestors have lived abroad, and no matter how you think of yourself. After all, China has been the centre of the world for a long, long time; so any non-Chinese in China is known as a 'foreigner', an ocean person (a person from across the ocean) or an ocean ghost (a ghost from across the ocean). Please note here that the term 'ghost' is not a compliment, for ghosts roam around in the underworld hungry and cold without a home; while the 'spirit' is one with a home, and enjoys sacrifices from his living descendants.

In addition to residents, short-term visitors from the Mainland flock into Hong Kong. The numbers have risen vastly since the introduction of individual as distinct from group visas.

According to figures reported by the accounting firm Deloitte, Touche, and Tohamatsu, of the 21.8 million tourists visiting Hong Kong in 2004, 56 per cent were from the Mainland. It is interesting that while Hong Kong shoppers go to Shenzhen and other cities of China in search of copies (mostly handbags and watches),

Mainland tourists come to Hong Kong to buy the genuine articles as they become increasingly brand conscious. A tourist was heard to remark in Putonghua at Pacific Place to her mates: "Why do you want to waste time in this store? I do not see anything with a recognisable brand name!" In order to raise the image of snob appeal, shopping malls such as Pacific Place no longer welcome tenants with middle class appeal. Mark and Spencer's had been told that its lease would not be renewed.

EXPATRIATES

The term 'expatriate', or 'expat' for short, defined in the *Oxford English Dictionary* as one who lives outside his own country by choice, may sound better than 'foreigner'. An expat is understood here as a resident of Hong Kong whose native culture is not that of a Hong Kong Chinese.

How will the locals view you? Regardless of your nationality, you will be a foreigner; but, if you are ethnic Chinese, you will also be a Chinese no matter how many generations of your ancestors have lived abroad, and no matter how you think of yourself. After all, China has been the centre of the world for a long, long time; so any non-Chinese in China is known as a 'foreigner', an ocean person (a person from across the ocean) or an ocean ghost (a ghost from across the ocean). Please note here that the term 'ghost' is not a compliment, for ghosts roam around in the underworld hungry and cold without a home; while the 'spirit' is one with a home, and enjoys sacrifices from his living descendants.

'Ghosts'

Thus, more informally, if you are Caucasian in appearance, you will be referred as a *gweilo* (a male devil or ghost) or as a *gweipo* (a female ghost) or *gweilzai* (boy ghost) or *gwenui* (girl ghost)—depending on your gender and seniority. Similarly, if you are African in appearance, you will be a *hagwei* (black ghost), and so on.

These terms when used in Hong Kong, however, are not necessarily derogatory. It has become a custom to think of ethnic non-Chinese in our midst in such terms. As a matter of fact, they can even be considered friendly salutations, used to show a sense of familiarity—when the Chinese are usually far less personal. This does not mean that you need to express gratitude and pleasure for this dubious distinction. Increasingly, expats in Hong Kong resent being called 'devils' or 'ghosts'. Perhaps they feel less secure than their predecessor.

As long as the local population does not live in close proximity with the expats, dealing with each other only in the office, so to speak, relationships will remain cordial. There is a language gap; so, when there are failures in communication, a feeling of resentment on both sides may be intensified. (If both sides think about it, though, they should realise that such failures are mainly linguistic but partly cultural; since they are not caused by hostility, they should not lead to hostility.) Alas few expatriates have managed to learn Cantonese, principally because the language is not easy to master but also because they have no use for it elsewhere. When they complain about the English language capability of a local individual, their attitude can be interpreted as condescending and is resented by the local. Now and then, letters appear in *Letters to the Editor* columns from expatriate residents about behaviour by the local population. Some of the complaints show the local offenders to be rude; others are funny, but, even the humour of the situation does not mitigate the embarrassment and hurt felt by the expat victims. So far, skirmishes have been minor. The local population, on the whole, has contained its resentment. As long as each side is willing to remain polite, clashes are avoidable, especially when you can keep in mind that even in your own culture, there are good and bad days for everybody.

Now that not all employers in Hong Kong are giving their expat employees fat packages, an increasing number of expats are living along side local Hong Kong Chinese. More often than not, the people involved here are young and single, and their egos are not boosted just because they receive financial support to enable them to live a life-style way beyond their local neighbours, and in many cases way beyond what they had at home.

THE EXPAT SPOUSE

In recent years, a spate of young and single expatriats described at the end of the last paragraph has poured out of universities or business schools to seek employment in Hong Kong. Most expats, however, are experienced executives and professionals, and many are sent by international companies. Few have left their families behind. There is intense pressure on them to produce profits, if for no other reason than to cover their salaries and overheads. The rule of thumb is: the higher the package, the harder the expatriate is expected to work. Often there is a great deal of regional travel. While it may be beneficial to accrue frequent-fly mileage, the hectic schedule can be costly in physical and emotional terms. Bebe Chu, now a judge who used to be a solicitor specialising in family law, reveals that temptations here are tremendous. It takes a special man or woman, and a very strong marriage, to survive Hong Kong.

There are more expat wives than husbands of expats. The latter species is increasing though. For instance, eight of the eleven spouses who attended a gathering of Heads of Mission representing the Swedish Government in this region, were male. For spouses of expatriate executives whose employments terms give them luxuries not always available at home, such a s domestic servants, club membership, prestigious addresses, private schools, annual paid home leave—which translates into international travel, or even spedable cash—life should be comfortable indeed. Most expatriate spouses adjust well to Hong Kong, many in inimitable style, and are taking advantage of life in Asia. Many women acquire skills they have always wanted. One woman we know gained a doctorate from the University of Hong Kong. Others are working on master's degrees or learning Chinese. One father takes his infant daughter to the office three days a week, while his wife works—actively shouldering fifty per cent of the child-care and household responsibilities. Perhaps under similar circumstances this man would do as much had he stayed in his own culture, but unfortunately not all foreign families overcome their cultural shock so satisfactorily.

Newly arrived wives tend to stick together with other expatriate wives, if indeed they manage to meet each other. Those with children find it easier because they see mothers of their children's school mates. It is difficult to make friends with the local Chinese, as a rule, even when the expat wife is of Chinese origin. It is also difficult for returned Chinese to pick up relationships they had before they left. Or they may find old relationships parochial or

As a foreigner, once you are plugged into the local expat network, you will find that life becomes easier as you go about your daily chores. An expat family buying their essentials at a warehouse shop.

stifling. To overcome isolation and cultural shock, you must patiently take advantage of all opportunities, to widen your circle of acquaintance.

Whether you have returned or are a newcomer, there are programmes designed to help you get to know the Hong Kong of today. The English-speaking Department of the YWCA in Macdonnel Road, the American Women's Association, and the various University faculties of Continuing Studies offer day-time lectures, tours and how-to programmes introducing you to the Hong Kong culture, and helping you acquire skills you may always have wanted but have not been able to try—accounting, Zen Buddhism, or shadow-boxing. At the very least, you will get to meet other people, whether they are newly arrived or have been long in residence. With luck, they will enrich your sojourn with physical, social and intellectual activities.

For more serious problems there are guidance and counselling services. According to Jane Rice, a counsellor on chemical abuse who has lived here so long that she considers herself a Hong Kong person, there is no need to feel despair. You are not alone, as a majority of expatriate spouses have difficulty in adjusting to life in Hong Kong, at least during their first few months, or immediately after the exciting first stage of moving into new homes. Wives are deprived of the supporting network they enjoyed before coming to Hong Kong, while the working spouses are too preoccupied with their jobs to pay attention to domestic difficulties. The Community Advice Bureau can point the way to guidance and counselling services, such as the one at St. John's Cathedral.

THE INDIVIDUAL WITHOUT A LABEL

It is difficult to find a person in Hong Kong without a label. It is also difficult, although not impossible, for a person who arrives without a specific affiliation to find a place for her or himself, even if Immigration allows you entry. It took a young man from Taiwan with extremely distinguished parentage—educated in the most prestigious American schools and universities, fully competent in English and

Putonghua—almost half a year to land a job (but it was a wonderful job that fully employed his talents, training, and connections).

In Hong Kong, you are introduced as the son or son-in-law of *Da Laoban* (Big Boss/Owner) or a grandson of *Lao Taiye* (Old Master); or, as an expatriate with no local relatives, you will be introduced as Charles Berendsen, the Managing Director of such and such company, or as Stephen Garvin, a rising young star of the Hushuo Badao Company. It would be strange indeed if you were introduced as plain John or Joan Robinson. Try to establish yourself as an individual is not the thing to do in Hong Kong. Your label is your legitimacy.

THE WORKING WIFE AND THE FILIPINA MAID

It is not our intention to tie the working wife to the Filipina maid concept. However, these English-speaking imported domestics, many of whom are educated working wives and mothers who have left their families behind, certainly have made it possible for many Hong Kong wives and mothers to hold jobs outside the home.

Unless you are a professional, especially in finance or related services, and are bi-lingual in English and Chinese, it is difficult to find a job here. Twenty years ago, your fluent command of English would have been an asset, but now you will be competing with young bi-lingual women with local knowledge and technical skills. Furthermore, Hong Kong is still a man's world. Few successful women have made it on their own. Behind almost every conspicuously successful women, especially business women, in Hong Kong—and fewer than a score can be placed in this category—you will find the financial resources of her father or husband. However, successful professional women are increasing in number. None of this means that you will not be able to find a job in your profession. As a newcomer, how would people know your talents are available unless you shout them from the roof top? Seriously, this is where your networking can come in handy.

The Immigration Department reveals that there are more citizens of the Philippines in Hong Kong than of any other nation. An overwhelming majority of them are here as domestic workers. Whether they are called domestic servants, housekeepers, governesses, nursemaids, household helpers, domestic helpers, maids or amahs, their presence has made it possible for the expatriate wife to enjoy activities outside her home. The disadvantage is that few of these maids speak Cantonese. The advantages are many. The Hong Kong Government's regulations on imported domestic help are clear and exact. They protect employers and employees alike, although from time to time either side may find these regulations a hindrance rather than a half. Recently, however, the introduction of a monthly four hundred dollars contribution to the Government by each domestic help more than boggles the mind.

THE MASSES OF HONG KONG

Although a handful of Hong Kong names are listed among the world's wealthiest in *Fortune* and *Forbes*, more than half of the masses live in public housing estates. They work hard and live frugally; they are not a part of the luxurious Hong Kong lifestyle. The overall population density was 6,039 per square kilometre in 2001 (15,770 per sq. mile), ranging between 50,086 per sq. km (15,770 per sq. mile) in the metropolitan area and 1,146 in the less congested communities.

Hong Kong's Gross National Product in the fourth quarter of 2004 was reported at HK$345.3 billion (US$44.67 billion) at current market prices, according to Government figures. Government statistics for 2001 show that the overall daily wage was HK$346 for craftsmen and operatives. They also show that wage increases had lagged behind the rate of inflation. To cover expenses, more than one member of a family needs to work, usually the father, and daughters when they reach the age of fifteen. Certain fathers work at two jobs, and for many of these the second is driving the evening-night shift of taxicabs. In theory women receive the same wages as men, but families still educate sons beyond the school-leaving age of fifteen and put their daughters to work.

There is no minimum wage, except for foreign domestic workers. In a move said to be 'necessary to weather

Hong Kong's economic recession at that time (2002)', the Governmentrequired each domestic worker to pay $400 per month from her salary. In fact, this requirement cuts the domestic worker's pay by four hundred dollars. Not trusting either the worker or her employer, the Government takes the total amount (24 months x $800) from the employer at the time of the signing or renewing of the contract.

A fruit-seller along Macdonnell Road: a human-scale market in a residential street.

As an expatriate, you will encounter the Hong Kong masses daily even if you do not live in a public housing estate or travel by public transport. The masses deliver your newspapers and letters, cut your hair, sell you fruits and flowers, ride the lifts in your building, and work in your office.

THE 'MIDDLE CLASS'

Until the 1980s, it could be said truly that the people of Hong Kong were divided into those who had and those who had not, with all the economic and social implications of those terms. Then public and private sectors began to hire local Chinese for professional and management jobs. For the first time, locally hired employees in private companies, and civil servants—as distinct from those recruited overseas—are able to rise beyond middle echelon jobs. An increasing number of local Chinese enjoy sufficient income to buy their own homes, send their children to fee-charging schools, run cars, and take holidays abroad. Second salaries enable families to enjoy the services of imported domestics, and the domestics allow mothers to earn the extra salary outside the home to free themselves from the drudgery of house-keeping. It is this group—hard pressed, but more 'have' than 'have not'—that demands greater political participation in public affairs. It is also this group that voices its insistence on a continuing Hong Kong identity.

SOCIALISING

With an open mind and persistent disposition, you will find yourselves socialising with the locals, perhaps at first only with your colleagues. Fitting into the local society is another matter. It is more a state of a mind, for Hong Kong is a heterogeneous society. Read on and see whether you are fitting in already by just being yourself. Immigrants to Hong Kong brought traditions, superstitions, religious beliefs and practices from their own cultures with them. Some of the festive celebrations, such as the Lunar New Year and Christmas, have become a part of the Hong Kong heritage and are observed as public holidays. Others, like the Hindu Festival of Lights and the Jewish Rosh Hashanah, are celebrated by the particular communities but have not become a part of the general culture of Hong Kong.

INVITATIONS FROM THE LOCALS

Chances for you to be invited to local homes are not many. If at all, you will be invited to dine in restaurants or clubs, and to weddings. Festivals are family affairs. You will be invited to weddings of your colleagues and their relations, however. Hence it is helpful for you to understand what these affairs, and your presence at them, will mean to the locals.

HONG KONG WEDDINGS

Hong Kong marriages may be made in heaven, but weddings are definitely earthly affairs. Not every couple's dates and times of birth are vetted by fortune-tellers nowadays, but the astrological calendar is still consulted for an auspicious date. The wedding itself is not a religious rite, but there is a ritual to the occasion. Most weddings take place in the Marriage Registry, to which you would not expect to be invited. However, you will be invited to the wedding banquet of every one of your colleagues who ties the knot during your time here, and very likely to those of their relations as well. These banquets are neither intimate nor exclusive affairs. The larger the banquet, the more face the bride and groom, or their parents, will garner. Literally hundreds of people are invited. Unless you are out of town, you must accept the invitation and attend the banquet. There will be very few Westerners present, but you will be seated with people you know.

There is no such thing as not being able to afford to put on a wedding banquet. Everyone brings a cash gift—in a red packet, of course—or you can buy a redeemable gift certificate from a bank, which the bridal couple can exchange for cash. The amount depends on your connection with the bridal couple, but should certainly not be less than what a good meal would cost for two people. Always give an even number of notes as well as dollar amounts—two hundred, six hundred, one thousand, two thousand; never an odd number—three hundred, five hundred, or nine hundred. In theory, it is the parents of the groom who foot the bill because they are the hosts of this feast celebrating their acquisition of a daughter-in-law, the mother of their future grandsons. In fact, depending on the financial circumstances of the families, the cash gifts help. Modern brides from families with no financial constraint have taken to registering their 'wedding lists' at local shops, but nobody objects to cash.

The wedding banquet takes place in a large, and therefore noisy, restaurant. There will be a photographer, who takes pictures of everybody posing with the bride and the groom, and as many candid shots as they can muster. Since everybody will be playing mahjong or card games, including the people from your office, you will not want to arrive early. This will be an extremely noisy gathering, because it is a good time to have friends and colleagues together in a relaxed non-office atmosphere. Everybody is supposed to be having a good time, and having a good time means making

A Chinese wedding is a gaudy occassion and the banquet hall is likely to be decorated with lots of red and gold. The stylised character on the wall stands for double happiness.

a lot of noise. While it is rude to bring your needlework or your laptop computer to while away the three or four hours before dinner is served, it is not impolite to time your arrival to the start of dinner.

At the banquet table you will see a bottle of brandy, and perhaps a bottle of Scotch whisky, and sweet soda pop in tins. At Hong Kong wedding banquets wine, especially champagne, seems to be reserved for the bridal table. While food is being consumed, the bride will change her clothes twice—from the rented Western-style wedding gown, to a traditional Chinese-style bridal gown, to a Western-style evening dress, perhaps also rented for the day. The bride and the groom will go from table to table to toast their guests. As soon as dessert is served, which normally consists of Chinese sweet cakes and oranges—symbolising many sons because, until the advent of Sunkist, oranges contained many seeds—the bride and the groom, with his parents, will be standing at the restaurant door to wish you a good night. There is no need to linger after the feast is finished.

Should the celebration be modern as distinct from traditional, a cocktail reception is held in a hotel or a club. If the marriage is between a Chinese and a non-Chinese, the scene is strangely revealing. You will see the Chinese guests attacking the food, while the Westerners home in on the booze.

A part of the wedding ceremony you will not be invited to witness, is when the new bride serves tea to all the senior members of the husband's family—that is, any one who is older than her husband. Relatives are served in rigid order of seniority; this order also determines the amount a person will give to the new bride as *laisee*, or lucky money. Junior members are to give a smaller *laisee* than the senior members so as not to be perceived to outshine the seniors. This social etiquette is clearly defined for other occasions as well.

HONG KONG FUNERALS
Funerals are important occasions in Hong Kong, as well. They are usually held in one of the two large funeral emporia, one on Hong Kong Island and the other in Kowloon.

However, despite the sometimes overlong wait for space to become available, even Christian services are seldom held in church.

A grand send-off gives tremendous face to the deceased and the family. You attend the service to pay your respects to a friend or a colleague, and you assume that everybody else is there for the same reason. However this, like other Hong Kong occasions, can be used by people to show other people that they and the departed were on intimate terms; but only if the departed was a person of social significance. The size of the attendance at a funeral is in direct proportion to the wealth and fame of the deceased, or of his sons. The placement of the wreaths, and the names of their donors, prominently shown for all to see, make interesting reading while you wait for the ritual to begin.

There is a set of rules for funeral services. Send a floral tribute ahead of time, although the practice of donating to charities instead of squandering on wreaths is beginning to catch on in Hong Kong. Ask your Chinese friends and colleagues whether you should opt for the latter. If they say nothing, send flowers. Wear dark clothing, preferably black, to the service. Do not worry about what to do once you get there. There will be professional funeral directors to give you specific instructions in English. Be prepared, however, to walk towards the deceased at the end of the hall and bow to the photograph of the deceased. The casket will not be wheeled in until the service has begun. It will be open. At some time during the service, the mourners are expected to walk round the casket to say farewell to the deceased. You can seat yourself away from the centre of the hall if you do not wish to circumnavigate the coffin.

You will be given a small white envelope which will contain a coin and a piece of sweet. The coin is a symbolic gesture to help defray the cost of your transportation to the funeral. The sweet is to help lessen your sadness. Sometimes there is also a white washcloth or handkerchief to help wipe away your tears. You can eat the sweet as you leave the service and spend the coin on your parking, or give it to the taxi driver. Do whatever you wish with the washcloth or the handkerchief.

There is no etiquette governing its disposal. Remember: funerals always start on time because the funeral operators must adhere to a strict timetable. there is no parking near both funeral homes. When in doubt, take public transport.

Christian funerals are like similar services that you know at home. Buddhist or Taoist services, on the other hand, are interesting to an outside observer. Eulogies and other laudatory remarks are not a part of the Buddhist or Taoist funeral rite because they concern the worldly achievements of the deceased, which are not important after he is dead. The presence of monks at a Buddhist funeral, and the rites that comprise chanting of *sutras*, burning of incense, and recitation of prayers, are to aid the transmigration of his soul. Your presence is sufficient to comfort the bereaved family. Unless you know the family well, there is no need to say anything to them at all. A simple bow will suffice.

The Chinese do not go home directly after a funeral, lest they are followed by the ghosts who linger around such a ceremony. So, they go somewhere, anywhere, as long as it is not home.

ALTERNATIVE LIFESTYLES

Homosexuality is no longer against the laws of Hong Kong. However, Hong Kong society is still fairly conservative and the sight of two men holding hands or kissing intimately in the street are still frowned upon and likely to attract stares.

There are a number of bars, restaurants and other facilities that cater to the gay community. These establishments can often be indentified by the rainbow flag or sticker placed in the window or at the entrance doorway.

The best way to find out what's happening in the local gay scene is to go online. One website address to try is http://sqzm14.ust.hk/hkgay. The links are extensive and a myriad of resources are available. They include everything from venues and counselling services to chat rooms and bulletin boards to events calendar and personal advertisements.

The other alternative is to ask a local gay friend to orientate you into the local (gay) scene in Hong Kong. Once you know your way, its easier to find like-minded individuals. But remember, be responsible and play safe.

CONCLUSION

The prevailing cultural traditions, superstitions and religions that you will see here are mostly derived from the Chinese and the British. The chances are that you will not find all of these celebrations completely strange; and, through understanding the background of each tradition, superstition or religious practice a little better, you will find yourself participating in Hong Kong ceremonies with sensitivity—and enjoying colleagues' celebrations with gusto.

SETTLING IN

CHAPTER 5

Mid pleasures and palaces though we may roam,
Be it ever so humble, there is no place like home.
—John Howard Payne (1792–1852)

MANY FACTORS HAVE MADE IT POSSIBLE for Hong Kong to enjoy its international position today. In addition to the presence of capital, labour, ingenious and daring entrepreneurship, and a political climate that supports laissez-faire capitalism, Hong Kong boasts a strong infrastructure, including highly efficient communication and transport systems which give instant access and rapid movement to all corners of the world. Freedom of the press, a printing industry and a large reading public maintain a copious flow of information. Here's what you need to know in order to settle in.

FINDING A PLACE TO LIVE

The first thing to do is to find a place to live. As you approach the housing agent, do bear in mind that few families live in houses and most people stay in apartments, small apartments. Compared to what you have back home, the apartments are likely to be really tiny unless you have a generous housing allowance.

Determine how much you want to spend on housing then make a list of your requirements for the agent. Do note that there is no preferred place to live. While many people choose to live on Hong Kong Island itself, the rentals here are the highest. Others prefer to live on the outer islands and commute to their office in Central by ferry, claiming a better quality of life. In general, just bear in mind that you will be able to get more space for the same price if you are agreeable to live further afield in Kowloon or the New Territories. Factors that affect your choice include where your office is, where your spouse's office is (if he or she works) and most importantly, do you have children of school-going age.

When checking the property ads, do bear in mind that the areas quoted are not the actual floor area you will get. In Hong Kong, the areas quoted include thickness of walls, window ledges and even parts of the lift lobby outside your apartment. What you should ask is what is the amount of usuable area. There can be a drastic difference.

Furnished or Unfurnished?

A furnished apartment will cost more but you are saved the hassle of furnishing it. Moving to a whole new enviroment, the last thing you want is to have to cope with buying furniture. If not everything provided by the landlord is to your liking, you can always negotiate with the agent. Try and ask for a separate dryer or an additional aircon unit for the study. Likewise, if you hate the colour of the walls, ask for a new paint job in the colour of your choice. Ensure that any of the landlord's furniture that you do not wish to accept is removed before you take over the apartment. With space at a premium, every bit counts.

If you prefer to go the unfurnished route, do remember that you will have to settle for a smaller space than what you have back home. That said, you have to consider carefully whether your existing furniture will fit into your new home and whether it is practical to ship the king-size bed over. More importantly, do remember that the contents of an average size house in the United States will not fit into a Hong Kong three-bedroom apartment, even if you have a large apartment. Be selective about what you bring and you will find that you can actually get by with a lot less than you imagined. For electrical appliances, check that your existing ones are dual voltage or you may need to get a transformer if you decide to bring them.

If you like home decorating, then opt for an unfurnished apartment. Go explore the home decor shops but do bear in mind what is permitted under the tenancy agreement.

Almost everyone in Hong Kong lives in an apartment. Although some apartment blocks offer splendid views, the trade off is that you will have to settle for less space than what you are used to.

Briefing the Agent

Give a list of your requirements to the agent and do indicate what can be compromised as the perfect home does not exist. Are onsite facilities important to you? If you are a fitness buff, then a condominium apartment with swimming pool and gym may be a good choice. Rather than traipse all over Hong Kong, ask to see photographs first then make a shortlist of places to visit.

When negotiating the lease, do check that the 'rates are included'. Otherwise, this means that you will have to foot the property tax. Do also check if there are monthly maintenance fees for your apartment and if these are included in the lease agreement. The security guards or even the doorman in your building have a cost and you want to avoid any unpleasant surprises.

Engaging a Domestic Helper (Maid)

One of the perks of coming to Hong Kong is the affordability of full-time domestic help. Many families engage a helper from the Philippines or Indonesia through an agency. The Filippina helper costs more but is usually able to speak English. Although any agency will be able to provide a selection for you to choose from, you may want to get recommendations from friends as not all agencies are equal and train the fresh girls in basic housekeeping skills.

While having someone do the housework and cooking is good, you will definitely have to sacrifice some privacy. Home is already smaller than what you are used to and a stranger underfoot 24 hours a day takes some adjustment.

Deciding what is the key role of your domestic helper will help in the selection process. Is she to care for the baby, focus on housework or assist in your elaborate parties? You can then match your requirements with her skill set and compromise on what is less important. Do you want a single girl or a married woman? Fresh candidates will need a lot of training but an experienced helper may have bad habits. Run through the files or videos provided by the agent and make a shortlist. Do take the time to interview the candidates carefully as she will be a part of your lives for the next two

Sunday is an off-day for most domestic helpers. In Hong Kong, they often gather at Statue Square to catch up with friends.

years. If there is any doubt, then she's not the right one for you. As always, trust your instincts.

When the helper arrives, take time to explain your lifestyle and your expectations. Explain exactly what needs to be done and how often. Draw up a simple roster for her to manage her time. For instance, sheets have to be changed once a week and the windows cleaned once a month.

What to Bring

Personal Documentation
- Passport with three years' validity
- Valid driving license
- Birth certificates
- Marriage certificate, divorce decree or any custody documentation
- Medical and Dental records
- Academic and Professional qualifications

Personal Items
- Prescription medicines—most medications are readily sourced but give yourself sufficient quantity to find a doctor you like
- Shoes larger than woman's size 38 / men's size 44 or clothing larger than woman's size 44 / men's size 52 are in limited supply, although there are a number of excellent dressmakers/tailors and shoemakers; the same applies to hosiery and under garments
- Your favorite drugstore personal care items—the same or equivalent may be sold in Hong Kong, but bring one or two bottles until you find them
- Self-tanning lotions—Hong Kong prefers whitening to looking tan
- Any special food a special diet requires
- Electronics, only if they are dual-voltage—take note that televisions in Hong Kong use a different colour system (PAL) from the USA (NTSC)

Even with an experienced helper, do explain how to operate your appliances—walk her through step by step on how to use the blender or mixer. Explain why you need to separate the whites from the colours when washing and how to tell what need to be hand-washed or dry-cleaned. You want to avoid any unncessary accidents or unpleasant incidents.

Foodwise, do show her how to cook or prepare dishes according to your family's tastebuds. She comes from a different cultural background and the references are obviously different.

When communicating with your domestic helper, the most important thing to bear in mind is clarity. Do give precise instructions. It's the vague instructions that lead to misunderstandings. While you trust her, you will need to be scruplous about minor things. Keep track of petty cash and get receipts if you send her out shopping. Do also be clear about working hours and free time. Although she may live with you 24 hours, she is not at your beck and call 24 hours a day. Determine what are the working hours, rest hours and tasks to be done.

Most importantly, remember that she is also human and a stranger adapting to a new land and living environment. While you have your spouse or family for emotional support, she is here all alone and likely to miss her family.

THE HONG KONG SCHOOLS

There is compulsory education in Hong Kong until the age of fifteen. All Government primary schools teach in Cantonese, with English as a subject. Recent Government policy permits some secondary schools to teach in English. Others must teach in Cantonese. The language issue is a serious one in Hong Kong as the command of English is seen as a necessary tool to employment in this international city, but language skills have deteriorated in recent years. English-speaking children are educated from primary to 'A' Level at the English Schools Foundation schools, where a modified UK curriculum is still followed, although a number of these schools, too, have adopted the International Baccalaureate programme in place of the traditional British A-level subjects. There are also a number of international schools, each using the curriculum of the country of origin—the French International School, the French schools curriculum, for instance; and the Hong Kong International School, the American curriculum. The French International School teaches in French and the German-Swiss International School teaches in German, but in each case there is also an English stream. Several international schools here follow the International Baccalaureate programme.

During the uncertain years of the 1980s many Hong Kong people emigrated to other parts of the English-speaking world. After a few years, the return of earlier emigrants with their school-age children led to the growth of the international school system in Hong Kong. When children have been away for two or more years, it is difficult if not impossible for them to return to the local school system, especially since they will have studied no Chinese while abroad. The system cannot accommodate students who weave in and out at different stages. However, some parents are unwilling for their children to give up Chinese completely. As a result, new schools have emerged to serve families who want their children to learn both English and Chinese. The Canadian Chamber of Commerce opened the Canadian International School and the Singapore Government opened the primary-level Singapore International School, which includes Mandarin as a subject. There is great demand for places at the Chinese International School, which in 1982 pioneered a curriculum in English and Mandarin; it requires students to study Chinese language, history and culture at all levels of the school.

TELECOMMUNICATIONS

The moderate monthly fee allowing the subscriber an unlimited number of local calls of any duration makes home telephones and fax machines commonplace in Hong Kong. Government statistics show 73 telephones and 38 fax lines for every hundred residents. When you count the number of instruments in your home and office, you may not feel that this ratio is impressive. However, the total number of telephones is 4.9 million, served by 3.9 million exchange lines. It is worth noting that the majority of the Hong Kong population is frugal, and usually there is not more than one telephone for each household.

At the other end of the scale, Hong Kong residents racked up 3.4 billion minutes of outward overseas calls in 2001. Through International Direct Dialing (IDD), you can reach more than two hundred countries, and to more than 1,000 cities in China, where people unable to obtain telephone lines are now available on mobile units.

Telephone rates are also much cheaper than before. Deregulation of the industry in 1995 helped consumers save an approximate total of US$2.5 billion in IDD calls. Today, ten years later, with several companies competing for your overseas call dollars, talking to your relatives and friends in your home country will cost you next to nothing. At this writing, talking to anyone in the United States during off hours on work days, and all through the weekends and public holidays, is a little more than a penny a minute.

Please remember, however, that there is still a difference of eight hours between Hong Kong and London, 13 hours between Hong Kong and New York, 16 hours between Hong Kong and the West Coast of North America, one hour the other way between Hong Kong and Tokyo, and two hours between Hong Kong and Sydney. Also watch for their Daylight Saving hours. As a result, your urge to speak to family and friends back home will need to be curbed considerably, lest they return the courtesy by ringing your telephone while you slumber.

The Internet

Like the rest of the world, the use of the Internet as a form of communication is growing so rapidly in Hong Kong that, except for the very old and the illiterate, it has become universal. As a result, numerous Chinese language and bilingual (Chinese and English) websites have been set up. These sites provide information on everything from pure entertainment to education and business news. Even the Hong Kong government has established an excellent website to provide information, such as 'live' footages of road traffic conditions. You can also download forms and save one trip to a particular government office, or in some cases, apply for what you need electronically.

Several retailers now allow you to buy groceries, books, electronics, book theatre tickets online, thus enabling the Hong Kong people to live up to their reputation of being on the go round the clock. And the connection speed is picking up as 95 per cent of businesses and households now have broadband access.

Hong Kong remains well-connected in IT terms. Visitors can easily log on and be online at one of the city's many Internet cafes

Usage of the Internet is becoming so commonplace that the Hong Kong Observatory's website crashed when too many users sought on-line the latest news of the typhoon that was in town, this despite round-the-clock reports on television and radio. During the same period, the Educational Department's website also crashed when over 50,000 students accessed the site for their examination grades as all the department's offices were closed due to the weather.

Mobile Telephones

The very high cost of mobile telephones in Hong Kong came down after March 1993, when the monopoly of licensed operators ended. The mobile telephone is now an essential feature of Hong Kong's daily existence. As the highest per capita users, Hong Kong people probably come closest to being on the go constantly, twenty-four hours a day and seven days a week; and the stress in their lives is enormous.

Nowadays, the mobile phone is so commonplace that it is unusual to see someone walking around without one. Several companies offer competitively-priced packages, thereby putting mobile phone costs within the budget of many, especially young students. The numerous offerings of different tunes in lieu of traditional ring tones means that you are greeted by a cacophony of electronic ditties from Bach's *Toccata* to the latest pop hit by Madonna.

Wireless Protocol Application (WAP) technology has also been introduced to Hong Kong, enabling users to check stock prices and email via their mobile phones.

The use of the mobile phone has become so widespread that several private clubs ban its use within their premises. It is also unfortunately uncommon to attend a concert, play, or event without a few discordant rings wafting from the audience. On the other hand, instant and constant access works well in a town where 'Time is money'—another adage seemingly coined for Hong Kong.

PUBLISHING AND PRINTING

Hong Kong is proud of the freedom of its press, which underpins the strength of the publishing and printing industry in the territory. Book publishing is mostly in Chinese, but English-language and bi-lingual Chinese/English publishing also thrive. There has been no effective labour union to impede the transition from manual to electronic control of setting and printing, and there is no shortage of expat spouses with editing experience, so the production of books and periodicals is relatively cost-efficient. In addition, the local printers' dual-language capability attracts major international academic publishers, such as Oxford University Press, to establish editorial and production offices in Hong Kong. Together with the local university presses, a large body of respectable scholarly and general works on China, Hong Kong and Asia at large, have been produced at fairly reasonable prices.

There are more than a million children in elementary and secondary schools in Hong Kong. Assume that every child uses at least one set of books in each category of subjects: reading, writing, arithmetic, mathematics, computer studies, general science, earth science, environment, civics, history, geography, biology, chemistry, physics, Chinese language, Chinese literature, English language, English literature— recognise that each set will have at least two volumes plus workbooks and related aids—and now add Chinese dictionaries, English dictionaries and bi-lingual dictionaries: the number of school books published each year leaves one groping for a mental abacus.

Popular non-fiction and fiction books are published, chiefly for the substantial Chinese-language readership.

The Press

Freedom of the press in Hong Kong means that there is no censorship before a newspaper or periodical is printed, but offending publications can be seized at newsstands. Journalists continue to complain that they do not enjoy complete access to Government information.

Two local English-language daily newspapers are the *South China Morning Post* (*SCMP*) and *the Hong Kong I-mail* (formerly known as *Hong Kong Standard*). The *SCMP* benefits from regional and overseas circulation, too, as emigrants

A streetside newsvendor in Central with both Chinese and English newspapers and magazines for sale.

from Hong Kong seek to keep in touch with what is going on here. Both newspapers publish online Internet editions. Despite competition from international daily newspapers, the circulation of these journals remains healthy. If you subscribe to one of these newspapers via a telephone call to the circulation department, the paper is delivered to the lobby of your apartment block, while a subscription through the local news agent brings the paper to your door.

The international daily journals are available in Hong Kong as if they were locally published. One of these, *The Asian Wall Street Journal*, is in fact put together and published in Hong Kong. *International Herald Tribune* and *The Financial Times* are printed here at the crack of dawn and can be available at your news agent or delivered to your home or office even before you sip your first cup or mid-morning tea or coffee. Seventeen of the Chinese-language newspapers cover general news. Others satisfy special-interest readers such as finance, entertainment news, and horse racing, but since these interests are general in Hong Kong, these newspapers enjoy a wide circulation.

A casual glance at any local newsstand reveals a large variety of magazines catering to special interests including cooking, computer and electronic technology, motor cars, music, the arts and antiques, film stars, Cantopop stars, lifestyles of the rich and the famous, *kungfu* and the martial arts including Ninja, astrology, horse racing and betting, as well as serious political and social commentaries such as *Zeng Ming*. Underneath the pile of respectable publications, there are what used to be called girlie magazines, in English and in Chinese, profusely and lewdly illustrated. Newsstands offering such publications usually also handle pornographic video tapes.

Publications deemed pornographic are taken away when the police decide to enforce anti-pornographic legislation. Sometimes the publisher is fined and ordered to stop marketing the offending magazine, but it is not difficult for it to re-emerge under a different name. For this reason, and because some magazines are insufficiently funded and do not survive more than a few issues, the number of periodicals in Hong Kong remains more constant than the list of their titles.

Foreign Correspondents

The importance of Hong Kong in the international arena is reflected by the presence of a large body of foreign correspondents, representing the world's leading newspapers and periodicals. Four hundred active correspondent members and 180 journalist members. Major news agencies, including Associated Press, Reuters, United Press International, Agence France-Presse, Kyodo News Service of Japan, Agencia EFE of Spain as well as LUSA of Portugal have offices here.

The Xinhua (New China) News Agency maintains an office with a large staff in Hong Kong. It has remained more than a news agency by continuing to be an official presence of the Chinese Government and its many quasi-public agencies here. The American Dow Jones Company owns a publishing company here, which produces mainly financial journals such as *Far Eastern Economic Review* and *The Asian Wall*

Street Journal. It also operates news wire and computer data retrieval services. So does Reuters.

Booksellers

English books in Hong Kong have mushroomed over the last decade. While Hong Kong Book Centre in its various guises once dominated the market, several other bookstores now exist, all of which provide a passable variety of reading material. The chain bookstores include Dymocks and Bookzine. All their sales people know their merchandise, and will order books not in stock. Hong Kong's first Internet bookseller, Paddyfields, can order any book published by a UK or US publisher; the shipping is free within Hong Kong. My favourite bookseller remains The Hong Kong Book Centre, nestled in the basement between Giordono's and Worldwide Building. It carries classics and best-seller fiction as well as professional tomes. The ambience is friendly and service efficient.

The larger Chinese-language bookshops, the Commercial Press in Causeway Bay and Joint Publishing in Central and Wanchai, also market English-language books. You are allowed to browse for as long as you wish and read to your heart's content. Elsewhere, alas, the Chinese practice of reading while browsing through the bookshops is a thing of the past. Books on display are wrapped in cellophane; considering the price of books in Hong Kong, who can blame the sellers? The Commercial Press also boasts a marvellous selection of stationery in its basement, but the service can best be described as indifferent.

Libraries

There are more than three dozen public libraries in Hong Kong. The catalogues of the libraries, including the reference Arts Library, are on-line and can be accessed via the Internet. The new Central Library opened in early 2001. It holds two million items of library materials. There are more than 400 public access terminals and microcomputers for readers to search local and overseas catalogues, multimedia programmes and on-line databases through the Internet. Meanwhile, to obtain borrowing rights, all you need is your

Hong Kong Identity Card and an address. Therefore, without further delay, please hike over to Victoria Park and find the Central Library!

Private libraries belonging to clubs are open to members only. The Helena May on Garden Road boasts perhaps the largest collection of leisurely reading and children's books in town. The university libraries are not open to the public, but if you are a research scholar you can gain access through faculty members you know.

RADIO AND TELEVISION

If you are a radio listener or a television couch potato, there is plenty on the local stations to keep you diverted.

Several radio stations cater between them to all tastes from classical music to current events, Cantopop and up-to-date stock market prices. If you are addicted to what goes on in the pop world at home, do not despair. Such broadcasts are transmitted here with no time gap. For myself and many friends, we stick to BBC Radio, between 670 and 680 on your AM dial.

The standard of local television programmes is a matter of personal judgement. During the recent past, the number of English-language programmes has declined, because audience demand is increasingly for other languages. Presentation that used to be in English is increasingly bi-lingual, in English and Cantonese. It is not having two languages in the same programme that annoys, so much as the pronunciation of English with a Cantonese accent and *vice versa*. Each of the two local television stations, ATV and TVB, broadcasts through two channels, one in Cantonese and the other (partly, at least) in English. The CBS and ABC Evening News comes in the early morning on the English-language channels. However, English-language broadcasting time is being usurped by programmes in such languages as Japanese, Korean, and Putonghua: further indications that non-English and non-Cantonese speakers are on the rise in Hong Kong.

Satellite television and cable television have invaded Hong Kong's peace of mind; both are widely available but the quality of the programmes is another matter. For English-speaking viewers, what used to be available on two channels can now be received on thirty or more, but it is difficult to find anything you really want to see. Horse racing and European football dominate sports programming.

More than ninety-eight per cent of Hong Kong households own at least one television set, and sixty-nine per cent own VCR or DVD players. The most popular programmes are the soap operas and variety shows on the Cantonese channels, opening a window for audiences in South China on life among the capitalists. Learn Cantonese quickly if your ambition includes merging into the local popular culture, for much can be gleaned through these programmes—including local colloquialisms, and people's attitudes, concerns and priorities.

CINEMA AND VIDEO/DVD/VCD

Hong Kong's film industry has come a long way from the days of Bruce Lee and *kungfu*, but whether this progress has a positive influence on the audience is a matter of opinion; authorities blame certain types of film for glamorizing criminal elements in our society.

Hong Kong films enjoy world-wide circulation, although most of them are made for Cantonese-speaking audiences. Recently, things are looking up as many of Hong Kong's cinematic talents, such as Jackie Chan, are gaining an international following through Hollywood films. The blockbuster *Crouching Tiger, Hidden Dragon* also introduced Chinese films to a wider audience.

There are fewer cinema theatres in Hong Kong (in 1993 there were 190 theatres, but in 2000, only 72) as residents opt for home entertainment. The new cinemas are comfortable and have satisfactory acoustics—a great improvement. Seats are pre-assigned. It is also nice to have smoking and eating banned. All films are classified into one of three categories: #1, suitable for all ages; #2, not suitable for children; and #3, suitable only for adults over 18. Even so, the censors wield their scissors freely. If you are partial to sex and violence on the screen there is no need to feel cheated, however, for a great deal of steam and blood remain.

Cinema sound is turned up sufficiently to waken the dead. So, if you are hard of hearing, do not let that keep you from going to the movies. Whatever the language on the sound track, subtitles are provided. If the dialogue is in Cantonese or Putonghua, English and Chinese subtitles appear. If the dialogue is in English, the subtitles are in Chinese. If you find the subtitles distracting, you will soon learn to ignore them.

If you do not enjoy going to the cinema, and find all television programmes abominable, there is no need to worry. There used to be a number of companies which delivered renting videos to your home, but it is a luxury of the past. VCD and DVD sales are big business in Hong Kong, and shops can be found in every neighbourhood and almost every shopping centre. Plonk down a sum of money, and the discs are yours.

COPYRIGHT LAWS AND PIRACY

Although piracy of the printed word is not a major concern in Hong Kong, it is perhaps because relatively little money is involved. Copyright infringement of popular music tapes, video tapes, computer software and TV games, infringement of somebody else's copyright is significant. The Government has started to come down hard on piracy and new laws with harsher punishments have been instituted. The Customs officers, especially at the Shenzhen-Lowu border, are enforcing laws against pirated goods more strictly with heavy penalties. So, even if your conscience does not trouble you, beware.

TRANSPORT

For a mostly privately owned but Government franchised system, Hong Kong's public transport works well. There is an exciting amount of variety, and the prices are right. Although some aspects of the service could be much improved, a venturesome individual like you should sample all of them, but I would suggest avoiding the rush hour. You must try the escalator from Central to Mid-Levels. At eight hundred metres, with a climb of 135 metres, it is the longest in the world. It goes down towards town until ten in the morning, after which it does what its name implies.

The Ferries

Hong Kong, after all, is a watery world—joined together by its ferries. They cross Victoria Harbour, between various points on Hong Kong Island, Kowloon, and the New Territories; and they thread through the South China Sea to the outlying islands.

Whether or not you always cross the harbour by the Star Ferry, you must try taking a boat to more than one outlying island. Even in the First Class, a ferry ride provides an interesting sociological study of the Hong Kong populace. Ferries that carry vehicles are alas no longer in service; but have no fear, others continue to carry passengers everywhere. In one way or another, you may find a place to walk, eat and drink at weekends that will seem not a thousand miles but a hundred years from Central.

For travelling to more distant places such as Macau and ports of South China, jet-foil hover ferries are safe, fast

The Star Ferry, in which a First Class crossing between Kowloon and Hong Kong is still very affordable.

and relatively free of hassle; their speed will not reduce your enjoyment of the scenery *en route*. Legend has it that aircraft jet engines require little adaptation before they propel hydrofoils across the Pearl River's estuary. On the longer routes there are conventional steamships. You can travel on deck, or sleep the night in your own cabin.

The MTR and LRT

To the Hong Kong travelling public, long used to being snarled in traffic jams, the rapid journeys provided by the Mass Transit Railway—underground—and the Light Rail Transit—on the surface—are akin to the miraculous. Starting in 1979, the public took a while to get used to the idea of this kind of transport. Once accustomed, they took to it with enthusiasm. In 2001, a daily average of 2.3 million passengers travelled on the MTR, with another 322,700 on the shorter LRT. The trains are modern, air-conditioned, convenient, efficient and clean—because eating, drinking and smoking are banned. Mobile telephones and pagers do not work underground, so the trains are also comparatively quiet. The MTR connects with the light railway, which has stops in the New Territories all the way to the Chinese border.

Trams and the Peak Tram

Electricity-powered trams have run on street tracks across the north of the Island since 1904. Today, Hong Kong Tramway Limited operates 161 double-decked cars: east-west, parallel to the coastline. In mid-2000 they carried 235,221 passengers daily. (You may hire one of the specially decorated trams, through the Hong Kong Tourist Association, as a novel setting for a private party. The tram will go along the tracks from its western terminus to the end of the line, finishing in a fruit and vegetable market.)

For ordinary commuting, it is direct and on street level so, if you do not mind crowded travel at a snail's pace, you will enjoy the ride. Get onto the tram at the back, work your way forward to pay your fare, and further forward to alight. You will have the unique sensation of being in the middle of the street, yet safe from the moving traffic. You can see

Trams still operate on Hong Kong Island and are a cheap and and efficient means to get around.

the shops on both sides of the street, as well as pedestrians rushing from place to place. The top deck offers the more interesting experience but, if you are over five feet eight inches tall, you will not be able to stand upright.

The Peak Tram is a funicular railway, hauled by cable from the lower end of Garden Road to Victoria Peak. At first privately owned, with the Kadoories as the largest shareholders, the Peak Tram is now controlled by the Hong Kong and Shanghai Hotels. The Peak Tram's construction accelerated development of the Peak as a residential area. It climbs 373 metres on gradients as steep as 45 degrees. The cars are parallel to the flat ground so, as you rise or descend, you see buildings at an angle.

The best place to sit is on the right side of the car to the rear as you ascend. When you descend, you will be sitting backwards; but there is no cause for fear. The Peak Tram has been in operation since 1888 without a single accident –despite the antics of young expatriate boys of bygone years climbing onto the back of the cars while they were moving. The line serves 9,000 passengers daily—tourists and residents.

Double-deckers and Minibuses

Of the almost six thousand public buses in Hong Kong, 5,512 are double-deckers. Buses carry an average of 4.35 million passengers daily. Originally blue or red and bought from Leyland Motors of Yorkshire, manufacturers of London Transport double-deckers, the Hong Kong fleets now include German and Japanese vehicles. Many of the buses have burst out in bright hues with advertisements on their exteriors.

Bus stops are places to test the Darwinian theory of survival of the fittest. At older bus stops, metal barriers have been placed to ensure order, but at the newer stops, it is still every woman for herself. We may further test our agility by trying to climb to the upper deck as the bus pitches and yaws through Hong Kong's steep and narrow roads.

Not all the roads are suitable for the double- or even single-deckers; hence the minibus, seating either 16 or 18 passengers. There are two species of minibus: with green

ORIENTAL
ARTS & JEW-
ELLERY CO
STONES—IVORY
CARVING JEWELRY
ANTIQUE WARE &
CLOISONNE WARE
IMPORTER EXPORTER
WHOLESALE & RETAILE
80 NATHAN RD ¾
TEL 3-68443

TAT HING IVORY-WARES
Manufacturers Exporters & Importers
80G NATHAN ROAD 94

D251

7

During peak hours, even
public transport such as
double-deck buses crawl
along at a slow pace
because of the traffic jams.

HK 4492

stripes or red, on a basic beige. The red striped minibuses are for private hire, so makes stops whenever a passenger wishes to get on or alight, while the green follow their pre-determined routes. The destination of each green minibus is displayed above the windscreen, as is the fare. The style is friendly and informal, but the standard of cleanliness varies.

When you discover the minibus route you want to use, it won't be long before you catch onto the routine. You wave at the driver to stop. Just before you want to get off, you yell 'stop'; or the same command in Cantonese, sounding like '*look chair*' but without the *k* and the *r*. It would be nice if you added a 'please' but, whatever sounds you utter, the driver will know that you want to get off. When you alight say 'thank you' to the driver in any language, especially if you are a regular rider. The gesture will be greatly appreciated—since his is a pretty boring life, and an exacting one, manoeuvring a bus through thick traffic day in and day out—and, eventually, he will remember you so that he can then be relied upon not to shut the door until both your feet are on the street.

Ride with the Octopus

If you will be travelling on public transport, get the Octopus Card. The Octopus is essentially a cashless means to ride Hong Kong's transport system. Just tap the stored value card on the scanners as you board the vehicle and again when you depart. The best thing is that you don't even have to take it out of your handbag or wallet. The cost of your journey is automatically deducted for a quick and hassle free trip. Your Octopus Card will work on the MTR, the Kowloon-Canton Railway (KCR), buses, trams (including peak tram) and ferries. Recently, the Octopus has been extended for use at supermarkets, convenience stores, vending machines adn even recreational facilities. You can add value to your Octopus Card at the machines located at any MTR station. There is also an automatic add-value service where the card is linked to your bank account and is topped up when it reaches a certain value. Just bear in mind that the card is anonymous so if you lose your card, anyone can use it.

Taxis

Taxis in the New Territories are painted bright green, and in Kowloon and Hong Kong Island are painted dark crimson. Licence fees are high, and the number of licences issued is limited. It is not true that taxi ownership is controlled by a syndicate. Many cabs are owned by individual drivers, who drive the cabs themselves during the day, then lease the taxis to other drivers for the night shift. If the night drivers seem to pay scant attention to the speed limit, it is probably because they are on their second job of the day.

The taxis are metered, and it is extremely difficult to cheat on the meter. At one time writers to *The Editor* expressed their concern about the compact size of the newer taxis, claiming that smaller wheels covered shorter distances each revolution, thereby making journeys more expensive—because the meters clicked on in proportion to the speed at which the wheels went round. More often than not however, higher fares are a result of traffic congestion as taxis are now allowed to charge HK$1 for each minute spent idling.

You are well advised to ask a Chinese friend or colleague to write your destination in Chinese for you as many drivers, particularly those who drive at night, do not always know the name of the building or street in English. Learning basic directions such as 'turn left or right', and 'straight ahead' would be to your advantage as well.

The drivers do go off duty, and the change of shifts takes place between three-thirty and five.

As in all major cities, when it rains in Hong Kong available taxis disappear. There are taxis, but not for you. You can call all the taxi numbers in the telephone book, but nothing will come. The offer of an extra ten dollars—now going up to twenty—will bring about a miracle, but you wouldn't want to become a part of the system spreading corruption would you? Here you are, a person needing to arrive somewhere within a short span of time: are you going to be guided by your principles of fairness, or are you going to play ball with the local system and not miss your appointment?

Driving in Hong Kong

A Hong Kong driving licence is expensive, but there is no need for you to go in person. If you have a licence valid in your own country—one acknowledged by the Hong Kong Government as requiring all licensed drivers to know how to drive—you can send a messenger to obtain the forms to apply for a Hong Kong licence. The messenger can stand and wait until your name is called, and pick up your licence when it is ready.

Unless you attend to these formalities yourself, however, you will miss the special experience of waiting for your licence at the Motor Vehicles Department—akin only to that of waiting for your identity card to be processed or your residence visa to be issued at the Hong Kong Immigration Department. There are 1,312,886 licensed drivers in the territory; and 'moving violations' can disqualify you from driving. Rushing through the red light or getting a jump before the green light actually comes on will earn five points, against you.

If you think that our roads are crowded, you have the Government's figures to support your contention. There are just under 300 motor vehicles per kilometre of Hong Kong's roads. Every car seems to be on the road at the same time and in much the same place as yours. Being native here, the drivers want to take advantage of every minute and of every inch of space. Therefore, as you politely wait in a long queue trying alternately to merge into one or another tunnel lane, other drivers will push ahead of you from all directions. While you remember the admonitions of your driving teacher to keep a safe distance from the car in front, do not be surprised if some other car cuts right in between. It is like getting into an office lift: you must be on your guard lest you lose your space.

Take the traffic regulations very, very seriously. They are strictly enforced at all times.

Buying a Car in Hong Kong

For those of you from North America, it seems impossible not to have a car, although this may not be a problem with Londoners and those coming from other European cities. In Hong Kong cars are often considered a status symbol and you actually have to pay a lot more than you do back home.

For starters, the cost of petrol is close to US$ 6 per gallon. You will also have to pay for parking space at your apartment and the equivalent of US$ 300 per month is not uncommon. As part of your employment package, the company may pay for your parking lot in the office. Otherwise, it's another cost as season parking in the city is not cheap. Outside of work, do also bear in mind that parking space is limited in many parts of Hong Kong. Add to this the severe traffic congestion and you may want to seriously consider buying a car.

Of course, there are also plus points that may convince you to get a car. If you do not live along the route of the MTR or have a straight bus route to the office, driving may cut by half the time taken to get to work in the morning. But of course the main advantage of having your own vehicle is that you can easily get away to enjoy the great outdoors, go hiking or play a round of golf. You are not at the mercy of public transport and strict schedules, just leave whenever the family is ready. And even better, you can pack in your toddler's stroller and a picnic basket with no fuss.

Living in Hong Kong, which is one of the main entry points into Asia from North America, you can bet that friends and relatives from back home are going to visit. Your own set of wheels means that you can meet the folks at Chek Lap Kok direct. It's a lot easier than trying to give directions for them to transfer to a taxi from the Airport Express and then instructions on how to get to your home when they don't speak Cantonese.

FINANCES

Hong Kong has one of the world's lowest taxation rates—a flat salary tax of 16 per cent. There is no capital gains tax so any profit you make on playing the stock market or speculating in property is yours to keep. However, a stamp duty is imposed on property sales. The fiscal year in Hong Kong is from 1 April to 31 March. Depending on your nationality, you may also have to pay taxes in your home country, so do your homework. US citizens have to pay taxes on income earned worldwide but there is an income tax exclusion if you live or work overseas. Do also check out tax credits if your home country has a higher tax rate than Hong Kong. See also Salaries Tax under Resources section on page 264.

Opening a Bank Account

There are over 100 foreign banks in Hong Kong so it is very likely that your home bank will have an office here. If this is the case, you can easily arrange to access your funds through a written arrangement. There will however be a service or administrative charge. Once you have an local address, you can open a Hong Kong bank account, just bring your passport and proof of address (such as utilities bill) to the bank. There is usually no mininum deposit required but policies differ from bank to bank. Remember to apply for an ATM (automated teller machine) card that allows you to withdraw money from these machines.

CONCLUSION

Come to Hong Kong with an open mind and a positive attitude. If possible do your "homework" before you depart. If you adopt the right mindset, this could be the start of a must fulfilling stay or it could be the start of a new adventure. Ultimately, it's you choice on how you choose to settle down in your new home.

Part of the secret of a success in life is to eat what you like
and let the food fight it out inside.
-—Mark Twain (1835–1910)

EATING OUT IS A MAJOR INSTITUTION in Hong Kong. So, one of the real reasons behind your decision to come to Hong Kong could be the urge to enjoy Chinese food.

You can go to restaurants by yourselves, or with non-Cantonese speaking friends, in the urban areas where English-language menus abound. As time goes by, learn to speak at least some Cantonese, by whatever means, and try the restaurants in out-of-the-way places. When you have achieved merely a few polite words and phrases, you will find a warm welcome everywhere. The Hong Kong people may giggle at your pronunciation and intonation, but underneath they will be so appreciative that you are trying to learn their language. It shows that you respect the local people and that you want to be their friends. At least you will be providing them with something to talk about for days to come. Nowhere will you see more evidence of their appreciation of your linguistic efforts than in the restaurants and shops you decide to patronise.

EATING OUT
Hong Kong people probably eat out more often than those of any other land. There are over thirty thousand restaurants in Hong Kong. All major cuisines of the world are represented—French, Italian, Mediterranean, Indian, Japanese and Korean—and all schools of Chinese cooking, such as Cantonese, Chiuchow, Sichuan, Shanghainese, and

the latest cusine to arrive us Xinjiang. Prices vary from the bank-breaking top of the market to fast food for less than twenty Hong Kong dollars per head. Happily, most of the restaurants come somewhere between. If you want to start with a safe bet, that long-standing institution, Jimmy's Kitchen, has branches on either side of the harbour.

There have been substantial rises in lower to middle incomes during the last dozen years: not enough to pay for luxury cars or foreign holidays, but enabling families to eat well and often in Hong Kong restaurants. Certainly some people eat out only once in a while, as a birthday treat or some other celebration; but there are people who eat all three meals in restaurants every day. Hong Kong parents do not appear to need to adjust their schedules to their children's bed-times, so you see whole families eating out even on weekday evenings.

HAUTE CUISINE TO FAST FOOD, WESTERN STYLE

The large number of Western restaurants reflects the cosmo-politan character of Hong Kong. Consult the young men and women in the international business world for insight into Hong Kong's eateries. There will be no cultural shock when you eat there; apart from the Chinese appearance of the waiters and waitresses, there is nothing to suggest that you are in such a faraway place as Hong Kong.

It is taken for granted that better Western food can be found in its native countries, but there is no need to apologise for the chefs of Hong Kong. That stand-by of many years, Gaddi's at the Peninsula; or the Grill at the Mandarin Oriental; and relative newcomers to the scene, Petrus at the Island Shangri-la or The Grissini at the Grand Hyatt: these cannot be surpassed in the quality of food, wine, ambience and service. In fact, luxury hotels try to outperform each other in their Western and their Chinese cuisines, and you can benefit from their competition. It is difficult for restaurants serving Western food to operate other than in hotels because of the high rents, but a number do provide exceptional food and thrive: such as Cafe Damigo in Happy Valley or M at the

Fringe. Prices in all restaurants have risen in recent years, but there are set-luncheon menus which should not offend either your pocketbook or your sense of fairness.

At the lower end, fast food has become a fad in Hong Kong. It is astonishing how the Chinese, who traditionally rejected both tomatoes and cheese, have taken to pizza, over-cooked hamburgers and french fries—in Hong Kong. This open expression of fondness for Western food is no longer solely a status symbol with which Hong Kong people try to show their modernity. They actually like these new-fangled comestibles. Sandwiches, however, are still thought of as snack food, not as a substitute for rice or noodles in a main meal.

The Jumbo floating seafood restaurant in Aberdeen is practically an institiution and is a must-visit for non Hongkongers.

CHINESE RESTAURANTS

It is almost impossible to find bad Cantonese food in Hong Kong. The Chinese restaurants, large and small, up-market or basic, all serve edible food, and more than a few serve great food. A number of restaurants have adopted the chic of *nouvelle cuisine*, arranging the food exquisitely to Western aesthetic standards; and many have given up *maijin*—monosodium glutumate, the chemical taste-enhancer that causes the *Chinese Restaurant Syndrome* of burning headaches and swelling limbs, symptoms which received widespread publicity in Europe and America a while ago. It is perfectly acceptable to ask the waiter to leave out the *maijin*. More likely than not the chef will bow to your wishes since the cost of *maijin*, imported from Japan, is on the high side. Make sure that the cook is asked to leave out chicken essence also, which is used as a substitute for *maijin*. If you read the contents on a chicken essence bottle, the first item you see will be *maijin*.

There is a newly opened chain of moderately priced restaurants serving substantial Cantonese food, albeit a little heavy on *maijin*. It is known for its soups and casseroles; indeed, the name of the restaurants is Ah Yee Liang Tong, literally meaning *Number Two's Terrific Soup*. Shirleen Ho tells the traditional story that Ah Yee, meaning Number Two, was the euphemism for a man's mistress, his wife being Number One. When the man visited the Number Two he had to eat something; but if he partook of a full meal his wife would suspect that he had eaten somewhere else, when his appetite was not up to its usual standard. And, if this state of affairs continued, the wife would know that he had a second household. Hence, he could only accede to the soup course at Number Two's, and the Number Two, of pleasing nature by definition, learned to make terrific soup.

Expatriate residents like to patronise a couple of large Beijingese restaurants where the noise is beyond tolerance but where good food is offered at reasonable prices. They also like the Sichuanese restaurants which offer almost exactly the same menu as certain other Sichuanese restaurants—say in New York's Upper East Side. There is nothing wrong with these restaurants, but you should try others also.

A Typical Family Style Menu featuring Cantonese food (Moderately-priced)

The courses are served at the same time (normally the number of courses is equal to the number of diners)

- Soup of the day
- Patter of sliced roasted meats: duck, goose, pork, jelly fish
- Boneless fish slices with vegetables
- Fried chicken
- A pork dish—rarely sweet and sour pork
- Bean curds with vegetables or shrimp
- Rice
- Dessert which is either a fresh fruit platter or a soup made with beans, sesame and peanuts, with a large quantity of sugar added to make the dessert very, very sweet. (Not surprisingly, the word dessert translated into Cantonese means 'sweet plate'!)

A Typical Banquet Menu featuring Cantonese food (Expensive)

The following courses are served, one at a time.

- Whole Roast Pig
- Stuffed crab claws or whole shrimps
- Whole lobster salad
- Sharks fin soup
- Abalone
- Mushrooms in oyster sauce
- Fried chicken
- Steamed fish
- Vegetable
- Fried Rice and noodles
- Dessert and fruit platter

EATING WITH CHOPSTICKS

You must learn as soon as possible to eat with chopsticks. The restaurants will provide you with a knife and a fork but, unless you suffer from arthritis, it is difficult to explain why

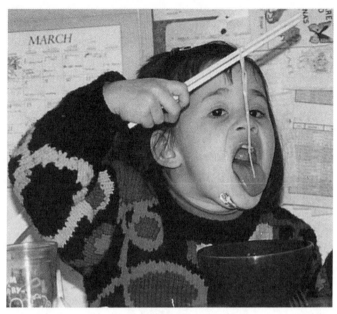

You cannot start too young: this Eurasian child has the hang of it ... in her own fashion.

a Hong Kong resident cannot handle chopsticks. You will learn easily and, once you have, it is like riding a bicycle: the skill is yours forever. On the other hand, it is better to be safe than sorry. Until you have mastered the art of eating with chopsticks, ask for the Western implements. Dry-cleaning is not as readily available as you might like and, as with the price of a silk tie, dry-cleaning costs have risen into the stratosphere.

THE ETIQUETTE OF RESTAURANT DINING, FAMILY STYLE

Your Chinese friends and business acquaintances rarely entertain at home. Unless they live in spacious quarters and enjoy the services of a good cook, they will invite you to dine at one of Hong Kong's many excellent restaurants serving Chinese food, some of which are in private clubs. It is not that they want to keep you out of their personal space, as with a stranger; but they might worry about losing face should you not like their home, or feel that it is too humble.

Entertaining in Chinese restaurants may take place in the general dining room, where it is less formal and where food is ordered from a regular menu. You will be asked by your host to choose something from this menu. Unless you know your host very well, let him order. The chances are that he will not select anything that is too exotic, unless he knows specifically that you are partial to duck's tongue or *brèche de mer*. If you are truly allergic to certain types of food, speak up and be absolutely firm that you cannot 'try a little bit' under any circumstances. You will be eating *family-style* in the sense that all the dishes will be for everyone to share. The dishes will be placed in the middle of the table, and all of you will be serving yourselves from them, unless the host takes this task upon himself or a waitress or waiter officiates.

Dipping your chopsticks into the serving bowl with aplomb when you dine with a family—or in the same style with any group—is going to be hard. (For a while, kind people will understand your difficulty and indulge you, as if you were not quite grown up.) Even harder to become accustomed to is everybody else at the table dipping into the same bowl with chopsticks which have been in and out of their mouths.

However, since the outbreak of SARS in 2003, standards of hygiene are beginning to take priority over the intimacy of sharing a meal family-style. The restaurants are providing an extra pair of chops—more often than not a different colour—to be used as serving chopsticks. It is all right to reach across the table, but choose the piece of food closest to you.

Most of the food will have been cut into bite sizes already. It is perfectly in order to bite into larger pieces with your front teeth, as long as you do not drag the portion that has been in your mouth out and onto your plate again. Let me share with you a secret: after scores of eating with chopsticks or fork, I still do not know what to do with a piece of fish bone caught between my tongue and teeth.

THE ETIQUETTE OF BEING ENTERTAINED IN A PRIVATE ROOM

Alternatively you might be entertained in a private dining room, reserved for your party alone. This is banquet dining, on a small scale. Food is ordered from a special menu in advance, and the meal is a great deal more expensive than in the general dining room. It is understood that shark's fin will be a part of the meal in private room dining. In a Cantonese restaurant, the meal will also include steamed whole garoupa or preserved abalone; in a Beijingese restaurant, the ubiquitous roast duck with pancakes.

In any case, in order to justify the specialised service and the privacy of the dining room, you are expected to drink alcohol, sodas or *fresh* orange juice; not merely water or tea. Whatever you order to drink will keep on coming all evening, unless you stop the waiter or waitress firmly. A word of warning must be added here. Somehow a persuasive salesman has managed to convince the Hong Kong public that a certain brand of distilled water is good for your health, so it is served everywhere, including hospitals where there are heart patients. If you do not wish to become a part of this scheme of drinking water without any character or mineral content, order boiled tap water.

> Fresh orange juice may look appetising, but since it was squeezed many more than fifteen minutes before, all the vitamins will have disappeared before it reaches you, leaving only sugar.

Your host will probably bring along a bottle of brandy, which he and the guests will drink neat, or have a bottle with his name on it already at the restaurant, indicating that he is a regular patron: another status symbol, to be noticed by the initiated. The territory boasts the highest per capita consumption of cognac outside France; nowadays, the status of the cognac is determined by the presence of the letters XO on the bottle. Wine has also become very popular.

The guest of honour is always seated furthest from the door. Today, men and women are usually seated at the same table, assuming that both sexes are represented. If so, your spouse will be seated next to you. Traditionally, Chinese women and men were seated in separate rooms or at separate tables; by putting spouses together, it is hoped that the guest wife will feel less awkward at this gathering of strangers.

The host will be seated closest to the door. It will always be a round table, in the middle of which a 'lazy susan' keeps the food circulating. When the waiter or waitress handles the serving, an equal portion of every dish will be placed on a small plate, and yours will be placed in front of you. Few diners have risen hungry from a Chinese banquet table. To reduce the chances of such a misfortune, the last course is apt to be the heaviest, but not necessarily the least interesting. The meal is over when the waiter places a bowl of flowers in the middle of the lazy susan. It is your cue to get up and say good night, if you are the guest of honour. Do not linger.

> There is no need to eat the whole lot unless you truly like it; and remember that there are at least ten courses at these dinners in a private dining room.

During the meal, the courses will be served one at a time. As your host gestures you to start eating, by extending his chopsticks and saying 'Please', you should raise your cup or glass and say 'Thank you' before you eat.

Confucius has always been quoted as saying that one does not talk while one is eating, and no doubt your mother would agree with him. In other words, do not talk with your mouth full. In between courses, of course, there will be conversation. After all, you have been invited to dinner so that you and your host can get to know each other less formally than across the desks of your offices. You will find, however, that only the guest of honour and the host exchange pleasantries. If you are junior to your host, do not speak unless addressed directly; and remember that serious subjects are rarely brought up. Please note especially that this is neither the time nor the place to show off your command of Cantonese, unless you speak it really well and the host has asked you to use the language. Nor is it considered macho any more to drink too much alcohol.

A Poem

You may find the following poem entertaining. It was penned by a Western trader at Canton, W C Hunter, who was given what appeared to be a sumptuous Cantonese feast by a Chinese merchant, and harboured his own private fears as one dish was uncovered after another. The poem was printed in *The 'Fan Kwae' at Canton Before Treaty Days 1825–1844* (London, 1882).

The feast spread out, the splendour round
Allowed the eye no rest;
The wealth of Kwang-Tung, of all Ind,
Appeared to greet each guest.

All tongues are still; no converse free
The solemn silence broke.
Because, alas! friend Se-Ta-Che [Western guest]
No word of Chinese spoke.

Now here, now there, he picked a bit
Of what he could not name;
And all he knew was that, in fact,
They made him sick the same!

Mingqua, his host, pressed on each dish
With polished Chinese grace;
And much, Ming thought, he relished them,
At every ugly face!

At last he swore he'd eat no more,
'Twas written in his looks;
For, 'Zounds!' said he, 'the devil here
Sends both the meats and cooks!'

But, covers changed, he brightened up,
And thought himself in luck
When close before him, what he saw
Looked something like a duck!

Still cautious grown, but, to be sure,
His brain he set to rack;
At length he turned to one behind,
And, pointing, cried: 'Quack, Quack.'

The Chinese gravely shook his head,
Next made a reverend bow;
And then expressed what dish it was
By uttering, 'Bow-wow-wow!'

THE FEAST MENU

At first, everything on the table will be new and exotic to you. Give it a try, you may like it. In time, you may become blasé and enjoy each dish for the texture and the flavour. Some things will never lose their appeal even after many years. An occasional Peking Duck is still exciting to behold, and even sweet-and-sour pork does not lose its freshness.

Actually, the most unusual items on the menu will probably be shark's fin and perhaps a whole roast piglet with head and tail. If you recognise the solitary brownish oval-shaped object on a plate as preserved abalone, and if you do not want to struggle with this rubbery delicacy, feel free to decline. As they may cost a thousand or more dollars apiece, the host is sure to forgive you for not taking one bite and leaving the rest on the plate. At such meals in Hong Kong today, the bill of fare is usually on the table in both Chinese and English, so that you will know what you are eating.

When you spy chrysanthemum petals, however, it is time to focus positively on what is being served. These flower petals always accompany snake soup, which is considered a nourishing delicacy during the winter months. It is harmless, and moderately expensive, so it would be impolite to decline.

THE TEAHOUSE: A HONG KONG TRADITION

Yum cha literally means *drinking tea*, or *to drink tea* when used as a verb. After thousands of years of tea connoisseurship the Chinese have yet to come up with a dripless spout. However, despite the introduction of coffee, soda and other beverages, tea drinking has remained an important tradition. Teahouses have existed in China since antiquity, serving a variety of teas, generally with watermelon seeds, or peanuts in their shells. It was the Cantonese who first introduced food into the teahouses; they became known as *yum cha* or *dim sum* restaurants. The food served in the teahouses never amounted to major meals, only *dim sum*: literally small pieces of meat or vegetable wrapped in pastry and easily eaten. Although *yum cha* and *dim sum* are used synonymously in Hong Kong, there is, properly,

Dim sum (above) are served in bamboo steamers or small serving dishes with each containing three or four servings. In traditional restaurants, the waitress calls out what she has on board the dim sum cart (below) as she pushes it round. Even if you do not understand Cantonese, just point at anything that catches your fancy. Sadly, the dim sum cart is a dying tradition and many restaurants now use a conventional menu.

a distinction—when you go to a restaurant to *yum cha*, you eat *dim sum;* or, when you *yum cha*, you drink tea and eat *dim sum.*

Until recently, before tablecloths were introduced into *yum cha* restaurants, women used to pushcarts of *dim sum* among the tables and sing out what was on their individual carts. The patrons indicated what they wanted by asking—or gesturing with their hands or their chins—which added to the informality of the atmosphere. Today, there is an order form (often bilingual) on the table for you to fill in with what you want to eat; or your order is taken by a uniformed waiter. The food is no less delicious, but *à la carte* is not so much fun as from the cart. Clearly, as restaurants go upmarket, so do the prices.

Dim sum restaurants in Hong Kong are informal places where business news is gathered and transactions are made. Certain restaurants are patronised by certain trades or professions. Property owners, for instance, meet at the Luk Yew Teahouse and have a table reserved for them every day. This is why in general there is no space for a casual customer until after two-thirty.

The Chinese way of making a business deal is not to negotiate in the presence of a legal team, but to talk about items of mutual interest in an informal place over tea and *dim sum.* Introductions are made and people and business are brought together. This old way of conducting business is also on the way out, as younger generations and hired managers take over.

THE GREAT CHEFS OF HONG KONG

Perhaps the most efficient and least costly way to sample the best international and Chinese cuisines is at a Los Angeles institution transplanted here, the *Great Chefs* of Hong Kong. Thanks to the generosity of the erstwhile Hilton, Conrad and Marriot hotels, this is now a much anticipated annual fundraising event.

More than twenty hotels and restaurants support their chefs in donating talent, time and special dishes to benefit the Heep Hong Society for Handicapped Children. In 2000, cuisines of the Australian, Austrian, Californian, Cantonese, French, German, Italian, Japanese, New Zealand, Swiss and Thai schools were represented at the *Great Chefs*: as truly international a collection of delicious mouthfuls as you can hope to eat standing up.

Champagne, still wines, mineral water, *espresso* coffee—and more—flow through the largesse of their local distributors. These included a Hong Kong Chinese architect educated at Harvard, and an Austrian lawyer trained in Vienna, serving beverages themselves in their inimitable styles and adding much to the convivial atmosphere of the occasion. Patrons walk around the Ballroom, drinking and eating what they want. If you would like a particular chef to cook a meal for you and your friends at home, you can bid for his or, indeed, her services at the auction that is a part of the *Great Chefs*. This grand charity function is open to the general public.

Alas, the Hilton Hotel has been demolished and an office building stands in its stead. Now the venue for the Great Chefs changes every year.

CONCLUSION

As you come to know Hong Kong and its people better, you will discover that eating out is not just a means to an end but is also a social experience to be enjoyed and savoured. What's more the sheer variety of dishes and cuisines available also make dining a pleasure.

LEISURE ACTIVITIES

CHAPTER 7

What is this life if, full of care,
We have no time to stand and stare?
—William Henry Davies (1871–1940)

SHOPPING IN HONG KONG

Shopping in Hong Kong is no longer simply hunting for bargains or counterfeit merchandise, or picking up a Chinese curio or two. In fact, there are few great bargains left. But as a resident you can find almost anything you need if you spend time and energy looking for it. Maybe you will not be able to locate a dozen maroon-coloured bath towels all at once; but you can accumulate all the ingredients you need for baking a Christmas fruit cake by visiting three or four special food shops—GREAT, Olivers, and City'super—or even your local supermarket.

Service standards in Hong Kong, especially in shops frequented by tourists, have improved vastly during the past decade, although here and there you may still face surly assistants—unless they have deduced somehow that you are about to spend a great deal of money. Following this line of thought, Japanese tourists and well-heeled Mainland patrons are in general served first in the boutiques with the most elevated prices. You can always walk out in a huff if you are not satisfied with the service. Otherwise if that particular shop stocks what you really desire, you will just have to persevere until you have secured the full attention of the staff and cajoled from them the merchandise you want to see. The staff are mostly underpaid women and whose self-assurance comes with the uniforms they wear. When all else fails, ask to speak with the manager.

Yes, there are unscrupulous shopkeepers in Hong Kong. Victims may have recourse to the Hong Kong Consumers' Council. The best way to approach any purchase of substance—whether a camera, a fax machine, a watch, or a diamond necklace—is to get someone who has been here for some time and has established *guanxi* (a special relationship) with certain shopkeepers, to go with you. You can then be more sure that you are buying a genuine article at a fair price.

The Shopping Malls

The one place in Hong Kong that are likely to make you feel at home is the shopping mall, if you are used to these standard facilities; but these malls have a distinct character of their own. There are restaurants, yes, including McDonalds and other fast food emporia, department stores and a variety of specialist shops, but the merchandise in the shops will be more international than you find at home. The advent of up-market malls—Lee Plaza, Landmark and Pacific Place—featuring the most elegant of shops, has led to the up-grading of older malls such as Ocean Terminal. There are other large malls, Festival Walk and those at Taikooshing and Times Square, for instance, which cater to a less well-heeled clientele. These malls also serve as air-conditioned indoor playgrounds for family outings at weekends and holidays, especially when the weather is too hot or too wet out of doors. There are exhibits, concerts and, lately, fashion shows to entertain lunch-time and weekend shoppers and sightseers. The Taikooshing mall even boasts an ice-skating rink.

Etiquette of Street Hawkers and Bargain Emporia

There are still factory outlets throughout Hong Kong, but you should be prepared to pick through a lot of imperfect factory rejects under the watchful eyes of untrusting proprietors. The sound of Cantopop is beyond the normal level of tolerance; but, if you know what you are looking for and know your labels, the prices are really superb. Stanley has become too chic for good bargains, but newcomers and

Hong Kong has specialised areas to shop. Stanley Market (above) on Hong Kong Island is a good place to find clothing bargains while the Jade Market (bottom) in Kowloon is know for the variety and quality of jade, an ornamental stone of the mineral jadite or neophrite that is often used to make jewellery.

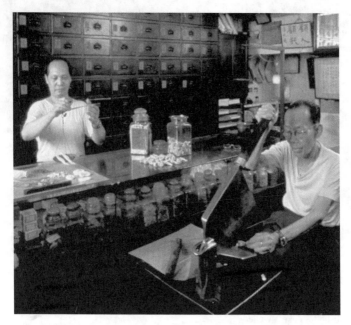

A shop selling traditional Chinese medicine. Just tell them your ailment and they will prescribe an appropriate cure—usually quite effective as these are based on centuries old recipes passed down from generation to generation.

visitors still find the market exciting. The etiquette allows bargaining. However, confronted with a proprietress with a cunning eye for profit, you are not going to get very far. The rules also allow you all the time you want to investigate the goods in the fixed premises but, since hawking on the street without a licence is illegal, partly because many items are counterfeit, you need to rush when you negotiate with a mobile hawker. Once money is paid, goods can not be returned. The flower and jade markets in Mongkok remain great for bargain hunters.

Antiques, Curios, Souvenirs and Junk

Hong Kong specializes in Chinese antiques, curios, souvenirs and junk. Sometimes it takes a knowledgeable eye or a trusted dealer to tell them apart. Usually the only items you will find made for non-Chinese taste are the China Trade pieces—things made in China for sale abroad or to Westerners who lived in China.

There are antique dealers in the shopping malls and other elegant establishments, including hotel arcades, but nothing has taken away the romance and adventure of hunting for antiques in Hollywood Road. If any object made a century or more ago is considered an antique (as defined by the United States Customs), then there are a great many genuine antiques in Hong Kong, from neolithic pottery to late Qing furniture. For portable but elegant items, visit Honey Church Antiques on Hollywood Road. You must remember, however, that age and value do not always go hand in hand. There are even more objects—better labelled as curios, souvenirs and junk—that pose as antiques. Follow the advice of the Tourist Association: patronize only stores sporting the HKTA logo. At least these antique dealers will not lie about the age and value of the piece that happens to attract your eye. No true connoisseur buys on sight without investigation; that is, long drawn-out discussions with dealers about date and origin— but not necessarily provenance—and of course price.

While the prices may be much lower than back home, try to curb your enthusiasim and bargain aggressively for an even better price.

Real antiques that you fancy might not be as expensive as you expect. Rare treasures, of course, command prices beyond ordinary pockets like yours or mine; and are auctioned at Christie's or Sotheby's, both of which maintain offices in Hong Kong.

Chinese tastes in antiques differ from those of expatriates, which is fortunate for you. Whereas you think a pottery figure pretty exciting—say, a fat lady in green and yellow glaze excavated from a Tang dynasty tomb—Chinese collectors would prefer not to own something intended for the dead. Neolithic pottery jars are no longer a dime a dozen but, because there are so many of them on the Hong Kong market, the prices are still affordable.

Expatriate residents in Hong Kong seem to have a partiality for Korean chests, and indeed these are lovely and are available everywhere, but most of them were manufactured in your lifetime. Go browsing in Hollywood Road and Wyndham Street when you have time. The antique shops are mostly family owned and managed. The dealers know and love their wares. Genuine collectors spend Saturday afternoons there, establishing *guanxi* with their favourite antique dealers. The dealers, many of whom speak excellent English, enjoy sharing their passion with the true connoisseur. Once in a while, however, you are expected to buy.

Clothing

The availability of ready-made apparel for men and women, and the rise in labour costs, have brought about the decline of clothing 'tailor-made in Hong Kong'. When European designers embarked on the course of producing more than one costume per design, Hong Kong jumped onto their bandwagon. When you can buy off the rack from boutiques featuring a selection of the world's most renowned names —which can provide you with style as well as a symbol of status—why would you subject yourself to some anonymous tailor who demands at least four fittings?

Good tailors are still around, of course, but they are expensive. Those who have not yet emigrated are getting old, and no younger generation wielding a mighty needle has yet emerged to take their places. More affordable clothing can be found in a myriad of department stores and boutiques, featuring garments made in Asia; and in the Chinese emporia selling clothes made in China. In general the Hong Kong population is conscious of the latest trends in style, and dresses well.

One area which has seen improvement in recent years in the retail rag trade is larger-sized clothing for the fuller non-Chinese figure. It is difficult to keep your cool when the saleswomen tell you that they do not stock clothes for fat people—extra offensive if said in Cantonese because the dialect uses the same adjective for fat people and fat animals. Or, if 'extra-large' sizes were offered, these would fit your eleven-year-old child. Happily, this kind of humiliation has come to an end. There are shops which cater for large men and women, though you have to look for them. Again, you will need to consult the grapevine.

Yaumatei: The Tradition of the Seafaring Populace of Hong Kong

Yaumatei (close today to the favourite expat shopping paradises: the Flower and Jade Markets) came into being primarily to serve the populace engaged in maritime shipping.

In 1860, the British Army had hoped to keep the newly accessed Kowloon Peninsula solely for military use. In fact, until 1970, when it was transformed into Kowloon Park, the Whitfield Barracks had separated Yaumatei and Tsimshatsui into two distinct districts for more than one hundred years. Tsimshatsui, immediately across the harbour from the City of Victoria, was to evolve into an area of sophistication, pandering to the tourists as well as an upmarket local clientele.

Yaumatei, on the other hand, with a relatively calm shore which could shelter ships during the typhoon season, amassed a populace living on boats. It also turned out to be a good place for lighters to unload and take on goods. A population of cookies came into being. A service industry to cargo ships developed. As a result, Yaumatei was to become a community of working men and women connected with the less glamorous aspects of maritime shipping.

Much of Yaumatei today is the result of two major land reclamation projects, the first lasting from 1887 to 1904, and the next phase in 1924. Until Nathan Road gained prominence as the leading commercial street in Yaumatei as well as Tsimshatsui, the town centre of Yaumatei was Shanghai Street, named after another leading seaport on the China coast.

Even before 1887, the streets of Yaumatei had been laid out in grids. Their names—Shanghai Street, Ningbo Street, Canton Street and Saigon Street—deriving from major port cities of Asia, attest to the maritime association of the neighbourhood from its very beginning.

During the the 19th century and the early twentieth century, Yaumatei was characterised by its hovels, derelict boats, and workshops serving the shipping trade. It was an industrial as well as commercial area, and a rough neighbourhood by any yardstick. The workshops were in clusters. Those on Canton Road, for instance, dealt in hand tools and accessories.

Shops and other facilities were there to cater to the needs and caprices of seamen while ashore but served the soldiers from the barracks as well. There were barbers, chandlers, tailors, shoe-makers, bath-houses, brothels, pawnshops, iron-mongers and tin-smiths, carpenters and woodcarvers, and coffin makers. Hawkers feeding people with little time and money operated in the open air, but with hot food and a roof to keep out the elements.

In time, families settled in Yaumatei so the neighbourhood became increasingly residential without giving up its commercial and industrial character. Shops to fulfil household needs, selling clothes food items, knives, scales, woks, bamboo steamers, ceramic ware,

(continued on next page)

(continued from previous page)

Chinese medicines, dried goods, and clothes, for instance, replaced some of the others on Shanghai Street. Structures of four to six or nine stories were built, with the upper floors as residences, especially if the buildings did not have elevators to make them unsuitable for business premises. The better buildings boasted two apartments per floor, but the less commodious were little more than sleeping cubicles for seamen or labourers rather than homes for families. A United Nations study on slums revealed that as late as 1977, although most households in Yaumatei enjoyed 'access to a flush toilet', having to share kitchen facilities was one major reason for 'frequent squabbles' among the neighbours.

The spiritual life of the seafaring population as well as the local residents had not been neglected in Yaumatei, as evidenced by the presence of a myriad of houses of worship which gave Temple Street its name. In matters of religious conviction the Chinese were not a discriminating lot, embracing all manners of deities which came their way without exclusion. Hence, a host of supreme beings occupied every altar. As befitting a seaside community, the Queen of Heaven, protector of the sea and all who sailed on it, venerated on the Chinese coast as well as the islands fringing the shores, enjoyed the place of honour in the temples at Yaumatei.

Temples were also erected to honour the City God, the Mother Dragon, the Bodhisattva Guanyin, all the individual gods of the Sixty Year Cycle, and a pantheon of deified historical personages including Judge Pao, General Guan, and Wong Tai Sin. The Earth God and the ancestors, too, were not forgotten. Questionable taste and incongruity of iconography not withstanding, the temple precincts were also inhabited by a handful of fortune tellers, candle, oil, and incense sellers.

In addition, Yaumatei was a world of hawkers, whom you encountered where'er you walked. The Temple Street night market as a phenomenon of cheap goods loudly hailed at stationary stalls did not come into being until after the Second World War. The conjecture that this bazaar was not managed in any formal sense, or that it was administered by the triad organizations, only serves to highlight yet again the grassroots character of Yaumatei.

Watches, Jewellery and Electronic Bargains of Yore

Once more, develop your own *guanxi* in shops that carry watches, jewellery, cameras and electronic bargains of yesteryear. The best way is for a friend already enjoying such a relationship to introduce you. You may then hope for the best possible prices without being cheated. The practice of unscrupulous traders trying to get rid of their out-of-date if not altogether bogus merchandise on unsuspecting customers is most prevalent in these markets. Distrust all 'great deals'. Always see that there is a guarantee as well as a warranty. Anything that needs plugging into an electric outlet should be scrutinized to ensure worldwide use, because dual voltage appliances should be universal today. Pay attention especially if you live in Japan and the United States where appliances are available for the single voltage of 110–120.

Computers, plus Software and Computer Games

All makes of computer, including IBM personal computers and Apple products, are available in Hong Kong. Clones made in Asia are also here, as is much pirated hardware and software. You will have to examine your conscience when you venture into the labyrinth of bargain computer supplies: Government agents still raid the shops from time to time for counterfeits. Be prepared to pay heavily for service and replacement parts. The facts that many young school children play hand-held computer games during break instead of kicking a ball, and that Triad-controlled computer game parlours can be found in various neighbourhoods, are of increasing concern to educational and law enforcement authorities.

CASH, CREDIT CARDS AND DISCOUNTS

Almost all your guidebooks tell you to bargain in Hong Kong. Indeed, bargaining was a part of the fun of shopping. Modernization of business practices, however, has led to the installation of price tags on all kinds of merchandise. Even so, most stores will give you a discount if you insist, and jewellers will give a higher discount than, say, Lane Crawford. Usually, discounts apply to cash sales only. Cheques used to be accepted everywhere, but since the advent of credit cards, paying by personal cheque is a thing of the past. A rule of thumb is: if the sales staff are surly and the service is bad, use whichever credit card takes the highest percentage for commission. When all else fails, bring someone skilful at handling recalcitrant shop assistants with you.

PUBLIC HOLIDAYS IN HONG KONG

Calendar of Public Holidays
Fixed Public Holidays

1 January	New Year's Day
1 May	Labour Day
1 July	Hong Kong SAR Establishment Day
1 October	National Day
25 December	Christmas Day
26 December	Boxing Day

Moveable Public Holidays

end Jan—mid Feb	First three days of Lunar New Year (Spring Festival)
early April	Ching Ming Festival
March–April	Good Friday
March–April	Easter Monday
April–May	Lord Buddha's Birthday
May–June	Tuen Ng (Dragon Boat) Festival
Sept–early Oct	Day after Mid-Autumn Festival
October	Chung Yeung Festival

On these public holidays banks, schools, public offices, and government departments close. Police, Fire, Emergency Services, and Speed Post, however, although with reduced services, remain open. Public holidays in Hong Kong are statutory, which means that you are legally obligated to give employees the day off as a paid holiday, or substitute it with another day if their services are needed on the public holiday. Note that Chinese festivals are observed according to the Chinese Lunar calendar and their dates vary every year, as are Christian holidays such as Good Friday and Easter. Festivals or holidays of other nationalities or faiths are not observed in Hong Kong as holidays for the public.

There are twelve statutory holidays. They are: the first day of the new year (one day), the first three days of the Chinese new year (three days), Ching Ming (one day), Labour Day (one day), Dragon Boat Festival (one day), Establishment

Day (one day), the day following the Mid-Autumn Festival (one), Chung Yeung Festival (one), Chinese National Day (one day), and Christmas Day (one day). The employees are also entitled to take every Sunday off.

Other public holidays, such as the Saturday between Good Friday and Easter, Buddha's birthday, and the day after Christmas, however, are also public holidays. This means that the date is shown in red colour on your local calendar. Since these holidays are not considered statutory holidays, legally, your employees are not entitled to a day off with pay. More humane employers, do not quibble in giving their Christian domestics Good Friday.

Closed to Traffic

On public holidays and on Sundays certain areas are closed to motor traffic to enable pedestrians to roam in safety. From time to time, events are scheduled to take place on these closed streets. Watch out for these events as they can get rather crowded.

CHINESE FESTIVALS

Five Chinese festivals are marked by public holidays in Hong Kong: the Lunar New Year, or Spring Festival, the Ching Ming Festival, the Dragon Boat Festival, the Mid-Autumn Festival, and Chung Yeung. Ching Ming is a time for remembering, and at Chung Yeung people climb to higher ground, an excuse to spend some time out of doors with the family; in Hong Kong it is also an occasion to visit ancestral graves. The other festivals are joyous occasions marked by great ceremonies and special foods.

The Lunar New Year—Spring Festival

The Lunar New Year is the most significant of the Chinese festivals, and is the most elaborately celebrated. Until after the mid-1980s, offices, schools, factories, shops and restaurants were closed for at least five days, some for as many as fifteen, because this was the time of the annual vacation for workers. In recent years, an increasing number of restaurants have even opened on the first day of the New Year, and more are

opening on the second or third day, probably to earn extra money to cover their overheads. Conservative employers, especially in cases when workers do not even take Sundays off, still allow their hirelings a more extensive respite for the holiday season. With the advent of Filipina domestic help, Hong Kong's household services, at least, no longer come to a complete halt—as they did when Chinese amahs used to return to their native villages and not re-emerge until the end of the month.

The buildings on both sides of the harbour are again neon-lit, but the greetings are now 'Felicitations and Prosperity', more suitable to the Chinese New Year season and the Hong Kong ethos. The population, the children at least, don bright-coloured clothing and enter into the spirit of the holiday. There are special dishes for the New Year, and the most conspicuous decorations in Hong Kong are the miniature orange trees and flowering peach branches. No unlucky word is supposed to be uttered; children are fed sweets constantly, to mollify the ill effect of any unfortunate word that might emerge from their mouths.

The nicest aspect of the Lunar New Year celebrations in Hong Kong is the firework display on the second day of the

Children receiving laisee at Chinese New Year's. Note the peach blossoms and the miniature golden orange tree.

year. Three boats are moored in the harbour. Wonderful fireworks are shot into the night sky, synchronized with music specially composed for the occasion. Usually, a major company sponsors this much awaited event. All traffic along the harbour stops during the display, and hundreds of thousands of the populace line the shore and the roads, uttering the ubiquitous 'Wah' each time anything rises from the boats. If you rent a hotel room with a harbour view in order to watch the display, do not count on leaving until well after the roads are reopened.

The single most important ritual for you to remember is to wish everyone 'Fat choy'. This concept, of gaining a large amount of money during the coming year, has become an integral part of the season's ritual. You hand out red *laisee* packets. You give one to everyone you see, almost: your household, the people who normally render you services such as the doormen in your apartment and office buildings, all the children you meet, and all the unmarried adults too. The office as well as household staff normally draw a thirteenth month's pay at this time, but you must not forget to give each a red packet on the first working day of the year. The amount in each envelope depends on your relationship to the recipient; bear in mind, though, that all paper currency feels the same inside a paper packet. So, unless you use different designs for the differing amounts inside, you will find yourself in a confused state of mind each time you hand out a laisee. To make the distinction even more evident, you can insert the same amount in each envelope and simply hand one to some people and more than one to others. Children used to be happy with anything, and indeed they are spoilt by the large number of laisee gifts they receive these days. The Hong Kong streets are littered with discarded red packets, while the bolder children sing the jingle 'Felicitations and Prosperity! Laisee is coming my way. I really do not want any that contain only one dollar, but I will welcome any packet with a ten dollar bill inside.' Inflation, we understand, has raised the ante of the children's disclaimer to 'ten dollars' and the minimum welcomed to 'one hundred'.

Grave Sweeping at Ching Ming

The Chinese commemorate their departed progenitors by visiting family shrines and sweeping ancestral graves, at Ching Ming in early spring. In Hong Kong, residents whose ancestral graves are not in the territory head for their home villages in a mass exodus to China.

Like other traditions, this practice of commemorating the dead has undergone many changes inside China. It has been declared superstitious by twentieth century reformers, and eradicated as an opiate of the people by Maoist modernizers; but these traditions have been faithfully observed outside China wherever there are large concentrations of ethnic Chinese. Southeast Asia, including Hong Kong, has become a rich repository of old Chinese traditions. Newcomers soon attune themselves, and flock back to family graves in China at Ching Ming and other weekends.

The tradition of honouring the dead means offering obeisance and food in front of the spiritual tablets; or, in

At ancestral graves in Hong Kong. Hillside positions optimise fungshui. Food, incense and flowers are offered. Photographs of the buried are baked into porcelain and set on the headstone.

the absence of such tablets today, before photographs of departed progenitors. The offerings are symbolic gestures to ensure that the ancestors continue to enjoy their sustenance in the nether world. Similar ceremonies are performed at the grave-side. Incense sticks are lit. Cooked cold food is offered and, here in Hong Kong, there is always a roast pig. For some reason that nobody could remember, even during the seventeenth century, no fire is lit in the kitchen at Ching Ming. Pieces of paper folded into shapes resembling silver and gold ingots are burned in furnaces in the temples, since fires are no longer allowed in the cemeteries. Today, on the assumption that inflation is not confined to this world, paper currency in $1,000,000 denominations is sent to the ancestors—also through the flames.

Dragon Boat Races

The Tuen Ng Festival takes place at the beginning of the summer, when the weather in North China is just warm enough for outdoor sports. It is marked in Hong Kong by dragon boat races, promoted by the Hong Kong Tourist Association into an international event. The races were a tradition of fishermen and boatmen of the rivers. The noisy dragon boats and glutinous rice buns, associated with this festival, are said to have originated during the third century BC by the local people to save the poet and official Qu Yuan from the fish in the Milo River. Qu had thrown himself into the river when he became despondent because his sovereign had not heeded his entreaties to rid the kingdom of corruption. With the drummer beating the rhythm and oarsmen rowing with all their might, the races have embraced participants from all sectors of Hong Kong. This is an occasion for expatriates and locals to play together. There are men's and women's teams. On another day, there are participants from other Asian countries as well.

Mid-Autumn Festival

The Mid-Autumn Festival celebrates the harvest moon. Taking place in the middle of autumn, on the fifteenth day of the eighty month of the lunar year, the harvest is over, the

Dragon boat racing in Hong Kong waters; reviving a traditional way to celebrate Tuen Ng.

sky is clear, and the moon is large and round. The family, old and young, gather around a table, enjoy fruits of the land and water (crabs), and recall all sorts of legends involving the moon. Children play with paper lanterns made in the shape of rabbits, for instance, one of the residents of the moon, with a lit candle inside its hallow. More often than not, the rabbit is burnt and the child in tears.

In urban Hong Kong, the day of the festival remains a working day. Since the celebrations take place in the evening, the day after the Mid-Autumn is a public holiday. After the celebratory dinner, which now takes place in a restaurant, the children parade their lanterns where there is still space, such as the Peak or Victoria Park on Hong Kong Island.

Alas, paper lanterns of legendary figures have been replaced by plastic structures of popular cartoons. The lit candles have been replaced by a bulb powered by a single battery. Nevertheless, children are happy and the new-fangled toys suit much better their new urban life-style, and their international aesthetic taste. For you, at least, these changes

A father helping his child choose a lantern for the Mid-Autumn Festival.

give you a chance to learn all about what is making Hong Kong's young children kick—namely, to get to know the comic characters, mostly of Japanese origin, they adore.

Chung Yeung Festival

This festival is celebrated on the ninth day of the ninth lunar month, when people climb the highest hill they can find or care to ascend. The legend of 'mounting the heights', dating from no earlier than the Han dynasty, celebrates the number nine. It concerns a fortune-teller who warned a virtuous scholar of an impending calamity and told him to take his family to the mountains for the day. When the scholar and his family returned in the evening, they found that disaster had indeed struck, and that all his livestock had died. Time went on and nobody paid much attention to this holiday, except for scholars; they went up into the mountains, drank, and perhaps flew kites. Along the Yangzi River, it was a holiday for tailors. Families which retained the services of tailors gave them the day off, and treated them to a banquet with chrysanthemum wine.

Somehow, in Hong Kong, early Chinese settlers convinced the British administration that this was an important festival. Perhaps it came from a legend of the Song dynasty connected with Tin Hou. Tin Hou was supposed to have been born in 960 AD; though descended from generations of well-known public officials, her father had chosen to live among simple fishermen on a small island off the Chinese coast. Tin Hou's birth was said to have been unusual: her mother, a devout Buddhist, had a dream during which the Bodhisattva Guanyin provided her with a pill; afterwards Tin Hou was born. At the age of seven she was showing exceptional intelligence. When she was thirteen a visiting monk, impressed by her unique qualities, taught her the secrets of transmigration of the soul. At Chung Yeung in the year 986, when all in China climbed to high ground, Tin Hou was said to have ascended higher and higher until she merged with the sky. From there she made appearances and saved fishermen and other sailors from death among the waves. She is much venerated in Macau.

CHRISTMAS IN HONG KONG

Christmas is a public holiday, celebrated by the entire population. Hong Kong takes on a festive air for the entire month of December and into January, when preparations for the Lunar New Year begin. Since 1998, the term "Boxing Day" for 26 December, is not be used in the official Hong Kong calendar anymore, but Christmas remains a two-day public holiday. The buildings along the Victoria and Kowloon waterfronts are aglow with neon brilliance. The decorations are not merely Christmas trees and colourful lights, they are large scenes depicting themes of Chinese and Western folklore. Restaurants and shops which are not normally closed on Sundays stay open during the Christmas holidays. Hotels offer traditional Western Christmas fare—huge buffets and music. Motor traffic is kept away, to enable pedestrians to enjoy the festive scenes on foot in Central and Tsimshatsui.

To many Hong Kong Chinese, Christmas has joined the Lunar New Year as an occasion for gift giving. With glaring

Friends celebrating Christmas in Hong Kong. Note the absence of the generations now overseas.

lights and blaring music, Christmas in Hong Kong has become as tinselled and commercialized as some of the most secular you might have left behind. Merchants with a keen sense for opportunities to make a fast dollar, were quick to promote Santa Claus as the moving spirit of Christmas celebrations. This is also the time for charity donations through the sale of greeting cards, and parties for handicapped children and indigent elderly. In this respect, the public celebration of Christmas in Hong Kong differs little from the genre you probably know. Being able to celebrate one more holiday in such style further reflects the economic well-being of a segment of the Hong Kong population. It also shows Western influences institutionalized by the commercial sector of Hong Kong.

However, in another sense, Christmas celebrations in Hong Kong are like nothing you have seen before. Instead of attending a church service and a family gathering, you may mark the birth of the Christ Child, Hong Kong style, at one of the myriad hotels on Christmas Eve, enjoying a sumptuous buffet dinner, or restaurant-nightclubs participating in an once in a life time ritual. If you really cannot suppress an urge to experience such an evening for yourself, be prepared for a unique awakening. You will marvel at the restaurateur's originality in incorporating elements from Western celebrations of New Year's Eve, by providing noise-makers and party-hats with a dinner of many courses. What may compel you to abort the evening will be the band's thunderous rendering of *Hark! The Herald Angels Sing* and *Silent Night* in rock 'n' roll rhythm – to which you will be expected to swing, and sing along too no doubt, with the karaoke machine.

KEEPING BUSY IN HONG KONG

As is the case in any metropolitan city, Hong Kong has many activities that can keep one occupied in the leisure hours. From active pursuits to more sedentary hobbies, the city has it all, the only difficulty is deciding what to do. Here are some suggestions to get you started,

One bit of advice, if you join any organization that begins with the phrase 'Friends of' (such as 'Friends of the Hong Kong Museum of Art' or 'Friends of the Hong Kong Philharmonic'...) , you will find yourself in the company of a group of enthusiastic and informed individuals on almost any topic about which you want to know more. In addition to favoured treatment for you to obtain tickets, these organizations plan and organize wonderful tours to all sorts of interesting places. In time, however, you may need to curb your wild desire to go everywhere and see everything, for, in Hong Kong, too, there are only twenty-four hours a day and 365 days a year!

Country Parks and Other Walks

Hiking in the country is a noteworthy Chinese tradition which you may wish to adopt. Its cost is low and, except when washed out by rain, the trails are there all the time. By seeing something outside urban Hong Kong, you will avoid the ultimate misfortune: leaving with half of Hong Kong's character still hidden from you. 'Get a good map and stay on the trail' is the Government's advice

Hong Kong has many outlying islands where the people still lead a traditional way of life. These are ideal locations where one can get away from the hustle and bustle of city-living.

to walkers. In addition, bring bottled water and your mobile telephone.

The best known, and the most demanding, of the country walks is the MacLehose Trail. Going east and west, the trail is a hundred kilometres long. It is not for novice walkers. But novices will find many easier roads and trails, throughout the green parts of the territory. without the nuisance of flying away for long holiday weekends. And you will avoid the ultimate misfortune: leaving with half of Hong Kong's character still hidden from you.

Whatever you choose, do not forget the Maipo Marshes—a nature reserve run by the Worldwide Fund for Nature. This sanctuary, on the border between Hong Kong and the People's Republic of China, is the last stopping place for migratory birds from as far away as Siberia and Mongolia on their way to Australia.

Alas, before long, the Maipo Marshes may be a thing of the past—a victim of urban pollution and development.

Urban Areas

There are historic walks in the urban areas. Hong Kong Tourist Association publications give you a wide variety of choice, according to your interests and inclination. Or, you can take off by yourself. Do not worry about getting lost. After all, this is Hong Kong, you will find somebody who understands your questions and can answer you in English! Once I took walks through some of Hong Kong's old neighbourhoods such as Sheung Wan in Hong Kong. Following are the notes I made at that time.

A Walk in Sheung Wan—Earliest Chinese Settlement of Colonial Hong Kong head

Sheung Wan came into being as a result of the establishment of British Hong Kong. From the outset, this community has been Chinese; its development and growth virtually isolated from the colonial government which nominally had jurisdiction over it.

After the Union Jack was unfurled in Hong Kong on 25 January 1841, the expatriate traders located their activities on the waterfront in Central and Wanchai. The Chinese, comprising traders, small

(continued on next page)

(continued from previous page)

shop-keepers, craftsmen, and coolies, who provided goods and services in Hong Kong, were not embraced into this international community. They settled on the outskirts.

The earliest Chinese immigrants to Hong Kong were Cantonese speakers from the Pearl River Delta. At first they were allotted land above Queen's Road, opposite the Central Market. When pressure for space intensified in early 1844, the Chinese were moved further west, and eventually to an area above Hollywood Road by 1851. This was the Taipingshan area, reputed so mysterious and dangerous that few outsiders, including the colonial authorities, intruded.

The community was urban and commercial. Topographical constraints as much as cosmological considerations dictated the positioning of the pathways and structures. The small one or two storeyed buildings were constructed of bamboo and wood, and later of local bricks. Business was conducted on the ground floor, with the back or upper storey as living quarters. Inhabitants who did not own property occupied rooms that were little more than sleeping cubicles. Drainage was poor. Sanitation did not exist. Fire was an ever-present danger. Life was hard and cheap. Opium addiction was commonplace. There was an inordinate number of brothels. Contagious diseases, including syphilis, once began, could not be contained.

Shortly after the Treaty of Nanking confirmed British sovereignty in Hong Kong in August 1942, merchants from other parts of China, such as Chiuchow (Chaozhou, Swatow), arrived to take advantage of of Hong Kong's geographical location and free port status, and they set up their operations in Sheung Wan. They traded in rice, Chinese medicines, ginseng, textiles, as well as processed and preserved sea foods. Objects of masculine fantasy to restore virility, for instance deer and rhinoceros horns and other body parts, were also important articles of trade. As wealth was accumulated and special relationships established, a class of the elite emerged in Sheung Wan as leaders of the Chinese community in Hong Kong. Among the wealthiest merchants were members of the guild of Nam Pak Hong (literally meaning South and North Trade), who traded between China and Southeast Asia. These guilds were the forerunners of the Chinese Chamber of Commerce.

In time, heavy demand for space led to land reclamation projects, first to Des Voeux Road and then Connaught Road. As Chinese commercial interests moved down hill, the Taipingshan area was left with only minor trades and crafts mostly associated with religious observances and funeral rites – incense, tapered candles, coffins, ritual paper money and other objects intended for the dead in the nether world.

On the flat land, the commerce of Sheung Wan continued to exhibit the characteristic of clustering of goods. Workshops processing and packaging ginseng are side by side, as are shops with open

(continued on next page)

(continued from previous page)

fronts displaying preserved foods, items deemed essential to properChinese entertaining. Adding much to the colour of Sheung Wan are rows of beige coloured whole shark's fin on the shelves, golden brown dried abalone and scallops, black sea weeds which looks like human hair and are prized because its name in Cantonese sounds just like fa zai, literally meaning amassing wealth. During the Lunar New Year's season, strings of salted fish which usually hang in the front of the shops with great aplomb are overwhelmed by pungent sausages and pressed ducks.

From the beginning, British officials in Hong Kong has adopted the stance that the Chinese could manage their own affairs. Furthermore, they believed that the secret societies, the triads, seditious and criminal at the same time, had moved into Hong Kong, hence it was better to let the Chinese handle their own problems. The merchants assumed the leadership of the community. Civic responsibilities included the settlement of disputes and social obligations led to patronage of temples and charitable organizations. The Man Mo Temple was built in 1847 by an individual trader who had amassed a fortune from provisioning the British during the Opium War and by controlling the pirates around Hong Kong. The temple renovations in 1851, however, were paid by the merchants of Sheung Wan. From then onwards, the merchants began to sit on the Temple Committee. Since the Man Mo Temple owned the land around it, the Committee wielded a great deal of influence and power. Chinese elite went on to found the Tung Wah Hospital for the community and to organise Po Leung Kuk to care for women and girls.

Social responsibilities embracing sponsorship of festival celebrations are continuing today. The birthday of the Earth God on the 18th day of the first month of the lunar year, is celebrated noisily and gloriously, including performances of Cantonese operas. In this sense, at least, old Hong Kong still lives in Sheung Wan.

The Royal Asiatic Society

Despite its somewhat cumbersome name, this Society is in Hong Kong a group of low-profile individuals whose common interest is Asia, in particular Southeast Asia, including Hong Kong: all aspects of its peoples, arts, customs, cultures, institutions, philosophy, history, societies, traditions and so forth. Membership is open to all. It is a friendly and welcoming society. Lectures are given by local and visiting scholars. Topics vary, but the lectures cater to an audience sharing an interest in the Continent without necessarily being specialists in any aspect of it. Museum curators and other qualified members arrange tours to sites of cultural and historical interest in China and elsewhere. Programmes are conducted in English. The Society publishes its *Journal of the Hong Kong Branch of the Royal Asiatic Society*, supposedly once a year but with some flexibility.

Other Societies

Whatever personal interests, you will be able to find like minded individuals in Hong Kong, perhaps already organized into a society, such as the Ceramic Society, amateur dramatic or singing societies, and many others.

Museums and Galleries

The Hong Kong Government and the universities maintain museums and galleries. Although the objects and the techniques of display are of high quality and international interest, the special focus of Hong Kong's collections is Chinese or pan-Asian. The historical museums, including The Hong Kong Museum of History, the Heritage Museum, and those on sites that have survived from the past, such as the Sam Tong Uk in Tsuen Wan, a restored walled village of the New Territories, will enable you to delve into Hong Kong's past. The Hong Kong Museum of Art shows touring exhibitions of masterpieces of Eastern and Western Art, such as the exhibition of exquisite artifacts from China, and the more recent attendance record breaking Impressionist paintings from Paris. Art galleries display works by masters and experimenters. Works of sculpture by Henry Moore dot the urban landscape.

It will take time to become acquainted with the museums, but as a resident you will have more than a day or two to explore them. The Friends of the Chinese University Art Museum and the Friends of the Hong Kong University Museum are particularly active, and welcome residents such as yourself as members. A newly established museum on Dr Sun Yat-sen, under the guidance of Dr Joseph Ting, a local historian who was the first curator of the Hong Kong History Museum, is about to open as this edition goes to press.

THE PERFORMING ARTS IN HONG KONG

Hong Kong is no longer a desert as far as the performing arts are concerned. Since the establishment of the Hong Kong Academy for Performing Arts, not only the performers in dance, drama and music, the training of artists in all aspects of technical theatre and cinematic arts has been brought up to degree level, to the most modern aesthetic and technical standards.

Chinese Music

Chinese vocal and instrumental music is appreciated mostly by an older Chinese audience, especially those newly settled in Hong Kong. All schools of Chinese opera from the different provinces of China tour Hong Kong regularly. Hong Kong has its own Chinese Orchestra; it holds concerts at the Cultural Centre and in halls throughout the territory.

Chinese music, perhaps much more than Chinese visual art, remains difficult for people not reared in the Chinese tradition to appreciate. However, Chinese instruments are being modernised and will be better attuned to the non-Asian ear. The seating of the players has been modified also, to reflect Western influences. The conductor stands in front of the orchestra with his back to the audience. The number of players has been increased, creating a larger sound to suit the modern concert halls. In 1994 the Chinese Orchestra joined the Hong Kong Philharmonic for a number of joint concerts.

Chinese Opera

Almost all genres of traditional Chinese theatre are available in Hong Kong, either touring Chinese companies or local performers in Cantonese opera. Watch for visiting as well as local troupes performing Cantonese, Kun Qu, Peking, or Sichuan operas. Chinese opera is extremely popular with the locals, so, buy your tickets early. There are background briefings before the performances to help increase the level of your comprehension and enjoyment. Furthermore, high-tech Hong Kong theatres offer sur-titles in English as well as Chinese, to enable you to follow the plots and dialogues all along the way.

Western Music

As more and more young people come to appreciate Western music, concerts in Hong Kong are well attended. A large cultural complex was built in Tsimshatsui, and some major urban centres in Hong Kong, Kowloon, and the New Territories as well, housing concert halls, drama theatres and museums. Choral music, traditionally, attracts a large following. Whereas learning an instrument costs money, choral work does not. So music training in Hong Kong schools is principally vocal. Training of young children in classical instruments has become an important part of extra-curricular programme for Hong Kong students. In addition to private lessons initiated mostly by ambitious parents who want their children to enjoy what they did not, children are given opportunities to learn musical instruments through the good will of the Music Office, now administered under the auspices of the School of Music of the Hong Kong Academy for Performing Arts. The Hong Kong Sinfonietta provides an opportunity for many young local musicians to perform under world-renown conductors since 1991. The Hong Kong Philharmonic Orchestra, with local and expatriate professional players, has, since the 1970s, enjoyed a stormy relationship with several principal conductors. But the orchestra also plays under the batons of world famous guest conductors and soloists. Both these orchestras also serve an important role in music education.

Visiting orchestras, ensembles and soloists have Hong Kong firmly on their East Asian tour programmes. Ethnic Chinese musicians who have won renown elsewhere enjoy a warm following here. The most popular of these is Yo Yo Ma. A number of new works enjoyed their premier in Hong Kong. The symphony *1997* was written by the renowned Chinese composer Tan Dun expressedly for the handover ceremonies. It was first played by the Asian Youth Orchestra on 4 July 1997. Local composers, such as Law Wing Fai, work in the Western idiom with a Chinese twist, receiving commissions from orchestras to premier their works.

Amateur music groups perform regularly. The Hong Kong Oratorio Society leads the vocal field, with several concerts each year. The Bach Choir is also excellent, as are the Hong Kong singers and Bel Canto. There are also church choirs and the Hong Kong Philharmonic Chorus. An amateur group specializes in 'ancient' music and 'original' instruments. Depending on your skill and your willingness to commit time, you will be welcomed by any of these groups as player, singer—or listener. Our record of attendance up to today is eleven concerts in two weeks.

Theatre and Dance

Theatre in Hong Kong has come of age. In addition to visiting performers and amateur groups, there are local professional companies which produce plays in English or Cantonese: the Chung Ying Theatre Company, the Hong Kong Repertory Theatre, the Exploration Theatre (which, founded by the American community in 1982, performs original works by local playwrights). There is also experimental theatre at the Fringe and community centres staged by young dramatists in Hong Kong. The Hong Kong Singers is an amateur group comprising mostly expatriate members. The group performances musicals, the latest was *Annie Get Your Gun* in March 2005. So, get in touch!

Dance aficionados and connoisseurs should not feel left out by the Hong Kong cultural scene. The Hong Kong Dance Company performs traditional Chinese dances. The Western genre is represented by the Hong Kong Ballet and the City Contemporary Dance Company. Jean Wong, a ballet dancer and businesswoman originally from Shanghai, runs a string of ballet dance studios throughout the territory, training young men and women in the art of ballet. To celebrate its tenth anniversary, the Hong Kong Academy for Performing Arts staged Stravinsky's *Petroushka*, reproducing choreography, sets and costumes of the original Paris production.

The Hong Kong Tai Tai and the Tango

The latest craze among the women in Hong Kong is ballroom dancing. The Hong Kong *tai tai* hires her own professional dance teacher to train her in the art and skills of ballroom dancing. A number of tai tais have also managed to convince their husbands to do the same. So, charity balls have become quite a spectacle, with the tai tais partnered by their teachers dancing the tango! The teachers hail from all parts of the world, some even under exclusive contract to a single student. At one time, the tai tais had focused on karaoke singing, but the best and the bravest have switched to ballroom dancing.

The Hong Kong Arts Festival

For about a month each winter, the Hong Kong Arts Festival attracts all genres of Western and Eastern performing arts to the territory. The Arts Festival has become an established institution in Asia since its founding in 1973. Audiences from abroad join Hong Kong residents in anticipation of this festival. The organizers take into consideration all styles of Hong Kong taste, and seem to know exactly which of the dozen or more locales is suitable for a particular group of performers. The Arts Festival brings in more than a thousand artists from abroad each year. Their programmes include drama in English and Chinese, opera, dance, orchestral and smaller ensemble music, mimes, magicians, Peking and provincial Chinese opera, plus Japanese and other Asian arts. Hong Kong's own Philharmonic Orchestra usually opens and closes the Festival.

The 2005 festival has been hailed the best ever in the sense of attendance and receipt. On a single day, for instance, the programme included the participation by the Polish National Opera in *Otello*, Béjart Ballet Lausanne in its fiftieth anniversary tour, Compagnia Thetrale Fo-Rame in *Johan Padan* and *the Discovery of America* by Dario Fo, and the *French Kiss*. On other days there was the *Eternal Love*, a nine-hour Kun Opera performed by the Jiangsu Kun Opera Company, as well as a recital by an eleven-year old gifted Hong Kong pianist who won a coveted international award in 2004. There was a jazz performance, plus others from the region. The variety of the programme bespeaks the cultural taste of the Hong Kong audience, as well as reflects the standard of the Hong Kong performance locales.

The Festival's programmes is announced each September, when you may order tickets by post. Tickets go on sale at the various box offices one month before the events concerned. It is easy to buy tickets in person, because all box offices are linked by something called URBTIX. A message of warning: do not be too enthusiastic and buy more tickets than you will be able to use. A rule of thumb: no more than two events a week—but it is hard to confine oneself to such a regimen.

Besides this major festival there are the annual Asian Arts Festival, film festivals of various kinds and in various languages, and festivals catering to more specialised interests.

Ordering Tickets by Telephone or Internet

Thanks to modern technology, you can now buy performing arts and cinema tickets through automated phone systems or the internet, for a small fee of course. For the cinema, you can order them two days in advance and collect the tickets at the door.

Concert tickets are usually sold by either the Leisure & Culture Services ticketing system or HK Ticketing. Both systems will post the tickets to you for a service fee, or you can collect from their box offices. (Pay attention to the timings as some theatres require you collect well in advance of a performance.) If the latter, you will have an up-to-date, thoroughly professional system. If the former, you will need to speak to a usually polite but not always well-trained salesperson. On the telephone you are well-advised to follow a set procedure. If you say what you want in your own way, you will say it many times. First, establish that you want to buy tickets, and wait to be asked step by step what date, which performance, where, the title of the show, how many tickets and at what price. On further prompting, give your name and the numbers of your credit card and your identity card or passport number.

Bring your credentials: credit and identity cards (or passport). When you collect your tickets, you may have to prove you are indeed you, before you receive your tickets.

GAMBLING

Gambling is a way of life in Hong Kong. Sanctioned by law or not, the Chinese bet on horse and dog races, soccer, play mahjong and fantan at home, on the street or at small stalls—or in clubs set up for the purpose of gambling—and buy lottery tickets literally by the gross.

Mahjong, a game of tiles played by four people sitting at a table, is a latecomer to Chinese gambling. The game was not played in China until the Ming dynasty. It used to be a social game for the leisured classes, but playing with money makes it more fun. In addition to the winners, people who gain financially from this game are the numerous restaurants catering to mahjong. On weekend evenings the noise from tiles is deafening. Of course we can argue that a peaceful meal at a Chinese restaurant is a contradiction in terms, but no old Hong Kong hand would venture into any such restaurant hoping to enjoy a half-way peaceful dinner.

Dominoes, dating back to the Tang dynasty, is a game more ancient than the mahjong; but it is less prestigious. It is played in the street because it is a faster game. The stakes are smaller. The Chinese call this game 'connecting dragons'. The most popular game in Hong Kong is fantan, a card game played by any number of players, with or without a board.

Hong Kong Jockey Club—Lotteries Fund

Charitable use of the proceeds from gambling began during the administration of Governor Sir Richard Macdonnell, during the late 1860s, with the appropriation of funds or a grant of land to establish the Tung Wah Hospital to take care of indigent sick Chinese. Horse racing had been imported into Hong Kong by the British, and the Chinese immediately cottoned on to the gambling aspect of the 'Sport of Kings'. The Jockey Club Charities is now one of the largest single contributors to Hong Kong charities. The 'Mark Six' lotteries are drawn every week. The money not given to the winners swells the Lotteries Fund, which is used to finance welfare services through grants and loans.

LEARNING CHINESE

An Ancient Language

China is a large country, with a people comprising a large number of ethnicities, called nationalities in Chinese law. In addition to the largest nationality, the Han Chinese, whose language is Chinese, there are more than fifty recognised nationalities With the exception of one or two, each nationality speaks a distinct language.

In addition, within the Chinese language, there are a multitude of dialects, most of which are not comprehensible to the others. Arguably, the most difficult of the Chinese dialects is Cantonese, which is the street language in .Hong Kong. Almost all the newspapers are published in Cantonese. Therefore, if you want to pick up the 'local' language to communicate with the populace, you learn Cantonese. On the other hand, Cantonese is not used anywhere else, so, if you want to be able to communicate elsewhere in China, you learn Putonghua. Confused? I don't blame you. One comforting thought: all the Chinese dialects share the same writing system. So, you can communicate by writing.

Even before the Shang dynasty (age of the bronze sacrificial vessels) 1766–1121 BC, the Chinese writing system was already well developed. There was a subject-verb-object syntax and the characters, as Chinese words are called. The characters may appear strange and difficult to you who are used to the alphabet, it may be of comfort to know that there is logic behind the Chinese characters.

The Chinese language began as pictures or symbols. The characters are formed with pictographs (pictures), abstract descriptive pictographs (ideas), and phono-pictographs (sound = pronunciation). The character of 'wood' (木), for instance, is made of a 'tree' in ancient China. Two 'trees' (林) side by side form the character for 'woods', and three 'trees' (森), one on the top and two on the bottom, form 'dense forest'.

Since no language can expand based solely on pictographs, characters representing ideas and concepts, and characters representing visions and pictures eventually came into being. Further examples: putting the character of the sun and that of the moon side by side, you have the character meaning light, or brightness, or understanding.

The Chinese language is not difficult, but it involves a great deal of contextual implications. For instance, unlike English, which you must know well since you are reading this book written in English, there is no different person or for Chinese verbs: no singular or plural persons, nor past, present, or future tenses. The only problem remains that there is so much to learn and to remember! One time, an English friend was learning Chinese in Hong Kong. She was trying to flatter me, who read classical Chinese, by proclaiming: 'Ah, you must know a thousand characters!' I did not have the nerve to enlighten her that I had mastered more than this number before entering the fourth grade.

The basic principles of the Chinese characters may be simple, and the character eternal, 永 comprises all the strokes you need to form a character, writing Chinese is an art. I met an American woman, who knew nary a word of Chinese, nor had she seen anyone write the characters "live", actually wrote a book on Chinese characters, albeit for children, and won an international prize!

The good news is that, some foreigners have managed to acquire sufficient knowledge to survive in Chinese-speaking communities, to conduct business, or even to pursue a scholarly career in Chinese Studies. Do not expect, however, to get the accent right within, say, the first few decades of your speaking the language.

Although we use the term learning Chinese in a general context, do note that in Hong Kong, the Chinese language usually refers to the Chinese dialect Cantonese which most of the people in Hong Kong speak. What is called "Chinese" by most other people is the language spoken by the mainland Chinese and which is called Putonghua in Hong Kong.

Learning Cantonese in Hong Kong

To be perfectly sensible, unless you entertain the ambition to become literate in Chinese, you should just learn oral Cantonese in order to communicate with the populace, by using Roman transliteration without entering the realm of characters. There is no law against your expending your time and energy while here to master another language, however. In Hong Kong, regardless what people say about the deterioration in the local command of English, it is still a useful means of communication. If you go across the border to China, you will need to speak at least a modicum of Putonghua in order to get around. Then, Cantonese would not be helpful.

Private Tutors

Chances are that your employer here would provide you with some form of language tutoring in your office: either Cantonese or Putonghua. How much you actually learn will depend on you. Learning a new language calls for total concentration and perseverance. How much time do you have for this endeavour depends on where you put your top piority. If you have a demanding job, which you must since the employer is spending a great deal of money to bring you to Hong Kong, unless it is essential for you to understand Chinese for your work, chances for your being able to spend time learning Chinese are not good. If your job does demand that you possess a knowledge of Chinese, chances are that the employer would have hired a person who already speaks Chinese! Your spouse, on the other hand, is a different matter. Having said all of the above, if you are offered a tutor, take advantage.

Learning with a Group

Other than personal tutors, there are language schools which teach Cantonese and/or Putonghua. Please remember that most of these schools are operating as businesses.

There are serious institutions, well, some more serious than others. Check the websites of the universities. These institutions are funded by the Hong Kong Government, but almost all of them operate something called 'extension courses', touting 'life long learning'. You pay a great deal of money, but for some of these courses you can even receive credits that enable you to receive associate degrees. Almost all of these institutions offer Chinese language studies.

Let me give you one example. The University of Hong Kong runs SPACE (School of Professional and Continuing Education) which runs a Centre for Language Studies. The languages taught there include English, European languages (French, German, Italian, and Spanish), and Asian Languages (Japanese, Korean, Putonghua, the Shanghai Dialect, and Thai). Please note that Cantonese is not one of the subjects. In other words, the focus of SPACE probably is probably on local Cantonese speakers, not yet. Still, check it out on the net at http://www.hkuspace.hku.edu.hk.

Serious Chinese Programme

At the Chinese University of Hong Kong in Shatin, there is the New Asia Yale-in-China Chinese language programme. You can learn Cantonese or Putonghua, but this is a serious programme aimed at university level academic study. It probably means you need to devote full attention to your language learning, but the hard work and devotion will yield results. The website is http://www.cuhk.edu.hk/clc.

OTHER HOBBIES TO PICK UP IN HONG KONG

Whatever the reason or reasons for your presence in Hong Kong, you will be working hard, but hardly twenty-four hours a day and seven days a week! If you conscientiously plan some of your leisure, you will be able to enjoy a variety of unexpected activities, perhaps even pick up an advanced academic or professional degree, a modicum of Chinese, or a skill that will stay with you for the rest of your days, such as golf, art or antiques collecting.

Pursuing a Degree

There are ten institutions in Hong Kong which award bachelor's, master's and doctorate degrees in the arts, humanities, science and technology, and in such professions as dentistry, medicine, law, journalism, education and architecture. To meet popular demand, programmes in business administration have been added. At the University of Hong Kong, founded in 1911 and following the British system, teaching is in English except for Chinese and Chinese history before the modern era. The Chinese University of Hong Kong came into being in 1963, when three colleges following the American system were amalgamated. Lectures are given in English, Cantonese or Putonghua, depending on the instructors and the students in each course. Classes began at the University of Science and Technology in 1991, with faculty composed of ethnic Chinese academics hired from North American universities. Concentrating their resources at the undergraduate level, these universities also maintain facilities for postgraduate studies and scholarly research.

Institutions funded by tuition fees as well as the Government are the University of Hong Kong, Chinese University of Hong Kong, Hong Kong University of Science and Technology, Hong Kong Baptist University, City University (the old City Polytechnic) and Hong Kong Polytechnic University (the former Hong Kong Polytechnic)—all of which grant bachelor's and higher degrees. The two polytechnic institutes, originally founded to train students from textiles production and hotel management to occupational therapy, were given university status, as has been Baptist University. Lingnan College, heir to the pre-1949 Lingnan University of Canton, became a degree-granting institution in 1991. Two signs that its Board of Trustees is taking the institution more seriously are the appointment of Professor Edward Chen, an eminent economist and public personage, as the new President, and the construction of a new campus. The other three degree-granting tertiary institutions are the Hong Kong Academy for Performing Arts, the Hong Kong Institute of Education and the Open Learning University.

Several of these institutions hold classes for adults in the evenings. The extra-mural classes did not begin as a part of any university curriculum, in the sense that credits accrued in this manner did not culminate in a degree. However, the evening schools have developed into something grander. The extra-mural studies department at Baptist College has grown into the School of Continuing Education, providing opportunities for Hong Kong residents to study for credits from overseas universities without leaving the territory. The extra-mural studies department of the University of Hong Kong, too, has been transformed into the School of Professional and Continuing Education.

The Open Learning University is different. It was established in 1989 as a distance learning tertiary institution. It is self-financing. Students do not attend classes, nor do they enjoy face-to-face teaching. Lectures or tutorials on mathematics and computer studies, for instance, are televised, typically on Sunday mornings, with video copies available in the study centres.

Students accumulate credits, usually at the rate of one a year, by capping each nine-month course with a three-hour examination.

The OLU provides an opportunity for Hong Kong working adults who wish to take tertiary-level courses or who wish to work for a degree on his or her own time-table.

In other words, for the first time, Hong Kong people who have not been able to go to a college or university for one reason or another, immediately after finishing secondary school, may now pursue higher education even if they hold a full-time job.

This is where you, as an expatriate in the community, can benefit. You may wish to work for a college degree while you are here. Or, if you already have a degree, you may want to pursue a more advanced or a more congenial one. And even if you have no degree in mind, you may take courses—interesting or useful or both—which might well include excellent language training.

Collecting

From world renowned auction houses Christie's and Sotheby's to street stalls, you can fine all manners of arts, crafts, and jewellery in Hong Kong. Of course Asian, especially Chinese, arts are prevalent, but other genres are available too, if you have the money and the interests.

Sports

There are plenty of facilities for sport and recreation in Hong Kong. You can, however, count on the public facilities being crowded when you want to use them, and on the private facilities being beyond your reach. But still, they are there. The South China Athletic Club is an institution to get to know. Facilities include a driving range, and the prices are comfortable. Here you must practise your sportsmanship before your golf and wait with great perseverance. Cricketers will find kindred souls in the Hong Kong and Kowloon cricket clubs.

As with music, Hong Kong is attracting big names to its tennis, squash and golf tournaments. This means, of course,

Tai-chi or Chinese shadow-boxing is a graceful way to fitness. There are many groups that organise regular sessions so its easy to find a group at a convenient location and ask if you can join them.

that the prize is right, but it also indicates that the facilities are of international standard.

There are public swimming pools with good hygienic standards. To sail, water ski or snorkel, however, you will need to spend a great deal of money. Windsurfing had not been noticed as a significant sport in Hong Kong until Lee Lai-shan won the first ever Olympics Gold Medal in windsurfing for Hong Kong in Atlanta in 1996.

EASY TRAVEL TO NEIGHBOURING COUNTRIES
By Boat, Plane, Train, Bus, Car and Subway to China
Travel between Hong Kong and China has become more hassle-free over the last decade. You can fly from here to all the major cities, and to a number of smaller cities that are not a part of the general vocabulary, such as Changchun in Manchuria or Chengdu in Sichuan; but planes may not fly so often as they do to Shanghai or Beijing.

It is possible to go by ferry or hovercraft to ports of the Guangdong province, or by water to Macau and cross the border there. The non-stop train to Guangzhou is easy and comfortable; and, if you want adventure, you can take the train, with changes of course, all the way from Hong Kong to London, via the Trans-Siberian Railway. Buses are now running between Hong Kong and nearby points to the north; some will take you to more than passable golf courses in the morning, and bring you home that very evening. All the while, fellow passengers will be using their mobile phones at the top of their voices.

With the appropriate licences, you are even allowed to drive into China by car.

The most unbelievable and least expensive way to travel to China—and most of the Hong Kong populace 'commute' in this way—is by MTR, and then transfer to a local train of the Canton-Kowloon Railway as far as Lowu; from there one walks across the border to China. During a holiday weekend, more than half a million enterprising souls will cross and return in this way.

Regardless of the route, you need to obtain a visa to visit China. If your business requires you to make frequent trips, a multiple-entry visa is issued by the Chinese visa office here for six months at a time. As a Permanent Resident of Hong Kong, you can obtain a visa of longer duration, depending on the nationality of your passport. Otherwise, single or two-trip visas can be obtained. Single-trip visa can also be obtained at the Shenzhen border.

Patience and perseverance are the key words in making your travel arrangements to China. Unless you plan long in advance, you will be lucky if you can get a seat on a plane during the busy months of spring, summer and autumn. In China, do not expect polite and efficient service from the ground personnel. These young men and women are so hassled that they behave as if they were doing you a big favour by checking you in at all. Furthermore, their command of English—and Chinese, come to that—has deteriorated so much that, since they are tired and are not willing to listen, you feel that you should be grateful if they issue you a boarding pass for the correct flight. Any special request is greeted with sullen silence, if not rude mumbling. They could not care less whether you lose or keep your temper.

MACAU

Only a comfortable jetfoil ride away, Macau has become a favourite place for Hong Kong residence to pass a day or a weekend. Your Hong Kong ID will suffice as travel document. Macau offers more than mere gambling. Residence of foreign traders and families since the seventeenth century, it has been a sophisticated international enclave for more than three hundred years. The then Chinese government did not know what to do with these foreigners in the midst, so they built a wall, in fact telling the foreigners that, on your side of the wall, we do not care what is going on, as long as you keep peace. Hence, unlike Hong Kong, there was no treaty giving the Portuguese right to Macau. Meanwhile, Portuguese and Jesuit influences had been strong, and even today there is a Mediterranean flavour if you search. The new Macau also boasts golfing and swimming facilities, as well as a first-class museum and concert hall. Meanwhile, Portuguese and Jesuit influences remained strong, and even today there is a Mediterranean flavour if you search.

The chief industry in Macau is gaming, but, since Las Vegas moved in, the new Macau also boasts golfing resorts, as well as a first-class museum and concert hall. As this edition goes to the printers, a major entertainment complex, to include 20 restaurants, is about to open.

SHENZHEN

This new town created in the late 1970s and 1980s, offers nothing but shopping. Reached by subway/train, you leave Hong Kong in comfort and find yourself in Lowu in less than half an hour. There you can walk across the border, go through Hong Kong Immigration and enter China within a few yards. Standing in queque may lengthen the entrance process a little longer, but, it is worthwhile—if your sole purpose for this visit is shopping! Young Europeans, both men and women, appear to be impatient in the queque, and are often rude to fellow passengers. Please remember, it is not their fault that you chose a busy time of the day and week to travel!

CHINA AND OTHER ASIAN COUNTRIES

You can visit various parts of China without too much hassle. Being right next door, so to speak, you can afford to see one place at a time. None of the seeing seven cities in as many days for you! Check the net for bargains which include flight, airport transfers, and hotels. For instance, we went to Shanghai for the 2005 New Year's: attended a concert to celebrate the opening of the Shanghai arts centre with the China Philharmonic Orchestra from Beijing and Shanghai's very own Opera Chorus in a fantastic rendition of Carmina Burana by Orf, joined the crowds on New Year's Day in the Chinese City around the Temple of the City God in the tradition of Shanghai Chinese for the past centuries; and found the hospital in the old French Concession where my husband was born years and years ago! We found the bargain package on the net, flew to Shanghai, stayed at the Four Seasons, had a wonderful time without breaking the bank.

There are several long weekends in the Hong Kong calendar, make plans, check your budget, and go to near-by places in Cambodia, Vietnam, Thailand and China, even India and Sri Lanka for history, art and culture; Japan for history, art and culture, and cherry blossom or skiing; Malaysia, Indonesia including Bali, and Thailand for sun and sea; a well as local cultures which are so different from Hong Kong's, and of course, shopping. When we first came to Hong Kong in 1975, I happened to mention to the 'decorator' that I liked batik. The decorator, of whose sense of reality I could fathom nothing, chimed: 'Of course you need to go to Singapore, Indonesia, Malaysia, and Thailand to choose what you like!' She is right. These countries indeed produce beautiful batik, but I was then living in New York. Ignoring her totally, I walked over to Macy's and bought a dozen king-sized sheets and covered all the windows in our apartment!

Anywhere you go from Hong Kong, except for Macau and other points of South China, perhaps, you need to take a plane. When you are used to flying in from Europe or America, or even Australia, the few hours it takes you to go to a resort in neighbouring countries—for the beaches, skiing, spas, or sight-seeing, will seem easy.

DISNEY

As this edition goes to press, Disneyland is opening in Hong Kong. You will be bombarded with data as you settle, especially if you have children.

CONCLUSION

Whatever the reason or reasons for your presence in Hong Kong, you will be working hard. If you conscientiously plan some of your leisure, you will be able to enjoy a variety of unexpected activities, without the nuisance of flying away for long holiday weekends. And you will avoid the ultimate misfortune: leaving with half of Hong Kong's character still hidden from you.

LEARNING
THE LANGUAGE

CHAPTER 8

'Cus I'm a soul caught up without a friend,
Solitary, all alone.
Yes I'm a soul without a friend,
But I can make it on my own.
—Kiera Elizabeth Garvin (b. 1990)

LANGUAGES AND SIGNS

Hong Kong is a bi-lingual society. Although the local use of English is becoming noticeably less orthodox, the language is still understandable if you listen carefully with patience and imagination. All street names, at least, are clearly marked in English and Chinese. There are good maps and directories in both languages. The Cantonese transliterations of the English originals tend to exaggerate on the side of auspiciousness, but they are charming and sometimes even clever. English translations of Cantonese originals, on the other hand, almost always make you stop in your tracks.

If you are Mandarin-speaking (Putonghua) and do not know the Cantonese dialect, you may run into trouble because the translated street names in Hong Kong can confuse Chinese readers. Non-Chinese readers will not have this problem, because to them, Admiralty is Admiralty. There is no confusion. For Chinese readers, however, the name of the Admiralty MTR station becomes 'Jin Zhong', meaning 'Metal Bell' (so named because at that time it was within hearing distance of the British naval headquarters which used a metal bell); but, when pronounced by the MTR in Cantonese, it sounds suspiciously like 'Gum Jones'. By sticking to English, a great deal of frustration can be avoided.

On the other hand, even when you stick to English, you may be confused if your language training followed the American idiom. You may already know that you stand in a *queue* instead of a *line* while waiting for a taxi, and take a *lift* instead of an *elevator* up to your office. The use of prepositions in British and American English differs; likewise the presence or absence of the article *the* before a noun. You do not go to the hospital, unless to visit someone firmly in a particular establishment; as a patient you will go to hospital —a change of status from not being in hospital, which is more significant than the change of address. You will also spell *neighbour* and *labour* with the *u*. Whether you realize or realise it, the *Oxford English Dictionary* spells realize with a *z* but the *South China Morning Post* still insists upon an *s*, as in *recognise* and *sympathise*. Fortunately for you if you come from North America, criminals are put in prison here; so you will not have to face the confusion between *gaol* and *jail*. At least everybody is a capitalist, and you can capitalize on your sojourn here by becoming an Asian specialist.

Pronunciation Guide

The Cantonese romanised script uses the standard developed by Christian Kisa, based on the International Phonetic Association's guidelines.

Consonants

In Cantonese, the consonants **m** and **ng** can form syllables of their own. The other consonants are: **b**, **d**, **dz**, **f**, **h**, **g**, **gw**, **h**, **l**, **n**, **k**, **kw**, **s**, **t**, **ts**, **y**, **w**. The consonants **p**, **t**, **ts**, **k** and **kw** are pronounced with a heavy puff of air. The pronunciation of the trickier consonants are as follows:

- **dz**   as the *d* in *ditzy*
- **gw**   as the *gua* in *guava*
- **kw**   as the *qu* in *quit*
- **m**   as the *m* in **mother**
- **ng**   as the *ng* in *king*
- **ts**   as the *ts* in *tots*

Syllables ending in **k**, **p** and **t** are pronounced in a clipped manner: fast and with a shorter vowel.

(continued on the next page)

(continued from previous page)

Vowels
- a   as the *a* in far
- e   as the *e* in *met*
- i   as the *ee* in *keep*
- o   as the *o* in *roar*
- oe   as the *ur* in *your*
- u   as the *oo* in *woo*
- ü   a rounded *ee* sound like when saying *oo-ee* with little emphasis on the *oo*

Short Vowel
- ɐ   a short half-open *uh* sound like the *a* in *hat*

Long Dipthongs
- ai   as *aye*
- au   as the *ou* in *bounce*
- eu   as the *ew* in *mew*
- iu   *ee-yoo*
- oi   as the *oi* in *oil*

Short Dipthongs
- ɐi   as *hide*
- ɐu   as the *ou* in *lout*
- ei   rhymes with the *a* in *hay*
- eoi (öü)   as the French *oui*
- ou   as the *oe* in *hoe*

Some of the sounds in the Chinese language do not exist in English. The above consonants and vowels are matched as phonetically as possible to an English equivalent.

SPEAKING CANTONESE IN HONG KONG
Unless you have had some lessons, speaking in Cantonese is generally not advised as many words with entirely different meanings can appear to have a similar pronounciation and you may accidentally end up cussing someone.

If you do intend to speak Cantonese, visit your local books shop and purchase a phrase book (the latest) with useful phrases in English, Cantonese and Putonghua. See Resource Guide for a Glossary of common terms and phrases.

One interesting point to note is that if you are Caucasian, the local person whom you are speaking to may not "appear to understand" even if you speak perfect Cantonese. It could be a mental block based on the rationale that foreigners do not speak Cantonese. I have witnessed this with a good friend who tried ordering our meal at lunch. The restaurant captain appeared clueless when she spoke flawless Cantonese but when she repeated the order in English, he immediately knew what we wanted and repeated the order in Cantonese!

Of course, foreigners who make an effort to speak Cantonese are often appreciated by the locals. Although they may laugh or giggle at your attempts, they will at least applaud the efforts you have made to fit into their culture.

Asian expats in Hong Kong may have a harder task. As long as you look Asian, the older folks you meet will try to speak to you in Cantonese—it doesn't matter if you have lived all your life in California or spent your formative years in London. Even in five-star hotels, after the prefunctory "Good Morning" the staff will likely lapse into Cantonese. Only when you address them in English will the reply be in English.

Despite their cosmopolitan outlook, many Hong Kong residents are still most comfortable speaking in Cantonese. A journalist friend from Singapore who speaks only basic Cantonese shared her experience. She attended a press conference where the CEO gave a presentation in perfect Queen's English. But despite being armed with degrees from Cambridge and Sanford, he chose to speak mainly in Cantonese at the luncheon he later hosted. When it was time for her one-on-one interview, she actually had to request that it be conducted in English as she was not comfortable with Cantonese business terms.

The Chinese Influence

In recent years, more and more people in Hong Kong are learning or have learned to speak Putonghua to cater to the growing number of Chinese visitors. Most shop assistants can speak Putonghua as well.

Although the basic characters are similar for Cantonese and Putonghua, there is a difference in pronounciation and language usage. Even if you know Putonghua, do remember that Chinese newpapers and magazines in Hong Kong are written in Cantonese, so you may have difficulty understanding some of the written text.

GETTING AROUND

There is no need to ask for directions in what you consider to be your best Cantonese. As mentioned earlier, street signs are bi-lingual in Chinese and English, as are names of MTR stations, for instance.

Furthermore, Hong Kong people are extremely reluctant to give directions. Bear in mind that if they spoke no English, how are you going to be able to understand what they are telling you in Cantonese? Culturally, chances are that the local people, whether they understand you or are unable to speak any English, would not allow you to get as far as asking a question. They would most probably have avoided all eye-contact the moment you approached them and hurried off on their way.

What then should one do when you are lost or trying to make your way to an appointment? The best bet is to ask the hotel concierge or the doorman in your building, or a Chinese friend or acquaintance to write down where you want to go, and show the address in Chinese on a card and show it to the taxi or bus driver, or whomsoever you manage to be willing to answer your queries. This is where body

Collect Calling Cards

Most restaurants and shops have calling cards with their name and address printed in Chinese. Everyone I know has amassed a collection of cards from their favourite restaurants. Keep them in a little card holder alongside laminated cards of common destinations written in Chinese. Whenever you take a taxi and have difficulty communicating where you want to go, whip out your card case and you will soon be on the way.

language, and I mean pointing, will come in handy. When all else fails, good luck.

CONCLUSION

Although it may appear that there could be a potential language problem in Hong Kong if you do not speak Cantonese or Putonghua, the truth is that most foreigners will be able to get by with some basic phrases. Most of the younger people in Hong Kong would have studied English in school and even if they are reluctant to speak it, are able to roughly understand what you are telling or asking them.

Besides, one key aspect of relocating to a different country is to experience a different culture and see how other people live. Some initial inconveniences are to be expected. If just wouldn't be the same experience if it was just like home.

WORKING IN THE COUNTRY

CHAPTER 9

Nothing is really work unless you would
rather be doing something else.
—James M Barrie (1860–1937)

In the final analysis, regardless of personal preferences, work comes first in Hong Kong. For those with leisure time, playing is important too. Keep in mind, however, that there is very little social entertaining in the pure sense. The adage that there is no such thing as a free lunch is perhaps more true in Hong Kong than anywhere else.

THE OFFICE HIERARCHY

Whatever the nature or size of your business, please remember that the office structure in Hong Kong, like its society, is hierarchical. Whereas a clear line of authority is good management policy in the West, it is essential in the Hong Kong culture. Any blurring of the line will lead to confusion and resentment sooner or later.

The office hierarchy is determined by position, but age and gender of the employees also come into consideration. The business aspects of the hierarchy are easy to handle because divisions and layers of line and staff functions can be defined. It is the other aspects of office life that are more difficult to delineate. It is easier if you have a small office, because most likely the staff will be sharing various aspects of the routine of the office in addition to their specifically assigned work—following your example, one hopes—but, if you have more than four or five staff in your office, pay attention to the hierarchy even if you are democratic by inclination.

Do not blur this line. Hong Kong office workers have a keen sense of which tasks are more menial than others and therefore beneath their dignified station in the hierarchy. You must be careful and respect the hierarchy.

You do not ask a junior clerk to give a message to the department head, especially if it can be interpreted as an order. You do not ask the secretary to go down to the post office, a job ordinarily done by messengers, or to change a light bulb, a chore always performed by a handyman. Another example: never go to the back office to make yourself a cup of coffee or tea, unless you want to give the tea lady a heart attack by sending the message that you are getting ready to dismiss her.

Problems of this nature are solving themselves, though, as tea ladies are a disappearing breed; while those that remain are getting so used to the antics of a group of younger expats in trying to do everything themselves, that they are no longer so easily upset by a single annoying act.

When in doubt, use your common sense and pass all your orders down the line through your secretary or personal assistant and the department heads. They will know what to do to preserve everyone's dignity and your composure.

There are sub-cultures in the office hierarchy, noticeable by their dress. The lower the rank, the more assiduously the women follow the latest Hong Kong fashion and the men adopt the mannerisms of the latest Cantopop star. You can always spot a messenger—male or female—by the not-too-loose blue jeans and running shoes, with a Walkman attached to the waist and ear.

Uniforms which shop assistants and bank tellers sport with pride are not a part of the job identification desired by office messengers. Do not offend the messengers, for they are the most difficult employees to hire. Their turnover is high, and advertisements for them often go unanswered.

Workers arriving for work at Central. During peak rush hour, pedestrian traffic can be very heavy.

The Job Description

Titles and job description are important to staff because they derive a sense of security from having their duties defined in black and white. The titles show the line of authority. The job descriptions tell each employee what his or her duties are supposed to be.

Until and unless a rapport is established, and sometimes not even then, staff will not perform any chore which they perceive to be below their status and which is not specified in their job descriptions. They will not tell you that the chore is not a part of their job, for they know that talking back to the boss is rude, and speaking one's mind openly is not a characteristic of the Hong Kong culture. They will grumble behind your back, sometimes within your hearing, but definitely not to your face. Moreover, they will ignore your request. Now you know why you hire a telephone-cleaning service: because nobody can decide whose job it is to perform the menial task of keeping the telephones clean. You also hire a cleaning crew to empty the wastepaper baskets, but shredding confidential documents at the end of the day is not considered a demeaning task.

Office Etiquette

Even if you work in a casual style and generally run the business in a low-keyed way, staff see the gap between you and them as being important. You can be pleasant and say 'good morning', 'please' and 'thank you'; and praise workers for a job well done.

Criticism, on the other hand, should be delivered gently, and it is more effective if sent through the proper channel. It is essential to keep your dignity, and a certain distance from your staff. It is fine to be friendly, but over-familiarity makes it difficult to maintain command in the Hong Kong culture.

Office workers today come from a wider background than they did a dozen or so years ago. With the reduction in factory jobs, and an increasing demand for workers in offices and in service industries, young men and women who otherwise would have been bent over machines are now working in offices, restaurants, airline counters or hotels—where they have to relate to people in a variety of unpredictable situations. These young men and women come from homes where all decisions are made by their parents. They buy lunch boxes to eat at their desks, and so lose their best chance for developing social skills. Very likely their social circle is confined to families and relatives. They live in housing estates, and return there to spend all their non-working hours. The expats in the office are probably the only non-Cantonese people they meet.

They know their places and, while working hard at their jobs and eager to please, they are reluctant to venture beyond the responsibilities specified in their job descriptions. They are inarticulate, they cannot cope with what they perceive to be insults or unjustified criticisms, and they sulk. Or they resign without telling you or their direct supervisor what is bothering them. When a staff member leaves because he is going 'for further studies in Canada', you should know that either he has found a better paying job with another firm, or he has resented something said or done to him.

Staff members do not have an overview of what you are trying to accomplish. Spending from 9:00am to 5:00pm or 8:30am to 6:00pm five days a week, with half an hour for lunch, and often working every other Saturday morning, performing narrow tasks, cannot be unmitigated fascination all the time. Do not expect any flexibility. Call it the failure of the Hong Kong education system if you will, but workers have not been trained to make decisions or to use their judgement. Some of them may be extremely proficient at operating the computer but they cannot read a manual, nor are they willing to learn anything new by themselves. If you tell them to take the manual home to study so that they can improve their knowledge, they are reluctant. They do not say no, they just do not take the manual home. Self-training from the manual during their time away from the office is not a part of the job description. Besides, the conditions at home may not permit quiet study. If you want them to learn anything new, they would like to attend a training course at your expense and during office hours. At the end of the

training course, there is a certificate, which is important for the employee's curriculum vitae—and future work.

While they stay with you, however, the staff are conscientious and work very hard. Productivity in Hong Kong is high. They are serious, well groomed, and cheerful. Perhaps they prefer a male boss to a female one, and take instructions better from men; but, in general, Hong Kong women are good administrators because they are good with details. Try not to lose your cool or raise your voice. You will scare the staff. They will leave you 'for further studies in Canada' and you will have to hire and train replacements.

Part of the perks of working in an office is the bubbly soda provided by you. The staff drink soda because they like its sweet taste, and because it is worth money. Consumption of one or two tins a day means that you spend on their behalf another twenty to thirty dollars a week—tantamount to a rise in pay.

A young Chinese-American woman we know worked for the representative office of an American bank here one summer when she was a college student. She was asked why she did not drink soda in the office, especially at nine o'clock in the morning. 'You can drink tea at home,' advised her Hong Kong Chinese colleague, 'and soda is expensive.' If you tell the staff that soda is not good for their teeth you only reinforce their conviction that *gweilos* are miserly. Chuck the cost to office expenses and be happy in the satisfaction that this is a cheap way to buy goodwill.

Start Work Laisee

Another red packet of *laisee* is to be given to each employee by the boss on the first day after the Lunar New Year holidays. This one is called the *Start Work Laisee*.

The big boss gives the *laisee* to everybody in the office, while you, if you are small fry, give it only to people under your immediate command. Do not overstep the boundary. Remember the office hierarchy. It is not obligatory to give this packet, but giving it brings you yet again a great deal of goodwill and makes a cheerful beginning to another year of working together. The Hong Kong Chinese term for working together is 'we co-operate'.

The amount in each packet does not need to be large. We know people who put in a two dollar coin. The employees will be happier if they know that the gesture has come from you personally, and is not just more largesse from the company.

The First Name Syndrome

Employees in Hong Kong are becoming lax, and a worker with good manners is increasingly difficult to find. For instance, strangers half your age are calling you by your first name. Few people in Hong Kong like this informality, and almost everybody is denouncing the Americans for bringing their casual style of mixing business and personal relationships. The Americans are certainly more democratic and do tend to treat everybody as equals, but you cannot put the blame on the Americans for the first name syndrome in Hong Kong. People in New York and Washington may address you over the telephone as 'honey', but they are still likely to call you by your surname preceded by a proper title.

Nor, probably, does much of the blame stem from each culture seeing the other as putting the last name first.

When a sales person representing your company telephones a prospective client to solicit business, calling the client by his or her first name is discourteous. It is adding further insult to injury when the salesman introduces himself as *Mister* Da. No client is going to react favourably when your salesman says over the telephone: 'Is this Mary? I am calling about renew the service contract in your computer (sic). My name is Mister Da of XYZ Company.'

Sales people are not the only offenders in Hong Kong today. Travel agents and secretaries have also taken to calling people they have not met by their first names. Perhaps they hear you calling your business associates by their first names and are following suit. Perhaps you allow them to call you by your first name, or you may even think that you are improving the office culture by having staff address the bosses by their first names. Whatever makes you comfortable is perfectly all right, because you must have your own style in running your office. Do remember, however, that the Hong Kong culture is much more formal. Do let your staff call you Bob if it makes you feel more comfortable, but make sure that they address your clients, whether in person or over the telephone, as Mr Wong or Mrs Chen, not David or Shirley. If your surname is unpronounceable, perhaps Tchaikovsky or even Ronan, have them call you Mr John, or Mr Bill, or Miss Katharine or whatever, but do make sure that your secretary refers to you as Mr Tchaikovsky to people outside and inside your office. Over-friendliness leads to sloppy business relationships. In the case of Mary and the computer, she did not renew her service contract, despite repeated telephoning from Mr Da, a Miss Lo and a Ms Bo—all addressing her as Mary.

THE EXECUTIVE SECRETARY

Good secretaries are a rare species; one may be the best friend you will ever have in Hong Kong. Since you are an executive, she likes to sport the title Executive Secretary. It is only fitting because she manages your business and social calendar, arranges your travel, interfaces between you and the rest of your office, and guards you against the outside world. She makes sure that your correspondence looks beautiful, and that all your files are organised. She also helps you and your family in a myriad ways because you know neither Cantonese nor the local way of getting things accomplished. She is loyal and protective: in time, she will anticipate your moods and put up with your idiosyncrasies. Above all, she pampers rather than challenges your ego.

Secretaries in Hong Kong are receiving higher salaries than they did a decade ago, but their earnings are still far below those of your other associates. Your secretary will make your tea or coffee or, rather, instruct people in the back office to make it for you. She will not mind running personal errands for you and your spouse, but would hate to be asked to shop for birthday presents for members of your family. What a secretary most dislikes is having to tell lies to cover for the boss when the boss is, for reasons for his own, unwilling to confront the caller himself. Experienced good secretaries are hard to find. When executives change jobs in Hong Kong, they usually take their secretaries with them.

THE ETIQUETTE OF THE NAME CARD

Calling (or business) cards are known as name cards in Hong Kong. It is a direct translation from the Chinese *min* (name) and *pian* (small card). The term that means *name on a small card* is actually more fitting than *calling card*, because these cards are not used to call on people any more, but in introducing to you a person you are meeting for the first time, and you to the person who is meeting you.

Your card should have your name, title, the name and address of your company, your office telephone and fax numbers, and e-mail address. In Hong Kong, the card also sports the logo of your company, for a logo is perceived as something inseparable from a worthwhile company.

An employee who represents your company to outsiders should have name cards. A name card identifies him as a member of the company, acknowledging that the company is proud of the association. It also gives his correct name and where people can find him. Always carry a supply of cards with you when you venture out of the office. If a person you meet gives you his name card and you do not offer one in return, it signals to him either that you do not wish to make his acquaintance, or that you have no status at all. Remember, a person with no label in Hong Kong is without legitimacy.

Your Name in Chinese

Expatriates here like to have their names rendered in Chinese. Your colleagues will do this for you, transliterating your surname into Cantonese. There may already be a Chinese surname that fits yours nicely, and Hong Kong Chinese are wonderfully clever in finding appropriate characters to suit the sounds of your name. The characters they find for you will have lucky implications. However, if you do not want the ordinary Chinese renditions of more common first names, such as John into Yo-han (which may sound like a now defunct Japanese department store), ask one of your more literary friends to organize a name for you. Avoid companies which transliterate names for a fee. They have no sense of humour and little literary heritage.

It is even more important that your Chinese name should sound acceptable in Putonghua. Whereas Hong Kong people will know you by your name in its original language or its English version—because everybody you meet will understand at least some English—in mainland China or Taiwan you will certainly be recognised only by your Chinese name. You will not want your name in Putonghua to sound rude or like something the cat might have dragged in. So, think hard and choose wisely; do not take the first name given to you. Consult everybody you know who understands Cantonese or Putonghua.

As a Sinologist, Lord Wilson possessed a Chinese name long before he was appointed Governor of Hong Kong in 1987. His surname in Chinese was Wei, a character with three radicals which could also stand separately. Two of the radicals, as it turned out, were unacceptable to the Hong Kong Chinese because by themselves they were the characters for *woman* and *ghost*. Lord Wilson had to select another character among the more than fifty with the Wei sound.

Office Christmas Cards

It is becoming a fad for companies to send Christmas as well as Lunar New Year cards to all business friends and associates. Use your own judgement whether you wish to join this merry throng. Find out the practice of your predecessors and listen to what your colleagues think you ought to do. A number of charities sell Christmas cards to raise funds, so you will have plenty of choice. Select the cards you like for their aesthetic quality or for the charity you wish to support. Ask your office manager to handle the card details or, if you do not have an office manager, ask your secretary. If you want to combine your office and personal lists, consult your spouse. The Post Office publishes date and weight information for overseas Christmas mail. To avoid squandering your or your firm's earnings on airmail you might manage a mass mailing in October. It might then suit the Post Office to send this surface mail by air at its expense. You may then be surprised by a flurry of heavily stamped return cards early in November.

FAST FACTS

CHAPTER 10

'They say the world has become too complex
for simple answers. They are wrong.'
--Ronald Reagan

HONG KONG AT A GLANCE

Official Name
Hong Kong Special Administrative Region, or Hong Kong SAR

Official Status
Hong Kong SAR is a special administrative region of the People's Republic of China

Area
1,095 sq km (422.8 sq miles) of land, 40 per cent of which is made up of 21 country parks. The highest point is Tai Mo Shan (957 m / 3,139 ft) in the New Territories.

Major Districts
Hong Kong Island, Kowloon, New Kowloon, the New Territories and the Outlying Islands.

Population
6.81 million (2003)

Ethnic Groups
Chinese 95 per cent; others 5 per cent

Religions
About 43 per cent participate in some form of religious practice.

Languages
Cantonese and English are the two official ones.

Education
Literacy—92 per cent (95 per cent male, 88 per cent female)
All children between six and fifteen must attend school.

Health (2003)
Infant mortality rate: 2.4 per 1,000
Life expectancy: 81.5 years overall with 78.6 years for males
and 84.3 years for females

Work Force (2003)
3.5 million people are engaged in the following industries:
wholesale, retail, and import/export trades and restaurants
and hotels (43.7 per cent); finance, insurance, real estate, and
business services (19 per cent); manufacturing (7.5 per cent).

Government Structure
Chief Executive of the Hong Kong Special Administrative Region
Heads the Government, but there is a Chief Secretary for
Administration who heads the civil service.

Executive Council
Appointed by the Chief Executive to help formulate policy.

Executive Branch
The Executive Branch of the Government in Hong Kong
is different from the Executive Council. The Government
departments carry out the policies of the Council. There are
many departments, authorities, commissions, and others.
See the Hong Kong Government 'year book' (latest edition);
it is published annually.

Legislative Council
Comprising 60 members, 24 of whom were elected by
geographical constituencies through direct elections, 30

members by functional constituencies, and six by an Election Committee comprising 800 elected representatives of the community. As the term implies, the Legco makes laws for Hong Kong, but is not independent of the Executive. The last Legco election took place in 2004.

Judiciary
The Court of Final Appeals is the highest court in Hong Kong. There are lower courts.

Suffrage
All permanent residents of eighteen or older, regardless of nationality, enjoy the right to vote.

Currency
The Hong Kong dollar is pegged to the US dollar at the rate of HK$ 7.80 = US$ 1

Gross Domestic Product
HK$ 158 billion (2003) with a real growth rate of 3.2 per cent. Per capita GDP in 2002 was HK$ 22,988.

Natural Resource
Excellent deepwater harbour.; skilled workers

Industry
Textiles, clothing, electronics, plastics, toys, watches, clocks

Exports
HK$ 223 billion: clothing, electronics, textiles, watches and clocks, office machinery

Imports
HK$ 232 billion: consumer goods, raw materials and semi-manufactures, capital goods, foodstuffs, fuels

Time Difference
Greenwich Mean Time plus 8 hours (GMT +0800)

MILESTONES

1514	First Portuguese settlement at Tunmen
1841	• British flag at Possession Point on Hong Kong Island
	• Jardine, Matheson and Company warehouses and counting houses to Hong Kong
1842	• Free port status for Hong Kong
	• Treaty of Nanking (Nanjing) ceding Hong Kong to Britain
1843	• Treaty of the Bogue, Chinese allowed free access to Hong Kong for trade
	• Sir Henry Pottinger, Governor of Hong Kong
1844	Sir John Davis, Governor of Hong Kong
1845	The *China Mail*, English-language newspaper
1846	The Hong Kong Club
1848	Sir Samuel George Bonham, Governor of Hong Kong
1849	St John's Cathedral
1854	Sir John Bowring, Governor of Hong Kong
1855	Last public execution in Hong Kong
1857	*Hong Kong Daily Express* published
1858	Treaty of Tientsin (Tianjin) ceded Kowloon and Stonecutters Island to Britain; legalisation of the opium trade
1859	Sir Hercules Robinson (Lord Rosmead), Governor of Hong Kong
1861	• Hong Kong and China Gas Company set up
	• Hong Kong General Chamber of Commerce set up
	• Botanical Gardens established
1863	Issue of Hong Kong silver dollars
1864	Gas street lighting introduced
1866	Sir Richard Graves Macdonnell, Governor of Hong Kong
1868	Tung Wah Hospital established
1870	Telegraphic cable link to China
1871	Hong Kong-Singapore cable link
1872	Sir Arthur Edward Kennedy, Governor of Hong Kong
1873	Missionary schools in Land Grant scheme
1877	• Sir John Pope Hennessy, Governor of Hong Kong
	• Ng Choy, first Chinese barrister admitted to Hong Kong bar

1879	Secular curriculum in Government and grant-in-aid schools
1880	▪ Telegraphic link with the Philippines
	▪ Ng Choy first Chinese non-official member of Legislative Council
1881	Government telephone system
1883	▪ Sanitary Board formed (developed into Urban Council In 1936)
	▪ Canton-Kowloon telegraph line established
	▪ Sir George Ferguson Bowen, Governor of Hong Kong
1884	Hong Kong Jockey Club
1887	▪ The College of Medicine for the Chinese set-up
	▪ Sir George William Des Voeux, Governor of Hong Kong
1888	Peak Tram from the Cathedral to Victoria Gap
1889	Hong Kong Electric Company set-up
1890	Public telephone system introduced
1891	Sir William Robinson, Governor of Hong Kong
1896	Pedder's Wharf (Blake's Pier)
1898	▪ Lease of New Territories and New Kowloon
	▪ Sir Henry Arthur Blake, Governor of Hong Kong
1900	Chinese General Chamber of Commerce
1902	Temple Ohel Leah
1903	China Light and Power
1904	▪ Sir Matthew Nathan, Governor of Hong Kong
	▪ Electric tramways on Hong Kong Island
	▪ Reclamation project in Central
1907	Sir Frederick Lugard (Lord Lugard), Governor of Hong Kong
1910	▪ Kowloon-Canton Railway
	▪ Opium dives in Hong Kong and the New Territories closed
1911	▪ Revolution in China
	▪ University of Hong Kong
1912	▪ Republic of China
	▪ Sir Francis Henry May, Governor of Hong Kong
1919	Sir Reginald Stubbs, Governor of Hong Kong
1923	Cenotaph

1925	• Sir Cecil Clementi, Governor of Hong Kong
	• Hong Kong seriously affected by labour unrest in Canton, lasting until 1926
1926	Sir Shouson Chou, first Chinese member of Executive Council
1928	Peninsula Hotel opens
1930	Sir William Peel, Governor of Hong Kong
1931	Anti-Japanese riots
1935	Sir Andrew Caldecott, Governor of Hong Kong
1936	Airmail service between Hong Kong and Britain
1937	• Second Sino-Japanese War began in China (July)
	• Sir Geoffrey Alexander Stafford Northcote, Governor of Hong Kong
1938	Sir Mark Aitchison Young, Governor of Hong Kong
1938	Canton fell to the Japanese, influx of 500,000 refugees to Hong Kong
1941	• World War II, Japanese occupation of Hong Kong (December)
	• Internment of civilians at Stanley, military at Argyle Street and Sham Shui Po POW Camps
1945	Liberation of Hong Kong from the Japanese Occupation (August)
1946	• Return of British administration to Hong Kong—return of Sir Mark Young (see 1938)
	• Roman Catholic Diocese established
1947	Sir Alexander William George Herder Grantham, Governor of Hong Kong
1949	• Communist victory in China, influx of refugees to Hong Kong
	• First double-decker bus service introduced
1950	Korean War starts
1951	UN embargo on trade with People's Republic of China
1953	Public housing scheme after squatter huts fire at Shek Kip Mei
1958	• Sir Robert Brown Black, Governor of Hong Kong
	• Completion of runway at Kaitak Airport
1960	Agreement with Guangdong provincial authorities to supply fresh water

1962   Influx of illegal immigrants from China

1963   Chinese University of Hong Kong

1964   Sir David Clive Crosbie Trench, Governor of
        Hong Kong

1965   Mrs Liu Shui-fu becomes first woman member of
        Legislative Council

1966   Lion Rock Tunnel

1967   Riots in Hong Kong

1969   Francis Chen-peng Hsu, first Chinese Roman
        Catholic Bishop of Hong Kong

1971   ▪ Social welfare scheme of public assistance
        ▪ Free primary education in government schools
        ▪ Sir Murray MacLehose (Lord MacLehose of Beoch),
          Governor of Hong Kong

1972   ▪ Hong Kong Arts Festival inaugurated
        ▪ New Towns Programme established
        ▪ Hong Kong Polytechnic (Hong Kong Polytechnic
          University) established
        ▪ Cross Harbour Tunnel (October) opens

1974   ▪ ICAC (Independent Commission Against Crime)
        ▪ Hong Kong Philharmonic Orchestra established

1975   Hung Hom Railway Station opened by Queen
        Elizabeth II

1978   Vietnamese refugees arrive in boats

1979   Mass Transit Railway established

1982   ▪ Sir Edward Youde, Governor of Hong Kong
        ▪ Sino-British negotiations on future of Hong Kong
        ▪ District Boards established

1983   ▪ Formal Sino-British negotiations on Hong
          Kong begins
        ▪ Linkage of Hong Kong dollar to US dollar

1984   Margaret Thatcher, British Prime Minister, signed
        Sino-British Joint Declaration in Beijing

1985   ▪ Elections for 12 Legislative Councillors by
          functional constituencies
        ▪ Legislative Council to renovated Old Supreme
          Court Building
        ▪ Unified Stock Exchange established at
          Exchange Square

1986
- Daya Bay nuclear power station agreement signed Regional Council established
- Death of Governor Sir Edward Youde in Beijing
- Sir David Akers-Jones becomes Acting Governor of Hong Kong

1987 Sir David Clive Wilson (Lord Wilson of Tillyron), Governor of Hong Kong

1988
- Sir Ti Liang Yang, first Chinese Chief Justice
- Sino-British Joint Declaration on Hong Kong
- Permanent office of Sino-British Joint Liaison Group established
- Screening of Vietnamese boat people

1989 Mass rally of Hong Kong people after Tiananmen Square (June)

1989
- British Government announces that right of abode in the United Kingdom would not be granted to all Hong Kong residents
- Eastern Harbour Crossing Tunnel opens
- Open Learning Institute (Open Learning University)
- Massive Port and Airport Development Scheme
- Hong Kong Cultural Centre and Hong Kong Convention and Exhibition Centre opens

1990
- Basic Law of the Hong Kong Special Administrative Region (HKSAR) promulgated by the Chinese National People's Congress
- Government announcement of finance to construct the Lantau Fixed Crossing leading to the new Chek Lap Kok airport

1991
- Tate's Cairn Tunnel
- First direct election of 30 per cent of the Legislative Council
- Sale of first Government Bonds
- Memorandum of Understanding between Britain and China on the new airport signed
- Hong Kong Hospital Authority
- Teaching began at Hong Kong University of Science and Technology

1992 Christopher Francis Patten, Governor of Hong Kong

1993 Anson Chan, first woman and first local Chief Secretary of the Government of Hong Kong

1993
- Disagreements over proposed electoral reforms causes deadlock in Sino-British talks
- Bank of China begins issuance of Hong Kong currency
- Opening of Mid-Levels Escalator

1994
- Agreement is signed with Beijing on financing Chek Lap Kok Airport and the Airport Railway
- Daniel Fung first local Chinese Solicitor General
- Peter Nguyen first local Chinese Director of Public Prosecutions
- Enactment of electoral reforms by Patten

1995
- First elections to the Regional and District Councils and to the Legislative Council under Patten's electoral reforms
- Royal Hong Kong Regiment (The Volunteers) disbands
- Agreement on the Final Court of Appeal signed by the Joint Liaison Group and endorsed by Legislative Council
- Donald Tsang becomes first local Chinese Financial Secretary
- High Court conducts first civil case in Cantonese

1996
- Preparatory Committee votes to replace Legislative Council on 1 July 1997 with an appointed Provisional Legislature
- First Hong Kong Olympic Gold Medal won by windsurfer Lee Lai-shan in Atlanta
- Preparatory Committee chooses Selection Committee to select the Chief Executive of Hong Kong after the change of sovereignty
- The last British Governor gives final address to the Legislative Council
- Tung Chee-hwa, Chairman of Orient Overseas Holding Limited, is selected Chief Executive of the 'Provisional Government' of the HKSAR.
- The Selection Committee also selects the 'Provisional' Legislature

	▪ Anson Chan accepts Tung's invitation to continue as Chief Secretary
1997	▪ Opening of Tsing Ma Bridge to the new airport on Lantau Island
	▪ Opening of Western Cross Harbour Tunnel
	▪ Change of sovereignty—official ceremonies followed by festivities (30 June–1 July)
	▪ HKSAR established (1 July)
	▪ Tung Chee-hwa officially becomes Chief Executive of HKSAR
	▪ Financial crisis in Asia and the world (Nov)
	▪ Bird flu scare becomes crisis (December)
1998	The North Point—Kowloon City vehicular ferry service terminates after more than 30 years in service
1998	▪ Hong Kong resumes importation of live chickens from the Mainland after imports were cancelled and more than 1 million chickens killed at the end of 1997 because of an avian flu outbreak
	▪ The Court of Appeal rules that mainland children, including illegitimate ones, who are born to permanent residents, have the right of abode in Hong Kong if they arrived before July 1
	▪ The Ting Kau Bridge officially opens, linking Ting Kau with North West Tsing Yi Island and part of Route 3
	▪ President Jiang Zemin opens the new Hong Kong International Airport at Chek Lap Kok
	▪ The Hong Kong Monetary Authority invests $188 billion to shore up the stock market in an attempt curb currency speculation. The Exchange Fund Investment Ltd is established to manage these shares
	▪ Hong Kong's unemployment reaches 5.5 per cent the highest level in 22 years
1999	▪ The second 3,800-m runway at the Hong Kong International Airport opens
	▪ The passing of the Chinese Medicine Bill, a regulatory framework to control the practice, use, manufacture, and trading of Chinese medicine

- Hong Kong's first fatal accident at Chek Lap Kok Airport when a China Airlines aircraft overturns while landing during a typhoon
- Announcement that a Walt Disney theme park will be built at Penny's Bay on Lantau Island
- Hong Kong retains its rating as the world's freest economy in the 2000 index of Economic Freedom released by the Heritage Foundation and The Wall Street Journal
- The Provisional Regional and Urban Councils are dissolved at the end of the year

2000
- Anson Chan, the first female Chief Secretary, retires after nearly forty years of service
- Implementation of the Mandatory Provident Fund (MPF), Hong Kong's version of social security, or retirement pension. Every employee must contribute 5 per cent of his salary into this fund, while the employer contributes another 5 per cent. The fund is handled by specific fund managers.
- Clarification of the Right of Abode; especially pertinent to those born in mainland China. A court decision ruled that children born in Hong Kong do have the right to abide in Hong Kong, but children born on the mainland who are adopted by Hong Kong residents do not.

2005
- Resignation of C H Tung as Chief Executive. He is succeeded by his deputy, Chief Secretary of the Hong Kong Administration, Donald Tseng in March. Tsang is appointed acting Chief Executive.
- On 25 May, Donald Tsang resigns as to stand for election as Chief Executive.
- Donald Tsang officially appointed Chief Executive of the HKSAR by the State Council of the Central People's Government on 21 June 2005,

HOSPITAL AND HEALTH CARE
Public and Private Health Care
The Government operates a good system of hospitals and clinics, which provides sound health care at very low cost.

The University of Hong Kong and the Chinese University of Hong Kong both have medical schools, and their personnel staff the Queen Mary Hospital and the Prince of Wales Hospital. Waiting lists for non-emergency services are long, and facilities are overcrowded. Since 1991, the newly established Hospital Authority has assumed responsibility for the management and control of Government hospitals. There are also private hospitals and clinics in Hong Kong, each with its own following. British residents appear to prefer the Matilda Hospital on the Peak, while Americans and Japanese patronize the Hong Kong Adventist Hospital—which runs an active outpatient clinic. The Chinese prefer the Hong Kong Sanatorium because it is comfortable and home-like. The Canossian Hospital is known for its orthopaedic care. The Ruttonjee Sanatorium, which had been used for tuberculosis patients, has been rebuilt as a hospital for thoracic and pulmonary diseases.

Partnerships of physicians and surgeons operate here as business corporations, similar to those in the United States. Individual doctors see patients in their offices. It is a universal practice of members of the medical profession not to stay on top of their appointment schedules, and Hong Kong is no exception. It is disconcerting enough to arrive at a doctor's office only to find at least three other patients sharing the time of your appointment; but when you discover the waiting room full, and the queue of patients stretching down the corridor all the way to the lift, it is time to change doctors.

Traditional Chinese Medicine

Traditional Chinese medicine is alive and thriving in Hong Kong. Chinese practitioners do not have degrees in medicine; their knowledge and skills are usually passed down from father to son, and from master to student. This is changing as the University of Hong Kong has just commenced a degree programme in Traditional Medicine.

The Chinese practitioners diagnose by feeling the pulse and checking physical signs of disease with their eyes. Although medicinal herbs are still cooked over a slow fire into a bitter brew, many Chinese cures now come in capsule or pill form. Sooner or later, when you are sufficiently settled in to want to know more about Chinese traditions, you will probably walk down Queen's Road, Central, not far from Lane Crawford and the Chinese Emporium, to stop at Eu Yang Seng, a traditional Chinese medicine shop. Eu Yang Seng moved out of its old premises to make way for the escalator that goes from Central to Mid-Levels. The brightly lit new shop, directly across the street, opens onto the pavement unhampered by any wall. It has counters for selling medicines as well as display cases of herbs and other oddities – dried seahorse, or deer horn, for instance – with their curative values explained in Chinese and English.

Qigong and Tieda

Qigong is different from *tieda*; calling the practitioners of either of these schools of cure 'chiropractors' is not exactly correct. *Qigong* began as a sensible method of proper breathing and exercise and is sometimes practised alongside herbal medicine, but practitioners use their hands to massage the patient's body. It is becoming increasingly popular in Hong Kong and overseas Chinese communities. Its practitioners use a combination of massage, chiropractic, feeling of the pulse, and examination of the general colouring of the patient, to cure various diseases, including orthopaedic problems. *Tieda* practitioners, on the other hand, are rarely more than simple chiropractors and masseurs, but they also apply hot poultices of herbs to painful areas of your anatomy. The only concession they make to modernity is in enclosing the hot herbs in plastic bags so that the substance does not leak out.

Acupuncture and Acupressure

Hong Kong is also a place for acupuncture and acupressure. Acupuncture involves needles penetrating the skin; acupressure does not. Sanitary standards have improved, but care still must be taken when you visit an acupuncture establishment. Insist on sterilized needles, for hepatitis is common in Hong Kong. Otherwise, this time-honoured way of curing pains enjoys a large and faithful following among the Chinese population, and attracts expatriates also. In general, neither traditional Chinese medicine nor its practitioners should be regarded lightly.

Veterinary Services

Hong Kong is much more caring as far as pets are concerned than you probably would have guessed. In fact, dogs are extremely popular pets. Quarantine of imported animals used to last six months, but now pets are kept in for only one month. There was a time when one veterinary surgeon looked after all the animals not belonging to the Jockey Club. Today, there are veterinary clinics throughout the territory. If you are fortunate, you will discover one personable and intelligent vet, an Irishman with a delightful sense of humour and a doctorate from the University of Edinburgh, even makes house calls. Get your grapevine to tell you who he and his colleagues are, or check in the yellow pages. The Society for Prevention of Cruelty to Animals is active here. The SPCA operates the only hospital for animals in Asia. Unfortunately, as ownership of pets becomes more popular, increasing numbers of pets are abandoned. Although the SPCA no longer accept abandoned animals in the first instance, it still has a large pound full of abandoned dogs and cats awaiting adoption.

ACRONYNMS

Hong Kong people, especially those whose command of English is not up to par, have a passion for acronyms, or abbreviations of names and terms of their own choosing. A 'mong', for instance, stands for a television or computer 'monitor'. The most commonly used acronyms are:

ADB	Asian Development Bank
CC	Cultural Centre
CCP	Chinese Communist Party
CE	Chief Executive
CEO	Chief Executive Officer
CFA	Court of Final Appeals

CJ	Chief Justice
CS	Chief Secretary
CSSA	Comprehensive Social Security Assistance
CUHK	Chinese University of Hong Kong
FS	Financial Secretary
GPO	General Post Office
KCR	Kowloon and Canton Railroad
HA	Hospital Authority
HK	Hong Kong
HKAPA	Hong Kong Academy for Performing Arts
HKIEd	Hong Kong Institution of Education
HKMA	Hong Kong Monetary Authority
HKSAR	Hong Kong Special Administrative Region
HKU	University of Hong Kong
HKUST	Hong Kong University of Science and Technology
HOME	Home Owner Mortgage Enhancement Programme
ICAC	Independent Commission Against Crime
ID	Identity Card
LEGCO	Legislative Council
MD	Managing Director
MPF	Mandatory Provident Fund
MTR	Mass Transit Railway
PA	Personal Assistant
PLO	People's Liberation Army
PRC	People's Republic of China
SAR	Special Administrative Region
SARS	Severe Acute Respiratory Syndrome
SMEIC	Small and Medium Enterprises Information Centre
TDC	Trade and Development Council
TST	Tsim Sha Tsui
WTO	World Trade Organisation

FAMOUS PEOPLE
Li Ka-Shing
Voted Asia's most powerful man by *Newsweek* and among the world's richest by *Forbes*, Li is a noted businessman. His flagship companies are Cheung Kong Holdings and Hutchison Whampoa. The Cheung Kong Group which has

business operations in 51 countries around the world has a market capitalization of approximately HK$707 billion. Li is also a well-known philanthropist and actively supports the arts.

Chow Yun-Fat

The star of over 70 films, Chow gained international fame in both comedy and drama before being associated with what are often called "heroic bloodshed" movies. His movie credits include *A Better Tomorrow* (1987), *The Killer* (1989), *Anna and the King* (1999) and *Crouching Tiger, Hidden Dragon* (2000).

Jackie Chan

A former stuntman who became a leading actor in Asia, Chan's movies such as *Half a Loaf of Kung-Fu* (1980) and *Drunken Master* (1978) are known for their well-choreographed fight scenes. He found fame in Hollywood with *Rumble in the Bronx* (1995) and also starred in *Rush Hour* (1998), *Shanghai Noon* (2000) and other films. Chan is also a spokesman for the Hong Kong Tourism Association and helps to promote its activities.

Lydia Dunn

A leading figure in both politics and the business community, she was raised to the peerage as Baroness Dunn, of Hong Kong Island in Hong Kong and of Knightsbridge in the Royal Borough of Kensington and Chelsea in 1990.

John Woo

Currently based in the United States, this leading director is known for his movies *A Better Tomorrow* and *The Killer*. which redefined Hong Kong cinema. Since moving to the US, he has continued to direct acclaimed hits such as *Broken Arrow*, *Faceoff*, *Mission Impossible 2* and *Paycheck*.

CULTURE QUIZ

Now that you have read the chapters on Hong Kong, have acquired a good deal of factual information, and are aware of some of the unique characteristics of its society and its people, you must think that you are ready to face all types of situations that living in Hong Kong can produce. This quiz gives you an opportunity to test how you would fare in various predicaments. Some of the scenarios are normal; you will meet them often while you live here. Others have been invented and may seem to you somewhat contrived. Laugh and wail in disbelief if you will—but these situations are based on actual occurrences. Remember, when you find yourself perplexed: keep your cool. Also remember that patience is a virtue, and will receive its just rewards. The Chinese character, *ren*—literally 'to endure' (you will see it everywhere)—suggests a good philosophy to emulate.

SITUATION 1
You have invited a few Hong Kong Chinese friends to your home to dinner. Each has brought you a present, intriguingly wrapped in a parcel tied with a ribbon. Should you:

Ⓐ Open the packages immediately in front of all the guests, praising each gift in elaborate language, and announcing how much you love it;

Ⓑ Thank the givers graciously and sweetly, and put the presents aside;

Ⓒ Hand all the presents back to the giver and insist that they take them home?

Comments
Option **Ⓑ** is your only choice. It is out of the question for you to reject a gift that has been brought into your home. If it is rally so valuable as to constitute an embarrassment as well as a bribe, you can settle the score the next day. Opening a present in front of everybody could humiliate the giver who

might fear, regardless of the pleasant noises you make, that you dislike the gift. And he would lose face if he thought his present modest in comparison with what the others had brought. Furthermore, the gift is for you to savour, not for everybody else to ogle. Gift giving is a personal matter, and the Hong Kong people are a suspicious lot. You do not want to provide the others with an opportunity to gossip about the motives of the giver. If the gift is too lavish, they may say that he is bribing you to gain an advantage; if the gift is too small, they may say that the giver is miserly.

Multiply this potential havoc by the number of guests bearing gifts, and settle with relief for Option **B**. However, when a gift is obviously a box of candies or a bottle of wine, it would be nice to open it to share with all your guests. But there may be more than one box of candies; or you may have already prepared the drinks for the evening—and plan to recycle consumable gifts… So it is up to you whether you open any of those. This is your decision, not a cultural one. If the chocolates are green from mould—and not because they are mint-covered—you put them aside and say nothing. Recycling hostess gifts is such a common practice, and you do not want to embarrass the person who brought the sweets. If you know her well, you can tell her about the green chocolate and you can share a good laugh. One of the leading chocolate importers in Hong Kong has been known to keep merchandise on the shelves a little too long.

Incidentally, unless it is a very large party, invitations in Hong Kong are initially given over the telephone. Invitations to dine at home always include spouses. The hostess will telephone her guests unless she has not met them, in which case the host will. Having secretaries telephone personal invitations to dine is arrogant and impolite. Of course if you and your wife are out of town when the [arty is being set up, your secretary will have top do the telephoning; always to the guest's secretary—if there is one. Always send a reminder near the date of the dinner. You can send an invitation card, or remind your guests by telephone or fax. This gesture shows that you are sincere in wanting your guests to come.

SITUATION 2

A friend or colleague invites you to dinner. The invitation card, or the hostess over the telephone, indicates that dress will be informal. Should you:

Ⓐ Show up in blue jeans and a silk shirt;
Ⓑ Appear in a coat and tie, with your wife in a nice dress;
Ⓒ Present yourself in a dinner jacket with a black bow tie?

Comments

Option **Ⓑ** is your choice. Actually, unless your host and hostess are particular about the outward appearance of their guests, it does not matter what you wear. Informal in Hong Kong, however, means coat and tie. It does not have to be matching coat and trousers, which is known as lounge suit. If your hostess wished you to appear in your best suit and your wife in her most elegant outfit, to go with her sterling silver and best table linen, she would have said lounge suit. If she wishes you to appear in casual attire, she will say casual, which is not the same as informal.

Do not let what you ought to wear worry you; no one except the most insecure host and hostess cares what you will wear. It is you they want to see, not the clothes on your back. Once, a birthday party was given for a young woman who was reaching the age of thirty. It was to be an outdoor barbeque at the height of Hong Kong's summer heat. The site of the festivities was a colonial-style house at Repulse Bay, which was soon to be demolished for redevelopment; so the people organizing the party thought that it would be a shame not to have a grand send-off for the house as well. The invitation said Gulf Attire, which meant black tie but without the dinner jacket, as is the custom in the Persian Gulf where the weather is perpetually hot. People showed up in black tie with and without the jacket, or in shorts as if they were going to play golf. A grand time was had by all. It did not matter what they wore. On the other hand you, as a newcomer, should probably pay attention to what the invitation card says and dress accordingly.

SITUATION 3

This situation would not arise had the lunch taken place at your club; but you invited a Hong Kong Chinese business associate to lunch in a restaurant. It was a wonderful lunch and both of you enjoyed the food as well as the conversation. As the waiter presents the bill, your business associate starts to grab it. Should you:

Ⓐ Let him pay the bill;

Ⓑ Start fighting him tooth and nail for the bill;

Ⓒ Say: 'This time please let me take care of the bill, because I invited you; you can be the host the best time'?

Comments

The correct answer is option **Ⓒ**. Your guests knows that you are the host, responsible for picking up the tab. On the other hand, for a Chinese it is the culturally correct thing to do to make a gesture to grab the bill. It will make you uncomfortable to fight for the bill because in your culture one does not offer to pay the bill if somebody else did the inviting, but you still must not let him pay since it is you who initiated the lunch meeting. The few words you will say, as in option **Ⓒ**, will stop his efforts at grabbing the bill. The waiter understands because it is part of the ritual of dining in a restaurant. Under no circumstance should you suggest a Dutch Treat.

Incidentally, there is a ten per cent service charge in almost all the restaurants you will patronise in Hong Kong, But an additional tip would be nice, especially if you have had good service from the waiter, or if you eat in the restaurant often. In the latter case, a *laisee* packet to the captain and your usual waiter during the Lunar New Year season will reap untold rewards during the ensuring year. It never hurts to say thank you with a tip after a good meal.

SITUATION 4

You have decided to invite a few ladies to lunch on a particular day. You make out a list and start calling the guests. Geromina Li or Simonella Beowolf, for instance, wants to know who else is coming before she even accepts or declines your invitation. Should you:

Ⓐ Give her the full list;
Ⓑ Say that it is none of her business whom else you are inviting, and bang down the telephone;
Ⓒ Mumble something to the effect that you are not yet certain who is coming because Geromina or Simonella is the first person you have called?

Comments

You resent having to reveal your guest list so you will not choose option **Ⓐ** even under torture. Geromina or Simonella, if course, is committing a faux pas. By demanding to know the names of your guests, she sounds as if she really would not come to your luncheon unless your other guests were worthwhile to her. As you may not indulge yourself with option **Ⓑ**, option **Ⓒ** is your only choice.

A word of warning, however. Since you are handling such an insensitive person as Geromina or Simonella, she will not receive your implied message and will probably continue to probe. Now you must weigh all your considerations. Do you need to know this woman for any particular reason? If so, you will have to bend backwards to be pleasant to her. This may not be a cultural issue, and similar situations may occur outside Hong Kong. It is just that there are so many women's lunches here (known as the *taitai* lunches). Household help is available, so women can afford the time to enjoy lunches away from home. Remember, there is no free lunch. You may therefore not want to become part of the taitai luncheon circuit, but it may be essential for you to accept and give luncheon invitations—for a variety of reasons which amount to building up *guanxi*.

Therefore, you will need to cultivate or tolerate Geromina or Simonella. Remember, keep cool.

SITUATION 5

You are in a shop which stocks the item you have been searching for all over town. The sales assistant is unhelpful. She is surly and refuses to bring out more of the same item, so that you can choose from a wider selection. Should you:

Ⓐ Walk out in a huff without buying what you want;

Ⓑ Ask to see the manager and have her wait on your behalf;

Ⓒ Swallow your pride and buy the item even though you are not happy with the colour or quality?

Comments

In this case, adopting option **Ⓒ** is not intelligent, unless you feel that the price justifies such a compromise. If you are reasonably sure that by looking through more items, you will be able to get what you want, by all means adopt option **Ⓑ**.

The logical thing, in this competitive world, is to adopt option **Ⓐ**. You will have to look elsewhere for the particular item of merchandise, but you will feel a lot better.

SITUATION 6

You have been invited to dinner in a Chinese restaurant, but you have not been told that you are the guest of honour.

When you arrive, your hosts asks you to sit on the seat of honour, at the had of the table, the seat facing the door, Should you:

🅐 Sit down as the host directs;

🅑 Make some noises in declining the honour for a few moments then sit where the host directs;

🅒 Sit somewhere below the salt and refuse to budge?

Comments

Option 🅑 is the correct choice. If you were not the guest of honour, your host would probably not have asked you to take the honoured seat. Choosing option 🅐, however, would show a lack of humility besides taking it for granted that you should be more important than anybody else at this occasion.

If the entertaining takes place in a private dining room of the restaurant, this situation will not occur because guests are seated away from the table until all have arrived. Your host, will then, seat the guests of honour first. Even so, demurring does not hurt.

SITUATION 7

A number of people are waiting for taxis, when you join the merry throng. Should you:

A Stay around and fight to be the first at the taxi door when it stops to discharge a passenger;

B Walk further towards the direction from whence come the taxis, so that you will be the forst to hail an empty taxi should one approach;

C Organise a taxi queue on the spot?

Comments

Everybody takes option **A** or **B**. However, option **C** shows signs of gaining ground. In fact, several regular taxi queues were started in this manner by some enchanting soul or others waiting in a non-queue. The institutionalised queues in front of the YWCA in Macdonnell Road, at the back of the Bank of America Tower in Central and in front of the entrance of M at the Fringe by the Foreign Correspondents' Club, for instance, were all started in this way. You can bet, however, that the individuals who started those queues were not Hong Kong Chinese.

In general, the culture of Hong Kong does not include fair play, nor showing politeness to strangers. Competition is so intense in every aspect of life that if you can improve your chances of getting a taxi by lessening those of your competitors, you will; perhaps by walking higher and higher on the one-way Wyndham Street, facing the coming traffic. So that you can catch an empty cab coming down before it reaches the other hopeful passengers. You can be certain, though, that someone else will walk higher than you. While the days of being pushed aside as you enter a taxi seem, happily, to be almost over, competitors still try very hard to get to the taxi door in front of you.

SITUATION 8

You have just arrived at your destination by taxi. The driver gas been playing his radio loudly, and paying no attention to your discomfort as he slammed on the brakes and increased speed each time he turned a corner. The meter shows nineteen-fifty. You give him two ten-dollar bills and he does not hand you the fifty cents change. Should you:

Ⓐ Forget the fifty cents and disembark;

Ⓑ Stay put like the Rock of Gilbraltar and demand the change that is due to you;

Ⓒ Say pointedly 'keep the change', get out of the taxi and leave the door open?

Comments

Regardless of your understandable feeling that you are being taken for another ride, forget the fifty cents. A tip of less than three per cent of the fare is not generous by any yardstick. So you should take option **Ⓐ**, and perhaps add a couple of dollars too. You will find the driver visibly grateful. He may not thank you aloud, but he will open the door for you since the passenger doors are linked to his foot by a mechanical device; and he will not drive away while you are still half in the vehicle.

Demanding your change may satisfy your sense of fair play, but it is just adding fire to an already aggravating situation. The amount is not worth the hassle. For the reason indicated, you are not going to inconvenience the driver by leaving the door open. Remember, passengers are a challenge to the drivers, too.

In many instances, however, the driver may decide to keep an extra dollar or two as a tip without your consent. You are, then justified in asking him to give you the correct change— radio or no radio. And that brings us back to unwritten options **D** and **E**. If the radio makes your head hurt, say you have a headache and ask for mercy; and carry enough in small denominations to pay what you want to pay.

SITUATION 9

You are eating out in a restaurant with a few friends, and the waiter is unhelpful. He appears to be uncivil, and service is slow. You have ordered the meal to be served family-style, but there is a long wait between courses. You have ordered a dish with a delicious gravy but the rice just is not coming. On top of it all, the noise level in the restaurant is intolerable, and your temper is rising. Should you:

Ⓐ Walk out in a huff leaving the meal unfinished and refusing to pay the bill;

Ⓑ Call the manager and ask him to remove the waiter;

Ⓒ Appeal to the waiter's better nature and ask him to hurry up the service?

Comments

There is no clear choice but option **Ⓐ** is to be adopted only under severe provocation by the waiter's behaviour and manner. By refusing to pay the bill, especially if you have already consumed a couple of dishes, you would cause a great deal of commotion. There would be an pleasant scene as you were leaving the restaurant, ruining your evening still further. You could modify option **Ⓐ** by offering to pay for what you have already eaten, and cancel the rest of the dinner.

Option **Ⓒ** is the least desirable, taking a long view, because it will involve your meeting the waiter halfway. You may not even want to lower yourself to plead for service, especially since you feel that what you want is your right and not a favour to be dispensed at the waiter's pleasure. However, by appealing to his sense of fair play you give him face, and he will be on your side in whatever battle there might be in the kitchen, to get your food served in the shortest time span he can muster. Ideally you negotiate for a hot delicious-dish replacement to come with the eventual hot rice.

Option **Ⓑ** is possible, and probably the most effective way to get your food on the table. However, you do not know the reason behind the slow serving. The bottleneck may be in the kitchen, upstream of the dining room service. If you succeed in having the waiter removed, you cause him to lose face in front of a restaurant full of people; you might cause him to lose his job as well.

SITUATION 10

You have been invited to meet the grandmother of a Chinese friend or associate for the first time. The old lady likes you. Despite the language gap, she has decided to make conversation. During the conversation, she asks for your age, why you are not yet married or, if you are, why you have no children yet. The conversation progresses inevitably to the amount of your salary. Should you:

Ⓐ Tell her to mind her own business and stop being so nosy;

Ⓑ Ask her to guess the answers to all her questions;

Ⓒ Ignore her questions and talk about something else instead?

Comments

It depends on how you feel. Obviously you cannot be so rude as to take option **Ⓐ**. Your friend, if he is sensitive at all, should have come to your rescue before this routine gets so far. Your friend should say something like 'Ah, Granny, foreigners do not like to be asked these questions!' But perhaps he is reluctant to dictate his grandmother's behaviour, and you are left to cope.

A compromise option **Ⓒ** is possible, for you are not unwilling to tell her your age, and say something completely nonsensical in answer to the other questions, by way of humouring the old lady. Remember, the Chinese do not like to say no, so she will understand that you are trying to evade the subject and talking about something else. The most polite option to choose, however, is option **B**. It will prolong the conversation, and lessen the awkwardness between you; there is no need for you to confirm or deny her conjectures.

SITUATION 11

You are an Australian woman traveling by yourself on the MTR. A well-dressed Chinese man of indeterminate age comes up to you and compliments you on your hair. Then he announces to the entire train that you smell like cow dung. Should you:

A Slap his face and tell him that he is unspeakable rude;
B Ignore him and find another place in the train to stand;
C Stay put; but, looking at your fellow passengers, twirl your index finger while pointing it to your temple, indicating that the man is crazy?

Comments

As soon as he has commented on your hair, which is a personal remark one does not make to strangers in any culture, you should find some way to distance yourself from him, which is a pre-emptive option **B**. Option **A** is not to be adopted under any circumstance. Neither is option **C**. Obviously the man is at last a little touched when he makes such as insulting remark aloud. By provoking him in choosing option **A** or option **C**, you only make matters worse. As it is, fellow passengers who understood his remark are already embarrassed at him. Those who do not speak English will be interested only if you react.

SITUATION 12

One of Hong Kong's senior men-about-town is sitting next to you at a formal dinner. He asks audibly whether you would mind him lighting a cigar. Since, in your opinion, such an act would emit smoke and aroma that not everybody would find pleasant, you reply in a dulcet but audible voice that yes, you would indeed mind. He lights up just the same, Should you:

A Tell him that you did say you would mind;

B Smile pleasantly and say nothing;

C Co to the ladies' room and cool off?

Comments

Yes, the man is rude and insensitive to ignore the clear wish of a neighbour, especially since he asked whether you would mind. Obviously he was not expecting a negative answer to what he considers a routine question, and thinks that the answer ought to have been an automatic 'Of course not, please go ahead'. Your frank response has made him lose face in front of the entire table of ten other persons. In this defiant gesture of lighting up his cigar, he clearly demonstrates to himself that there is no need to accept dictation from a woman.

What would have been the culturally correct response from you? Perhaps, had you merely smiled and made an inconspicuous gesture with your chin, you would have conveyed the message that it was not a good idea to smoke at a public gathering. Had your husband been this man's boss, of had he wanted something from your husband very badly, he would have heeded your understated wish; but not otherwise. This is a no-win situation. Go to the ladies room to cool off and avoid smoke; or grin and bear it.

SITUATION 13

You have decided to buy a basket of fruit to take to a friend, and have chosen a posh shop instead of using the van which carries fruit and vegetable to your building twice a week. You buy three mangoes at twenty dollars each, six peaches at ten each, two nectarines at fifteen each, six oranges at five each, and a bunch of bananas at twenty dollars. The basket is fifteen dollars. You hand him a five hundred dollar bill and wait for your change. Now you are mathematically gifted and have been trained to add in your head without a calculator. So, when you hear the vendor say 'that will be three hundred and forty dollars', you know that he is trying to cheat you. Should you:

Ⓐ Tell him that he is a cheat, demand the return of your five hundred dollars and walk out;

Ⓑ Pay the amount he asked without murmur;

Ⓒ Tell him that his total is incorrect and add together with him until you reach the correct number?

Comments

It is doubtful whether option Ⓐ is an option at all, because the vendor will never return the money no matter what names you bring to bear. If his skin is thick enough to want to cheat you, for certainly that is his intention, he is not going to be shamed into giving back your money. Never give any merchant your money until you have agreed upon the price.

Option Ⓑ is not an option either, because it is not the correct amount. Therefore, you are left with option Ⓒ. It is troublesome, but you must spend as much time as it takes, while controlling your temper, so that you pay the right amount, and not one dollar more.

SITUATION 14

You are with a group of Hong Kong natives and you are discussing all kinds of subjects, from money and politics to personal matters. You have told them all about your family, your father and mother—where and when they were born, where they went to school, how they earn their living—and even about your grandparents. Suddenly you notice that one of your friends has said nothing about his parents. Should you:

Ⓐ Probe—with specific questions about the friend's parents and their pedigree;

Ⓑ Announce that you are not going to say anything more about your family unless he returns the compliment;

Ⓒ Change the subject of conversation?

Comments

Options Ⓐ and Ⓑ are not tactful. Hong Kong family relationships are complicated. For one reason or another, your friend may wish to hide his ancestry. His parents might not be educated, which would not bother you but could upset him—especially if you have described your parents' illustrious degrees. Perhaps his father holds a menial job; or his mother may be a concubine and your friend is ashamed of the relationship. So choose option **C**. If you are really good friends, he will reveal all in time—when he is sure that you will not despise him because of his family background.

SITUATION 15

You ring a business associate in his office, and somebody answers the telephone. You ask for the person by name. The voice answers 'Mr Lee hasn't come back yet.' Should you:

A Assume that Mr Lee has come into the office already but has gone out temporarily;

B Leave a message for him to return your call, thank the voice, and hang up;

C Pursue further the whereabouts of Mr Lee?

Comments

The phrase 'hasn't come back yet' can have a host of meanings. It could mean that Mr Lee has not come to the office today, or that he will be out of town for the rest of the week. Under no circumstances should you choose option **B**; you must ask more questions to find out when you can expect a call from your friend. Option **A** is almost never justified because it usually means that Mr Lee has not so far come into the office.

Option **C** is your best choice. Unless you keep on asking questions, you are not going to find out the whereabouts of the person you want or when you can communicate with him. Our favourite answer to this sort of probing is 'Mr Yang hasn't come back yet. He is in the toilet.'

SITUATION 16

You are walking your silent Yorkshire terriers on Bowen Road and a family of father, mother and children come from

the other direction. The father barks 'Wow! Wow! Wow!' at your dogs, and your dogs go berserk. The children are visibly frightened. The father goes 'Tsk, tsk, tsk! Bad dogs!'. Should you:

Ⓐ Tell the father that he is an imbecile;
Ⓑ Shorten the leashes and pull the dogs closer to you;
Ⓒ Say something soothing to the children while glaring at the father?

Comments

Option **Ⓐ** is based on a true premise, for no sane person would go out of his way to tease a strange animal, but it is not the right time or place to educate a grown man. You should have begun option **Ⓑ** as soon as you saw the family approaching, in any case; and now you must say in your gentlest tone something to calm the children.

Hong Kong children have been taught to be afraid of animals, especially dogs since dogs are viewed as guards rather than pets. In this case, where the father has behaved so immaturely, it is up to you to assure the children that your dogs are harmless.

DOS AND DON'TS

It is difficult to compile a list of do's and don'ts based solely on cultural considerations. I remember that, after reading a Dos and Don'ts publication given to me by an international airline, which told me not to point at anybody or anything with my feet in Thailand, I had to curb my desire to do just that every time I am in Bangkok! Use your common sense!

DO'S

- Do Tip generously when you feel that the services provided warrant it. Remember, waiters, tax drivers, doormen and washroom attendants all depend on tips as a part of their salary.
- Do bring a gift to whatever occasion. If you do not know the recipients well, fruit, chocolates and flowers are always nice; and red wine is increasing in popularity.
- Do present your gift with both hands.
- Do have your calling cards (name cards) printed in both languages, and present to people you meet with both hands.
- Do have your destination address written in Chinese and give it to the taxi driver.

DONT'S

- Don't tip the postmen or the police. They are public servants, tips are defined as 'advantages'. Accepting tips, no matter how small, will get them into trouble with the ICAC, and you, the tipper, will be an accessory.
- Don't start any unpleasant topic such as illness or death, especially in the morning. In fact, do not use unpleasant words or terms on any social occasion, especially birthday and wedding celebrations.
- Don't wear black clothes when attending a funeral or a wake.
- Don't under-dress. When in doubt, wear a jacket and tie, you can always remove them if nobody else is so garbed.

On the other hand, trousers for ladies, especially as a part of an ensemble, are accepted everywhere.

- Don't ever take for granted that you can show up at any occasion, including outdoor barbecues, in sneakers (tennis shoes) and blue jeans.
- Don't give people clocks as gifts. Watches are alright. The word 'giving a clock' in Cantonese sounds like 'the end' meaning 'death'.
- Don't give apples to the ill. 'Apple' in Chinese, a two character term, sounds like 'death from disease' in the Shanghai dialect.
- Don't litter! This is not cultural, but legal. Even if you drop your keys or cigarette ashes on the ground, the law of Hong Kong considers the act 'litter', with a HK$5,000 fine
- Don't take your mobile telephone to a private club, especially if you are a guest. Most clubs have strict regulations against using mobile telephones with serious consequences for offenders (or their hosts).
- Don't point the spout of a teapot at anybody, unless you want to pick a fight with that individual.

GLOSSARY

COMMONLY USED WORDS AND PHRASES
Terms of Address

noi si/fu yen	madam
siu dze	miss
tai tai	missus
sin sang	mister

Greetings and Goodbyes

nei hou	hello
hai	hi
nei how ma	how are you
zou san	good morning
nei hou	good afternoon/ good evening
zou tau	good night
dzoi gin	goodbye
dɒng zɒn gin	see you later
ting yat gin	see you tomorrow
M goi sai	thank you
M sai hak hei	you're welcome

Numbers

yɒt	one
yi	two
sam	three
sei	four
m	five
luk	six
tsɒt	seven
bat	eight
gau	nine

sap	ten
sap yɒt	11
yi sap	20
yɒt bak	100
yɒt tsin	1,000
yɒt mun	10,000
sap man	100,000
yɒt bak man	1,000,000
yɒt bun	half
sam fɒn tsi yɒt	one-third
sei fɒn tsi yɒt	one-quarter
yɒt da (sap yi go)	a dozen
dai yɒt	first
dai yi	second
dai sam	third
dai sei	fourth
dzeoi hau	last
yɒt deoi	one pair

Days

sing kei yɒt	Monday
sing kei yi	Tuesday
sing kei sam	Wednesday
sing kei sei	Thursday
sing kei m	Friday
sing kei luk	Saturday
sing kei yat	Sunday
gam yat	today
ting yat	tomorrow
kum yat	yesterday
dzau mat	weekend
dzau yat	weekday
li go sing kei	this week

| seong sing kei | last week |
| ha sing kei | next week |

Time

dzung m sap yi dim	12 noon
ye man sap yi dim	12 midnight
dziu dzou	morning
ha dzau	afternoon
man soeng	evening
ye man	night
lai ming	dawn
yi ga	now
an d	later
yɒt dzeng gan	in a while
Yi ga gei dim?	What time is it?

Measurements

lei mai	centimetre
mai	metre
gung lei	kilometre
ping fong mai	square metres
ping fong gung lei	square kilometres
gung king	hectare
hak	gram
tsin hak	kilogram
lup fong mai	cubic metre
gung sing	litre

Colours

mai sik	beige
hɒk sik	black
lam sik	blue

hok sik	brown
gam sik	gold
luk sik	green
fui sik	grey
tsung sik	orange
dzi sik	purple
fan hong sik	pink
hong sik	red
ngan sik	silver
wong sik	yellow
bak sik	white
tau ming	transparent

Weather and Climate

hong seoi mai	flood
geoi fung	hurricane
gwai fung	monsoon
yü/luk yü	rain/raining
süt	snow
bao fung yu	stormy
tsing long	sunny
toi fung	typhon
tseon tin	spring
ha tin	summer
tsau tin	autumn
dung tin	winter

Transportation and Getting Around

fei gei	airplane
tse	car
dou leon	ferry
sün	ship

fo tse	train
ging gung hei tse	bus
gau tung dong	traffic light
yon hung dou	zebra crossing
kiu	bridge
tin kiu	overhead bridge
gung tse dzan	bus station
fo tse dzam	railway station
on tsün dai	seat belt
si gei	driver
ga tsiu	driving license
ga yau zam	petrol station
teng tse	parking
gung on	policeman
gau geng	traffic policeman

Directions

dzou	go
teng	stop
man	slow
fai	fast
li dou	here
go dou	there
dzo	left
you	right
dzo dzün	turn left
you dzün	turn right
dzün wan	round the bend
toe tse	reverse
tsik hang	move forward
U yang dzün wan	U-turn
M goi hoi man di	Please slow down

M goi hoi fai di	Please go faster
M goi hvi li dou dvng ha ngo	Please wait here for me
Ni dou ting	Stop here
Ngo gon si gan	I'm in a hurry

Food and Drink

min bao	bread
tsao fan	friend rice
min tiu	noodles
tong min	soup noodles
tsuk	porridge
tong	soup
sai tsan	Western dishes
hon bou bau	hamburger
dza yü pin	fish and chips
tou dao nei	mashed potato
pei sa beng	pizza
ngau pai	sirloin steak
tou si min bao hang	toasted bread
gvi dan	egg
ngau yau	butter
zi si	cheese
ngau lai	milk
sün lai	yoghurt
fvn yuk	bacon
fo teoi	ham
ngau yuk	beef
gvi yuk	chicken
ngap yuk	duck
dzü yuk	pork
yoeng yuk	mutton
hoi sin	seafood

hai	crab
yü	fish
lung ha	lobster
doei ha	prawn
swai yu	salmon
so tsoi	vegetables
mo gu	mushroom
to dau	potato
hou yau	oyster sauce
fan ke dzap	tomato sauce
hung lat dziu	chillie
sün tau	garlic
yoeng tsong	onion
tong	sugar
yim	salt
wu ziu fɒn	pepper
seoi go	fruits
ping go	apple
hoeng dziu	banana
bo loh	pineapple
si do be lei	strawberry
sai gwa	watermelon
hoeng bɒn	champagne
be dzau	beer
ga fei	coffee
tsa	tea
kong tsin seoi	mineral water
tsanf dzɒp	orange juice
dzao	wine
dong ning mung tsa	ice lemon tea
go dzap	fruit juice
dung ge	cold

yid ge	hot
sang ge	fresh
m san san ge	stale

Shopping

ngan hong	bank
seon yung ka	credit card
tsin	money
svu geoi	receipt
sai dzoeng ge tsin	small notes
dai dzoeng ge tsin	large notes
ngan bvi	coins
bou dzi	newspaper
tsui kvp si tsoeng	supermarket
doi	bag
hoeng yin	cigarettes
tong go	sweets
fa	flowers
dzü bou	jewellery
sü	book
soeng gei	camera
gu lung seoi	cologne
fan gan	soap
ngat sat	toothbrush
nga gou	toothpaste

RESOURCE GUIDE

WEBSITES

For general information about Hong Kong on the Internet
- http://www.english.hongkong.com
- http://www.info.gov.hk

EMERGENCY AND HEALTH

Dialling 999 in Hong Kong will connect you to the police, fire, ambulance and other possible emergency services. When you dial 999, do specify which you are asking for.

MEDICAL EMERGENCIES

There are more than forty public hospitals and a handful of private hospitals in Hong Kong. When you call 999, it will take you to the nearest public hospital. Public hospitals in Hong Kong are under the umbrella of Hospital Authority.
- http://www.ha.org.hk/.

In addition to the 999 emergency service, St. John's Ambulance provides free ambulance services for non-emergency cases. The have different telephone numbers for various locations in Hong Kong:
- Hong Kong Island
  Tel: (852) 2576-6555
- Kowloon
  Tel: (852) 2713-5555
- New Territories
  Tel: (852) 2639-2555

Hospitals that offer 24-hour accident and emergency services are as follows:

Hong Kong Island
- Pamela Youde Nethersole Eastern Hospital in the Eastern district
  Tel: (852) 2595-6111

- Queen Mary Hospital in the Southern district
  Tel: (852) 2855-3838
- Cheung Chau Hospital in Cheng Chou
  Tel: (852) 2981-0378
- Tang Shui Kin Hospital in Wanchai
  Tel: (852) 2291-2000

Kowloon
- Caritas Medical Centre in Sham Shui Po
  Tel: (852) 3408-7911
- Kwong Wah Hospital in Mong Kok
  Tel: (852) 2332-2311
- Princess Magaret Hospital in Kwai Chung
  Tel: (852) 2990-1111
- Queen Elizabeth Hospital in Jordan
  Tel: (852) 2958-888
- United Christian Hospital in Kwun Tong
  Tel: (852) 2379-4000

New Territories
- Alice Ho Miu Ling Nethersole Hospital in Tai Po
  Tel: (852) 2888-2888
- North District Hospital in Fanling
  Tel: (852) 2683-8888
- Pok Oi Hospital in Fan Ling
  Tel: (852) 2478-2556
- Prince of Wales Hospital in Shatin
  Tel: (852) 2632-2211
- Tuen Mun Hospital in Tuen Mun
  Tel: (852) 2468-5111
- Yan Chai Hospital in Tsuen Wan
  Tel: 2417-8383

Outlying Islands
Call 999

If all else fail, call your doctor and a taxi, then head to where your doctor tells you to go. Take a Cantonese-speaking (or Chinese-speaking) friend with you to the nearest hospital.

Some **taxi companies'** numbers are:
- (852) 2574-7311 in Hong Kong Island
- (852) 2760-0411 in Kowloon
- (852) 2475-0417 in New Territories

There is a nominal surcharge for such telephone booking services.) If the patient cannot travel by taxi, call 999.

NON-MEDICAL EMERGENCIES

If you lose your passport, call your government's consulate in Hong Kong or call 1081 for the English-language **Directory Assistance** and ask for the emergency telephone number of your consulate. (Be patient when calling; the Directory Assistance service operates on a trilingual basis, with English being the last language on the automated system. Listen very carefully in order to push the correct set of buttons.)

OTHER HELPLINES

The Samaritans: this helpline in Hong Kong operates on a 24-hour basis.
Tel: (852) 2389-2222 (for English speakers)

Electricity

CLP Power Hong Kong Limited supplies electricity to Kowloon, New Territories, and Outlying Islands (except Lamma Island)
Tel: (852) 2728-8333

Gas

The Hong Kong Electric Co. Ltd. (servicing Hong Kong Island and Lamma Island),
Tel: (852) 2880-6999

Telephone Services

Tel: 1000

Water

Government Water Supplies Department,
Tel: (852) 2824-5000

HEALTHCARE

Most medical doctors in Hong Kong, especially those from overseas, are incorporated into business groups, normally known as 'partnerships'. Local doctors, many of whom are trained in Hong Kong, work in their 'private clinics'.

Private Hospitals with Outpatient Services:

- **Hong Kong Adventist Hospital**
  Tel: (852) 2574-6211
- **Matilda Hospital**
  Tel: (852) 2849-0111
- **Hong Kong Sanitorium**
  Tel: (852) 2572-0211

Wherever the doctor you wish to see is located, you make an appointment, go to the office, clinic, or hospital, give the receptionist your name, and wait, and wait. Hong Kong doctors, like their colleagues elsewhere, cannot seem to keep to their schedule. Therefore, take with you reading materials, your embroidery or knitting and be prepared for a long wait. On the bright side, there are many General Practitioners (GPs), and all of them speak English. Get your friends and acquaintances to recommend one. The GP can then recommend specialists.

Remember to check your insurance policies if you have a local health insurance policy. Insurance agents in Hong Kong favour certain medical practitioners and pay a more generous portion of your bills. The website for the **Hospital Authority** is:

http://www.ha.org.hk/

Chinese Herbalists, Qigong and Tieda Practitioners and Acupuncturists

Get recommendations from friends, but remember that it is rare that any of the above will be able to communicate in English. A rare specie has been found! One *tieda* specialist with excellent English, 360 Queen's Road West, tel: (852) 2546-7867. Open daily from 9:00 am. No appointment is needed.

Pharmacies or Drug Stores

Pharmacies or drug stores in Hong Kong are known as chemists or dispensaries. They are attached to the major hospitals where you pay cash but the prices are lower than at independent pharmacies. Private doctors whom you visit also sell medicine. Therefore, it is not necessary for you to take prescription in hand in search of a suitable pharmacy. Meanwhile, there are many pharmacies everywhere in Hong Kong anyway which, like their counterparts elsewhere, sell everything from tooth paste to perfumes. Pharmacies with solid reputations include Mannings and Watson's (with branches all over Hong Kong). Remember to bring your doctor's prescriptions. In Central, try also Victoria Pharmacy and Fanda.

Dental Clinics

There are dental clinics in Hong Kong, but most dentists and dental surgeons work privately.

The two major universities—Hong Kong University on Hong Kong Island, and Chinese University in the New Territories—boast excellent dental schools of international standard. Their clinics treat the populace and a number of selected patients as the professors are primarily involved in training future dental surgeons. For emergencies, call the hospitals listed at the beginning of this section and ask if they provide dental services.

The website for the **Hong Kong Dental Association** is : http://www.hkda.org/

LOST AND FOUND (LOST PROPERTY)

- **Police Lost and Found**
  Tel: (852) 2860-2000
- **Airport Lost Property**
  Tel: (852) 2181-0000
- **MTR**
  Tel: (852) 2861-0020

PICKPOCKETS AND MUGGINGS

Although muggings are not everyday occurrences in Hong Kong, they still happen. Pickpockets, however, are more common.

FACILITIES FOR THE PHYSICALLY DISABLED

Most facilities in Hong Kong cater to the needs of the physically disabled; taxis drivers are friendly towards wheelchair-bound passengers and street crossings provide ramps for wheelchairs. Theatres and concert halls are equipped with wheel chair facilities, as are toilet facilities open to the public, such as those at the Culture Centre and the museums.

There is a free *Hong Kong Access Guide for Disabled Visitors*. It advises that you call ahead to find out if certain facilities are user-friendly. For residents, transportation for wheel chair passengers is available. Contact **Community Advice Bureau**, tel: (852) 2815-5444. For visitors, consult your hotel concierge.

If you find help for the disabled to be inadequate, you can lodge a complaint with **Equal Opportunities Commission,** tel: (852) 2511-8211.

FACILITIES FOR THE MENTALLY ILL AND MENTALLY HANDICAPPED

The facility for mental or psychiatric care in Hong Kong is the **Castle Peak Hospital**, [tel: (852) 2456-7111, website: http:www//chanmf@hk.org.hk]. In cases of emergency, telephone 999.

CHILD CARE

Teenagers in Hong Kong do not babysit. If you are a visitor and are staying in a hotel, consult the concierge or list of hotel services. If you are a newly-arrived resident, consult a friend who has children. If all else fail, call **Community Advice Bureau,** tel: (852) 2815-5444.

MAIDS

Part-time maids are available in Hong Kong. Consult your neighbourhood grapevine or call the **Community Advice Bureau**, tel: (852) 2815-5444.

BUDGET ACCOMMODATIONS

Do consult guide books that are designed for the cash conscious traveller. Here are some suggestions:

Hong Kong Island

- **Garden View International Hotel**
  Tel: (852) 2877-3737
  Offers rooms with a view of the Botanical Garden.
- **Harbour View International House**
  Tel: (852) 2802- 0111
  Rooms that overlook the Harbour.

Kowloon:

- **Salisbury Road YMCA**
  Tel: (852) 2268-7000
- **YMCA Waterloo Road**
  Tel: (852) 2388-5926
  Near tourist attractions and shopping.

For more choices, you may visit the following websites:

- http://www.megahotels.com.hk/,
- http://www.hongkongnet.net/,
- http://www.discoverhongkong.com/
- http://directrooms-hongkong.com/ for more choices.

CURRENCY

One Hong Kong Dollar is equivalent to 100 Hong Kong cents. Notes come in denominations of 1000, 500, 100, 50, 20 and 10 dollars. Coins are in denominations of 10, 5, 2 and 1 dollars, as well as 50, 20 and 10 cents.

You can change foreign currency in the usual places: banks, hotels and bureaux de change. Some shops also accept traveller's cheques.

Credit Cards

Almost all restaurants and shops you patronise will take credit cards. Some people pay everything with credit cards, including plane tickets and income tax, instead of writing cheques, in order to accrue 'points'.

Cash

ATMs can be found everywhere. Some of them accept international bank cards (e.g. those bearing the VisaPlus or

Cirrus logo), so you can retrieve cash any time in Hong Kong. Plan ahead during holidays and weekends in case the ATM runs out of cash since the demand for cash by the public on these weekends can be extraordinary. You will still need cash for petty items like bus fare or newspapers. Taxi drivers do not accept HK0 $1,000 notes; bus drivers demand exact change.

Octopus Cards

Stored-value 'Octopus' Cards are available at the MTR. It is the pay-now, ride-later plastic card which you can place in your wallet and operate the turnstiles without having to take it out. You can use the 'Octopus' Card for almost all forms of transportation.

DUTIES

Do not be taken in by the assertion that Hong Kong is a free port, and therefore there are no taxes imposed on the goods you purchase. Taxes are hidden and are a part of the prices you pay. In fact, high import duties are imposed on alcohol, cosmetics, tobacco and automobile (including petroleum). Companies pay company tax and individuals pay income tax. Do take note of the rules and regulations.

Salaries Tax

There is no tax withholding, but there are certificates you can buy in order to keep your cash handy for the **Inland Revenue** people. Furthermore, Inland Revenue takes credit cards. When in doubt, consult Inland Revenue, [tel: (852) 187-8088, website: http://www.info.gov.hk/ird/].

The **MPF (Mandatory Provident Fund)** is Hong Kong's response to charges that its citizens do not enjoy social security or retirement benefits. It is legally obligatory that 10 per cent of your salary (5 per cent paid by you taken from your salary and 5 per cent by your employer) is paid into a MPF account.

Whether you care to understand the management methodology of this fund or not, just make sure that you pay your share and that your employer pays his.

Also, watch out for unscrupulous employers who try to fleece you by telling you that they are hiring you as an 'independent agent' so that you need to pay for your own MPF and insurance. (See the next section.)

INSURANCE
Pay close attention to your insurance coverage. Your employer is required by law to take out certain insurance policies for you, especially those covering injuries incurred during work. Many employers also provide medical insurance, with or without premium contributions from employees. Check your entitlement before signing your contract.

If you are a visitor, make sure that you carry adequate travel insurance before you leave home. Your home country may not have reciprocal arrangements with Hong Kong.

ENTERTAINMENT AND LEISURE
Ignoramus would complain that Hong Kong is a cultural desert. It is not!! There are a large number of complimentary publications that provide information on entertainment and leisure activities. The daily newspapers as well as the media (radio, television) will not allow you to miss all the exciting happenings in every genre of the arts and entertainment in Hong Kong. If you insist on a DIY (Do It Yourself), check the following websites:
- http://www.hkevents.net/
- http://www.scmp.com/
- http://www.timeout.com/hongkong/

Restaurants and Cafes
Since this is not the kind of guide that lists eating places in Hong Kong, let me just say that no matter what type of food you fancy, at whatever price, it is available in Hong Kong. Consult tourist publications, your hotel concierge, your daily newspapers, and check the website http://www.food4hongkong.com/home/.

All restaurants boast a 'business luncheon' or 'daily specials' menu, this is a great deal since it costs less than what the same meal would cost in the evening.

Wine is becoming increasingly popular. Prices range from under US$ 10 to several hundred a bottle.

Fast food of both Eastern and Western genre is available. The restaurants are crowded, and extremely noisy.

'Food by Fone'

If you live on Hong Kong Island, you can dine in style at home or your office. The 'Food by Fone' people bring restaurant food to your home or office—45 minutes after you place your order. Call for a menu or check what you want from their website. You can order what you want by telephone, or by fax. You cannot, however, order from more than one restaurant each time. Depending on the size of your order, payment can be made by credit card.

Tel: (852) 2868-6969, fax: (852) 801-4385
Website: http://www.foodbyfone.net/

Shopping Districts

There is no such item as specific districts for shopping in Hong Kong as the entire place appears to be one huge shopping centre.

However, you my want to heck out the **Fleet Arcade** on the waterfront in Wanchai. Originally founded for the convenience of American servicemen on R & R Leave during the Vietnam War, the shops in the Arcade also welcome local residents. Besides a restaurant with outdoor seating by the sea on the ground floor, there are shops, selling souvenirs, jewellery and watches, musical instruments, camera, wine and cigars, suits and shoes, the most delicious sausages in the world, health food and golf balls. The shop that will interest you would be the one on the top floor, selling books, magazines, and videos and DVDs at US prices.

Night Spots

Lan Kwai Fong, a L-shaped area just above Central, together with its adjunct, **Soho**, continue to attract the young, and some not-too-young expatriate residents and visitors. Prices are not for the budget conscious.

Elsewhere, there are the standard bars and taverns: **Dickens' Bar** (Excelsior Hotel in Causeway Bay), **JJ**'s (Grand Hyatt in Wanchai North), and the **Fringe Club** (Ice House Street) that is known for the beer it serves. If money is no object, check out the hotel lounges and drinking places.

Areas such as **Wanchai** (reminiscent of the Suzy Wong-era) and 'Nightmarket' at **Temple Street** are not to be visited unless you are accompanied by local friends who speak Cantonese.

Libraries

Hong Kong's collections of printed materials, including books and journals in Chinese and other languages, have recently been enriched by other materials, such as audiovisual and electronic resources. As long as you hold a Hong Kong Identity Card and can prove that you have an address, you are entitled to borrow books from the various public libraries, including the much heralded **Central Library** opened in 2001. The **Library catalogue via web** can be accessed at:

http://libcat.hkpl.gov.hk/webpac_eng

All public collections, as well as collections of tertiary institutions are accessible through the Internet at:

http://www.hkpl.gov.hk/.

Other libraries open to the public include:

- **Goethe Institute Library**
  Tel: (852) 2802-0088
- **Alliance Française library**
  Tel: (852) 2730-9258

Private clubs include in their facilities libraries, but they are for club members only.

The **Library of the Helena May Club** on Garden Road, tel: (852) 2522-6766, holds perhaps the best collection of books for leisurely reading and for children in Hong Kong. Now that its racially-restrictive policies are no longer in force, you will probably find the dues affordable, and the library is definitely worth a visit.

The Family History Centre of the Church of Jesus Christ of Latter Day Saints (Mormons) in Hong Kong provides extremely rich resources on geological studies. The library is open to the public, but do make an appointment first, tel: (852) 2712-4788.

For commercial information, try the:

- **Trade Development Council** at the Convention Centre
  Website: http://www.tdctrade.com/
- **American Consulate Commercial Section**
  Website: http://www.usconsulate.org.hk/fcs/

CULTURAL AND SOCIAL ORGANISATIONS
National Associations

These are but a few example of cultural and social organisations which bring their national presence to Hong Kong. Membership is open and all of these organisations give language lessons.

- **American Women's Association**
  Tel: (852) 2526-0165
- **The British Council**
  Tel: (852) 2913-5012
- **The Alliance Française de Hong Kong**
  Tel: (852) 2527-7825
- **The German Goethe Institute**
  Tel: (852) 2588-1169
- **The Italian Dante Alighieri Society**
  Tel: (852) 2573-0343
- **Community Advice Bureau**
  Tel: (852) 2815-5444
  This is probably the most useful institution which will answer all sorts of questions. If they do not know the answer to your question, they will find out.
- **Caritas Hong Kong**
  EMA Hot Line, tel: (852) 2537-7247
  This group of Catholic centres provides a wide range of services to everyone in Hong Kong, from adult education, to day care, to hospitals and services for the elderly.

Fraternal organisations providing social services in Hong Kong include:

- **The Freemasons**
  Website: http://www.masonicasia.com/
- **The Rotarians**
  Website: http://www.rchkiw.org.hk/.

Women's organisations with programmes to help English-speaking newcomers adjust to Hong Kong living include:

- **American Women's Association**
  Tel: (852) 2865-7737
- **YWCA English-Speaking Members Department**
  Tel: (852) 2524-0639

Expat Clubs

Many of these clubs have long waiting lists. Your employer who brings you to Hong Kong will deem whether it would be worthwhile to include your club membership in your total compensation package.

- **Aberdeen Boat Club**
  Tel: (852) 2552-8182
- **Aberdeen Marina Club**
  Tel: (852) 2555-8321
- **American Club (Town)**
  Tel: (852) 2842-7400
- **American Club (Country)**
  Tel: (852) 2813-3200
- **China Club**
  Tel: (852) 2521-8888
- **Clearwater Bay Golf and Country Club**
  Tel: (852) 2719-1595
- **Discovery Bay Golf Club**
  Tel: (852) 2987-7273
- **Dynasty Club**
  Tel: (852) 2824-1122
- **Foreign Corresponds' Club**
  Tel: (852) 2521-1511

- **Hong Kong Club**
  Tel: (852) 2525-8251
- **Hong Kong Country Club**
  Tel: (852) 2552-4488
- **Hong Kong Cricket Club**
  Tel: (852) 2574-6266
- **Hong Kong Football Club**
  Tel: (852) 2882-7470
- **Hong Kong Golf Club**
  Tel: (852) 2812-7070
- **Hong Kong Jockey Club**
  Tel: (852) 2837-8111
- **Jewish Community Centre**
  Tel: (852) 2801-5440
- **Kowloon Club**
  Tel: (852) 2369-2816
- **Kowloon Cricket Club**
  Tel: (852) 2367-4141
- **Ladies Recreation Club**
  Tel: (852) 2522-0151
- **Hong Kong Golf Club**
  Tel: (852) 2670-1211
- **Royal Hong Kong Yacht Club**
  Tel: (852) 2832-2817
- **Shek O Golf and Country Club**
  Tel: (852) 2809-4458
- **South China Athletic Association**
  Tel: (852) 2577-5805
- **United Services Recreation Club**
  Tel: (852) 2367-0672
- **World Trade Centre Club**
  Tel: (852) 2577-9528

Special Interest Clubs and Societies

- **Asia Society**
  Tel: (852) 2103-9511
- **Friends of Hong Kong Cultural Centre**
  Tel: (852) 2734-2009

- **Friends of Hong Kong Museum of Art**
  Tel: (852) 2734-2196
- **Friends of the Art Museum (CUHK)**
  Website: http://www.cuhk.edu.hk/lcs/friends/
- **Hong Kong Anthropological Society**
  Website: http://www.cuhk.edu/hk/ant/others/anthro.html
- **Hong Kong Artists' Guild**
  Tel: (852) 2519-0102
- **Hong Kong Bird Watching Society**
  Tel: (852) 2377-4387
- **Hong Kong Cellarmasters Wine Club,**
  Website: http:www.asiawines.com/hk
- **The Museum Society (HKU)**
  Tel: (852) 2241-5500
- **The Royal Asiatic Society**
  Tel: (852) 2813-7500

VOLUNTEERING
Call the **Community Advice Bureau**, tel: (852) 2815-5444

WOMEN'S CLUBS AND ASSOCIATIONS

- **The Australian Association, Women's Group**
  Tel: (852) 2530-4461
- **CLARES St. John's Cathedral**
  Tel: (852) 2530-2129
- **Helena May**
  Tel: (852) 2522-6766
- **Hong Kong Association of Business and Professional Women**
  Tel: (852) 2535-9198
- **Hong Kong Association of University Women**
  Mailing address: GPO Box 11708
- **Women's Corona Society**
  Tel: (852) 2264-0004
- **Women in Publishing Society**
  Tel: (852) 2526-0206
- **YWCA—English Speaking Department**
  Tel: (852) 2522-4291
- **Zonta Club**
  Tel: (852) 2895-2250

TRANSPORT & COMMUNICATIONS
- **MTR,** tel: (852) 2881-8888
- **KCR,** tel: (852) 2602-7799
- **LR,** tel: (852) 24687788

Public Buses
- **Citybus,** tel: (852) 2873-0818
- **Kowloon Motor Bus,** tel: (852) 2745-4466
- **New World First Bus,** tel: (852) 2136-8888

Trams
- **HK Tramways,** tel: (852) 2548-102
- **Peak Tramway,** tel: (852) 2849-0668

Ferries
For other ferries to various parts of China, contact your travel agent.
- **Star Ferry,** tel: (852) 2366-2576
- **Discovery Bay Ferries,** tel: (852) 2987-7351
- **Outlying Islands Ferry,** tel: (852) 2131-8181
- **Macau Ferry,** tel: (852) 28593333

Taxis
There are several companies but these are the largest.
- **Hong Kong Island,** tel: (852) 2574-7311
- **Kowloon,** tel: (852) 2760-0411
- **New Territories,** tel: (852) 2475-0417

LANGUAGES
Chinese (Cantonese being the preferred mode of communication) and English are the two official languages used in Hong Kong.

How to Overcome Language Impasses
Hong Kong is not a place where natives appreciate your trying to speak their language. But, you may feel desperate as nobody around seems to understand what you want. So it's useful to have the address where you want to go written

in Chinese on a piece of paper to show the taxi or bus driver. Carry with you a phrase book, such as *Instant! Cantonese* by Bill Loh and Nick Theobald, available in all book shops.

In any case, I would feel pretty stupid to ask some one if he spoke English in very poor Cantonese. If the person speaks English, he would understand what I am saying in English, wouldn't he?

RELIGION & SOCIAL WORK

For English-language Christian services, see Saturday newspapers, especially the SCMP. Here are contact numbers of a few religious institutions.

- **Anglican/Episcopal**;
  St John's Cathedral, tel: (852) 2523-4157
- **Catholic**
  St Joseph's, tel: (852) 2522-3992
- **Interdenominational**
  Union Church, tel: (852) 2522-1515
- **Lutheran**
  Church of all Nations, tel: (852) 2812-0375
- **Mormon**
  Mormon Church, tel: (852) 2559-3325
- **Orthodox**
  Orthodox Cathedral of St Luke, tel: (852) 2573-8328
- **Quaker Meeting**
  Religious Society of Friends, tel: (852) 9192-3477
- **Islamic**
  Kowloon Mosque & Islamic Centre, tel: (852) 2724-0095
- **Jewish**
  Ohel Leah Synagogue, tel: (852) 2549-0981

GENERAL INFORMATION

Hong Kong is not a Third World country, therefore sanitary and health standards are excellent. However, Hong Kong health authorities do recommend vaccinations against both types of Hepatitis. Common sense dictates that you be vaccinated against other infectious and tropical diseases, such as smallpox, measles, and polio.

Government Internet Search Engines
General and Tourist Advice Bureau and websites
- http://www.info.gov.hk/
- http://www.discoverhongkong.com/

Immigration, Residency and Nationality Issues
Remember to carry either your Hong Kong Identity Card (HKID) or your passport all the time. For any questions, send an email to enquiry@immd.gov.hk

BUSINESS INFORMATION
Business Organisations: Chambers of Commerce
- **American Chamber of Commerce of Hong Kong**
  Tel: (852) 2526-0165
  Website: http://www.amcham.org.hk/
- **Hong Kong General Chamber of Commerce**
  Tel: (852) 2529-9229
  Website: http://www.hkgcc.org.hk/
- **Hong Kong Trade Development Council**
  Tel: (852) 2584-4333
  Website: http://www.tdctrade.com/
- **Hong Kong Convention and Exhibition Centre**
  Tel: (852) 2582-8888
  Website: http://www.hkcec.com.hk/

Individual countries have trade representatives in Hong Kong. The **City of Vienna (Austria)** even boasts a **Representative Office** in Hong Kong, tel: (852) 2521-8913.

LEGAL AID AGENCIES
Hong Kong law provides that any person who has reasonable grounds for taking or defending a legal action' can seek legal aid for civil and criminal suits.
- http://www.info.gov.hk/lad/.

CHINESE LANGUAGE STUDY
You will find literally scores of 'schools', 'classes', or 'private tutors' teaching Chinese Putonghua (Mandarin)

and Cantonese. For more formal or serious students, try calling:

- Hong Kong University's **SPACE** (School of Professional and Continuing Education)
  Tel: (852) 2559-9771
  Website: http://www.hku.hk/space/
- **Yale-in-China Chinese Language Center**, Chinese University of Hong Kong
  Tel: (852) 2609-6727
  Website: http://www.cuhk.edu.hk/lac/

OTHER STUDIES

If you like studying alone or tetiary-level academic credit, try the **Open University of Hong Kong** [tel: (852) 2711-2100, website: http://www.oli.hk/].

If you want to be trained as an office administrator or hone your secretarial skills, try **Sara Beattie College** [tel: (852) 2507-9388, website: http://www.sarabeattie.com].

If you are interested in Asian culture and want to lean 'how to' acquire a variety of skills from cooking Indian curry to Chinese shadow boxing, try **YWCA English-Speaking Members Department** [tel: (852) 2524-0639].

FURTHER READING

Books on Hong Kong are available at local bookshops. They are instantly recognisable because almost all of them show 'Hong Kong' in their titles. Shop managers obligingly place them where they will catch your eye as you enter the door, or in a section clearly marked 'Local Interests' or 'Hong Kong'. The list which follows is by no means exhaustive, but I have added some of the large crop of pictorial publications geared to capitalise on public interest in Hong Kong's past. The books cited here are my personal choices, what I have found useful and enjoyable. It does not mean, however, that books I have left unmentioned are all humdrum. You will have to browse through the bookshops yourself to choose those you like.

BILINGUAL STREET GUIDE

Before you even start to browse, however, you must buy at once the latest issue of *Hong Kong Streets and Places* by Hong Kong Government Publications. Even if you do not drive, you will need to consult a street map from time to time. This publication is more than a guidebook, it can be a lifesaver. The names of the streets are indexed in English and Chinese. If you point to the street you know by its English name, where it is listed in alphabetical order, a taxi driver, say, will be able to find its Chinese equivalent and take you to your desired destination.

FICTION

Most novels are undemanding, although physically they may be weighty. Several bestselling novelists have found Hong Kong a dramatic background for their work. As long as you do not confuse historical fiction with historical fact, novels can give you the flavour of a bygone era. Still in print are perennial favourites with more editions than can be counted on all your fingers and thumbs. James Clavell's

Taipan (Dell, reissued 1986) taking place in the Opium War era with Canton, Macau and Hong Kong as background, is truly a good yarn with almost no glaring historical *faux pas*. The characters are strong and the ambience of early Hong Kong is convincing. A later novel that takes place during the 1960s, *Noble House* (Dell, 1984), with the typhoon and landslide as backdrop and boardroom battles as a major theme, disappoints; but a good read nevertheless, since Clavell is such a master craftsman.

Robert Elegant's *Dynasty (*McGraw Hill, 1977*)* depicting Hong Kong's leading Eurasian family and its ups and downs, is pure fiction without any pretence of resembling what really happened; but a good aircraft or poolside companion, nevertheless. Richard Mason's *The World of Suzy Wong* (1959), racist and sexist though it is, and dated to boot, depicts the sentimental as well as the seamier side of old Hong Kong.

Other books in this category include: *Hangman's Point* by Dean Barrett (Village East Books, 1998), a fast-paced mystery/thriller and historical fiction with mid-19th century Hong Kong as its background. *The Bourne Supremacy* by Robert Ludlum (Bantam, 1987), an exciting thriller set in Hong Kong, China, and Macao of the Cold War era; *The Monkey King* by Timothy Mo (1993) is a witty account of a young Portuguese man who marries into an eccentric Chinese family living in Hong Kong. Nuri Vittachi's contribution to this genre, *The Fung Shui Detective*, operating in Hong Kong, first introduced in 2000, has been developed into a proper series (Thomas Dunne Books, 2004)

Speaking of crime, perhaps you should also look at *Hong Kong Murders*, based on fourteen actual cases of homicide, by Kate Whitehead (Oxford University Press, 2001).

In a more literary direction, I have always found the writing of John Le Carré somewhat formidable, but have enjoyed thoroughly his *Honourable School Boy* (Hodder & Stoughton, 1977) with recognisable but hybrid characters running in and out of the Foreign Correspondents' Club of an earlier period. Two recent novels that take place in

Hong Kong are *Foreign Correspondents Club* by Anthony Spaeth (Secker & Warburg, 1990) and *Kowloon Tong* by Paul Theroux (Mariner Books; reprint edition, 1998).

ANTHOLOGY

Barbara-Sue White has extracted 60 pieces of writings on Hong Kong from 1844 to the present from biographies, diaries, letters, novels, poems, short stories, speeches, and even postcards. The result is *Hong Kong: Somewhere Between Heaven and Earth* (Oxford University Press, 1996). The writers range from the mighty of the 19th century, like Queen Victoria, to the luminaries of the 20th, such as Richard Mason (*Suzy Wong*), Austin Coates, Anthony Lawrence and Elsie Tu. It is a comprehensive and highly enlightening reading in one single volume.

GENERAL HISTORY

There are many scholarly works on various aspects of Hong Kong's history—political, social, economic and so forth. Pre-eminently, you should consult *Research Materials for Hong Kong Studies* published by the Centre of Asian Studies, University of Hong Kong, with over 300 resource pages—but only if you are writing a monograph of some sort on the territory.

The best book from which to learn some of the history is *A Borrowed Place: The History of Hong Kong* by Frank Welsh (Kodansha America, 1993). Despite its length of more than 600 pages, this is a highly entertaining book. Welsh, a merchant banker who used to live in Hong Kong, has conducted research meticulously and seriously, but has not allowed pomposity of historical personalities and decisions to stand in the way of his witty presentation of events. The standard history of Hong Kong, by Endicott, is again in print.

A much less ambitious work, albeit more readable when time is limited, is *The Hong Kong Story* by Caroline Courtauld and Mary Holdsworth (Oxford University Press, 1998). A chronicle of Hong Kong's history from its misty beginnings to the present day, this book covers the interwoven sagas of the family dynasties and business emporia which controlled Hong Kong from its beginning to the end of the 20th century.

TODAY

Taking 1997 as the focal point, the date when Hong Kong turned from a British colony into a Special Administrative Zone of China, a topic of current interest is *Hong Kong and China, For Better or For Worse*, by Frank Ching, author of *Ancestors*, published by the Foreign Policy Association in New York in 1985. The information in the book may be not up to date, but the succinct analysis of issues involved in the handing of Hong Kong to China in 1997 has remained valid. Subsequent events have proved Ching to be an astute observer of the China-Hong Kong scene.

There is also *The End of Hong Kong* (John Murray, 1993) by Robert Cottrell, another astute observer of China and Hong Kong. A British publication on this subject is Sir Percy Craddock's *My Experiences of China* (1994). Sir Percy was a member of the team that negotiated the agreement returning Hong Kong to Chinese rule in 1997.

Other books in this category include *The Future of Hong Kong, Towards 1997 and Beyond* (1987), edited by Hungdah Chu, Y C Jao, and Yuan-li Wu, and *Economic Future of Hong Kong* (Lynne Rienner Pub, 1990) by Miron Mushkat. I recommend to you books on this subject written for an international readership primarily because, as a newcomer to Hong Kong, you will find them more user-friendly than local publications which take for granted familiarity with names, terms and events. You should also try to find *Hong Kong, Epilogue to An Empire* (1988) by Jan Morris.

To be brought wholly up to date with developments, you only need to open a newspaper or a journal—any of the local English-language newspapers and some of the overseas newspapers with international coverage—or any weekly journal such as *The Economist*, *Time Magazine* or *Newsweek*.

If you work in the field of high technology and would like to find out how to translate your talent and knowledge into cash, then read *A Choice Fulfilled: the Business of High Technology* (Palgrave Macmillan, 1991), by Charles K Kao, the retired Vice Chancellor of the Chinese University of Hong Kong. He is renowned as the 'Father of Fiber Optics', the basis for our telecommunications revolution, and is an authority on such undertakings. Written with the interested general reading public in mind, this book traces the development of intricate technologies for practical use in the age of information.

For SARS, the epidemic which closed all of Hong Kong's schools and universities for almost a month in 2003, there is *Twentieth-first Century Plague—the Story of SARS* by Thomas Abraham (The Johns Hopkins University Press 2005).

THE GOOD OLD DAYS

Old-timers in Hong Kong have written about their experiences. Austin Coates, a graduate of Oxford and son of the composer Eric Coates, wrote *Myself a Mandarin, Memoirs of a Special Magistrate* (1968), reminiscences of his life as a colonial administrator in the New Territories before villages were turned into new towns. It is written with compassion, a feeling of frustration, and a great sense of humour. Coates belongs to a generation which is literate as well as learned, and he is a master of the English language. If you read only one book on old Hong Kong, this should be your choice.

Anthony Lawrence, a journalist now in his 90s, retired from the BBC but from little else, has traded his microphone for a typewriter. He has been most prolific on Hong Kong for two decades. Of his books, the one most interesting to readers here is *The Taipan Traders* (Formasia Books, 1994), comprising China Trade paintings of old Hong Kong. His latest, *The Fragrant Chinese* (Columbia University Press, 1993) is full of insight and wit. He is preparing his diary from his early days in Asia, covering such events as the funeral of Gandhi and the landing of American forces in Vietnam. You will also find Colin Criswell's *The Taipans, Hong Kong's Merchant Princes* (1981) informative.

Meggie Keswick's *The Thistle and the Jade* (Octopus Books,1982) was compiled to commemorate the 150th anniversary of the founding of Hong Kong's premier *hong*, Jardine Matheson, and Austin Coates wrote the delightful and informative *China Races* (1983) to commemorate the centenary of the Royal Hong Kong Jockey Club.

Mary Holdsworth's *Foreign Devil, Expatriates in Hong Kong* (Oxford University Press, 2002), was further enhanced with added text by Caroline Cartauld. The dead have not been neglected. As a foreign settlement, Macao (Macau) predates Hong Kong. In *An East India Company Cemetery: Protestant Burials in Macau*, Sir Lindsay and Lady Ride, describe the Portuguese settlement of Macao which had welcomed all manners of foreign traders before the Opium War. The work started by Sir Lindsay, Vice-Chancellor of the University of Hong Kong, and his wife May, was edited by Bernard Mellor, Registrar of the University (Hong Kong University Press, 1996).

PEOPLE AND CUSTOMS

Hugh Baker's *Hong Kong Images, People and Animals* (1979) is so much in demand that it has been issued several times since as a paperback. Dr Baker informs and entertains readers interested in the Chinese tradition as practised in Hong Kong.

Michael Harris Bond's *Beyond the Chinese Face, Insights from Psychology* (1991) is the 'all-time bestseller ever published by an academic press', in the words of its publisher. It is a scholarly work, intended for the general reader like you and me as well, a series of articles explaining what makes the Chinese what they are.

Wang Gungwu's *The Chineseness of China* (Oxford University Press, 1992) explores the theme of Chineseness in greater depth, from a historical perspective. *Turbans and Traders, Hong Kong's Indian Communities* (1994) by Barbara-Sue White is still generally available for you to learn more about some of the people of Hong Kong who are not ethnic Chinese.

Tales and insights within Government House can be found in a single book on the wives of successive governors of Hong Kong, *The Private Life of Old Hong Kong* (Oxford University Press, 1991), by Susanna Hoe. At the other end of the social ladder, there is Maria Jaschok's *Concubines and Bondservants* (1988), a sociological study—but short and readable. These books should be on the essential reading list of all women and their men in Hong Kong.

The Moon Year by Juliet Bredon and Igor Mitrophanow (published 1927, reprinted in Hong Kong 1982) is the fountainhead of all non-scholarly books on Chinese festivals, containing every bit of information you'll ever care to know about festivals and customs from one month to the next throughout the whole lunar year—ancestors, gods, beliefs, superstitions, dragon and lion dances, the lot; but it is a weighty undertaking, not to be digested at a sitting. A more portable work is *Chinese Festivals* (1982) by Joan Law and Barbara E Ward, which is confined to practices in Hong Kong.

PERSONAL MEMOIRS

A number of memoiras have been published during the past few years by people who grew up or lived as adults in Hong Kong. Sir David Akers-Jones, who speaks fluent Fukienese (Fujian dialect), Cantonese, and Putonghua, penned his memoir, *Feeling the stones: Reminiscences* (Hong Kong University Press, 2005). From Wales and Oxford this British civil servant started in Hong Kong as a district officer and later rose to be Chief-Secretary of the Hong Kong Government, serving also as Acting Governor in the 1980s. Sir David enjoys the respect of the Chinese on both side of the border.

Elsie Tu's memoir, *Colonial Hong Kong in the Eyes of Elsie Tu*, emerged in 2003 (Hong Kong Univeristy Press). Another volume, the love story between Elsie, who came out from her native Britain to Asia to be a missionary, and Andrew, a refugee from Mongolia, shows how they found each other, the joys and tribulations in establishing their school for children whose parents could not afford to send them to other schools that charged a fee, and their personal life.

On the Chinese side, Adeline Yen Mah, an Oxford-educated physician, wrote about her childhood and life in Shanghai and Hong Kong, *Falling Leaves*, subtitled 'the true story of an unwanted Chinese daughter' (Boradway, 1999), became a best seller and the author has continued the theme subsequently into a series of further accounts. All of these books are available in the bookshops.

Another woman author, Christina Chingtsao, a little older than Adeline Mah but whose work came out a little later, also wrote about her childhood and life in Shanghai and Hong Kong. *Shanghai Bride: Her Tumultuous Life's Journey to the West* (Hong Kong University Press, 2005). Both authors reflect their triumph over the hardships enforced upon some Chinese daughters. Their frustrations and feeling of neglect, however, seem to give the impression that all daughters in Chinese families are not well-treated. Of course it is not the case.

PICTURE BOOKS

Picture books on Hong Kong's past and present are legion. Some of them are exquisite and others merely commercial. You will just have to browse and pick out the ones you like for yourself.

Two of my personal favourites are: *Hong Kong Heritage, A Personal View,* by Elyse Parkin (Oxford University Press, 1979), with charming watercolours; and Alan Birch, *Hong Kong, the Colony That Never Was* (Odyssey Publications, 1992), with contemporary photographs.

Several books published by Hong Kong's Form Asia—*Great Cities of the World Hong Kong* (1990), *Above the Barren Rock, Spectacular Hong Kong From the Air* (1994)—are of high quality. As is *Skyline Hong Kong* (2000) by Peter Moss, which comes in three sizes, to suit your pocket or coffee table. All are beautifully printed.

Two small volumes of delightful drawings of today's Hong Kong by an expatriate painter, Lorette E Roberts,

Sights and Secrets: Sketches and Paintings of Hong Kong (2003), and *Sketches of Soho* (2005), are almost 'mandatory readings'.

FAUNA AND FLORA

A revised and enlarged edition of Clive Viney's *Birds of Hong Kong* (1989), illustrated by Karen Phillips, can still be found in the bookshops. It is comparable in utility with Roger Tory Peterson's guides to American birds. B M Walden and S Y Hu, *Wild Flowers of South China and Hong Kong*, two volumes (1977, 1987), will become constant companions on your walks through the country parks. Check with Government Publications: there are other books on Hong Kong's fauna and flora, which include butterflies, fishes, and reptiles.

A Popular Guide to Chinese Vegetables (1982), text by Martha Dahlen and illustrations by Karen Phillips, has been reprinted several times. Embracing Chinese cooking utensils and simple recipes, this book is more than a guide to vegetables. Armed with it, you will be well able to venture into the Chinese markets; and to put their food on your dinner table with aplomb. Further, you will gain a deep understanding of the vegetables as food items and as nature's works of art.

OUT-OF-THE-ORDINARY GUIDEBOOKS TO INTERESTING PLACES

There are many good books in this category, too, and in general guidebooks today are of high quality. You will just have to find for yourself the one you like best. Hong Kong Tourist Association publishes maps and little guide folders, mostly *gratis*, and you can have them for the asking in their office at the Kowloon side of the Star Ferry.

Other publications include *Another Hong Kong, An Explorer's Guide* (1989), edited by Alan Moore, and Sally Rodwell's *A Visitor's Guide to Historic Hong Kong* (1991): wonderful books carefully researched and beautifully presented. You will want either or both in your library. The most portable though the most detailed book of this genre is *Historical Hong Kong Walks: Hong Kong Island* (1988) by a group of ladies led by the indefatigable Madeleine Tang. These women are curious to know all the details about everything they see, and so have provided you with factual and legendary answers to every question you can possibly have as you traipse along the routes of Hong Kong's historical past and its ever-changing present. I also enjoy *Discovering Hong Kong's Culture* (2002) by Patricia Lim, and *A Tale of Two Villages—the Story of Changing of Life in the New Territories* by Lee Ho Yin and Lynne D Distefano (2002).

There is a very, very large number of guidebooks on all aspects of Hong Kong. They more or less cover the same grounds, but this does not mean that you should not go the book shops, browse, and choose one or two you like.

SATIRE, AND GENTLE HUMOUR

The current guru of satire in Hong Kong is Nury Vittachi who used to pen the weekly 'Travellers' Tales' in *Far Eastern Economic Review*. His old columns from the *South China Morning Post* have been gathered in a single volume, *Only in Hong Kong* (1993). Political cartoons by Templar (Christopher Young) are also available in a single volume, *The Best of Basher* (1993); as are those cartoons still appearing daily in the *South China Morning Post* by Harry Harrison, collected into a single volume, *Harry's View* (2004). Larry Feign's *The World of Lily Wong*, the trials and foibles of a local woman married to a *gweilo*, no longer appears in the *South China Morning Post*, but it should not matter to you, because these cartoons are collected into single volumes and are still available in the local bookshops. Another Feign, *Banned in Hong Kong*, 'featuring cartoons you weren't supposed to see' (1995) has also been resurrected and is available in the bookshops.

While you are looking, also pick up Feign's *Aieeyaaaa*, which allows you glimpses into the Cantonese language in a hilarious way. To delve further into the mysteries of Chinese characters involving food and culture, look for *Swallowing Clouds* by A Zee. A Zee, according to the book jacket, 'was born in China, reared in Brazil, educated at Princeton and Harvard', and is a man.

Books to Commemorate the Final British Years

While books to welcome in the new order may be dated when this edition of *CultureShock! Hong Kong* is released but you may find a couple of publications specially written to commemorate the final British years informative and enjoyable. Jonathan Dimbleby of BBC made a television documentary on the years of the last British governor, and the text in print is *The Last Governor: Chris Patten & the Handover of Hong Kong* (Little Brown & Co, 1998). Among the dry text, you can find the juicy bits that led to charges that Patten had violated the Official Secrets Acts, but as a whole the book contains valuable information on the Sino-British negotiations during the heady days before July 1997. If it is light gossip you want, *Beating the Retreat: Hong Kong Under the Last Governor* (1997) by Tim Heald, a buddy of the Pattens from their undergraduate days at Oxford, comprises principally insiders' information with a lot of name dropping.

CHINESE WORKS, TRANSLATED INTO ENGLISH

Note from author: By the time you finish these pages, and when you have browsed once through the shelves of the bookshops, you will have found books not on this list that are much more to your liking. Well done! Do not forget to browse through the libraries as well. Remember, in addition to the public libraries, any private club you are lucky enough to join will have its lending library; and all will have books on Hong Kong. For instance, to update this section of *CultureShock! Hong Kong*, I passed a couple of days browsing the bookshops and libraries, and found two treasures by Louis Cha, the most popular martial arts novelist of the 20th century, *The Deer and the Cauldron* (1997–2001) in three volumes translated into English by John Minford, and *The Book and the Sword* (2005) translated by Graham Earnshaw, both titles are from Oxford.

Happy browsing, and happy reading.

ELECTRONIC RESOURCES

For those who prefer to 'click' their way to enlightenment, may I suggest the following websites?

The Economist City Guide to Hong Kong
- http://www.economist.com/cities/hongkong

General Information about Living in Hong Kong
- http://www.hongkongcalling.com

English Newspapers
- http://www.scmp.com
- http://www.hk-mail.com

Hong Kong Government Information Centre
- http://www.info.gov/eindex.html

Hong Kong Government Interactive Services Directory
- http://www.igsd.gov.hk

Hong Kong Tourist Association
- http://www.discoverhongkong.com

Hong Kong Trade Development Council Intro to Hong Kong
- http://www.firstchoicehongkong.gov.hk

American Chamber of Commerce in Hong Kong
- http://www.amcham.org.hk

Appliance and electronic store (Fortress)
- http://www.fortress.com.hk

Supermarkets
- http://www.parknshop.com
- http://www.wellcomehk.com

Specialty Groceries and Sundries
- http://www.citysuper.com.hk

Information for Vegans and Vegetarians
- http://www.ivu.org/hkvegan

Hong Kong Based Internet Bookshop
- http://www.paddyfield.com.hk

Hong Kong advertising magazines, excellent sources for goods and services of all kinds
- http://www.dollarsaver.com.hk
- http://www.hongkongtowncrier.com

Children's Concerns
- http://www.geobaby.com
- http://www.hkwithkids.com

'MUST-SEE' CHINESE FILMS

My daughter gave me this list for those interested in watching Chinese movies. If you buy them on DVD, make sure that the copy comes with English subtitles.

- *Balzac and the Little Seamstress* (2002) is set in the middle of the Cultural Revolution. It takes place in a 're-education centre' where three friends conceptualise an amorous and literary plot through the medium of literary classics which they read in secret.

- *Crouching Tiger, Hidden Dragon* (2000), is based on a period martial arts epic with themes based on honour, duty, betrayal, and revenge.

- *Farewell to My Concubine* (1993) is set during the Cultural Revolution, and evolves around two Peking Opera performers and the woman who comes between them.

- *Hero* (2002) is set in feudal China before it was united as an empire in 221 b.c. The movie is a historical tale of love, loyalty, jealousy, and intrigue.

- E*at, Drink, Man, Woman* (1994) is a comic depiction of a father and three grown daughters trying to live within the framework of a traditional Chinese family while pursuing their own interests.

- *Ju Dou* (1990) is set in the 1920s rural China within a rigid feudal system where tradition takes precedence over individual wills. This movie was considered to be critical of the prevailing political system and censored by the Chinese Government.

- *Raise the Red Lantern* (1991) is set in the 1920s and is an account of the tension in the household of a powerful man and his wife and concubines.

- *The Wedding Banquet* (1993) is full of comedy and pathos. The movie shows the cultural conflicts created when a young Chinese man of the modern world tries to please his traditional parents.

- Any Jackie Chan movie in Cantonese

ABOUT THE AUTHORS

Betty Wei is Honorary Research Fellow at the Centre of Asian Studies, University of Hong Kong. She also holds honorary appointments as Professor at the People's University in Beijing, and in the History Department of the University of Hong Kong. She is also active in the community, serving on the boards of several educational and welfare organizations. A graduate of the Chapin School and Bryn Mawr College in the United States, Professor Wei is a research historian focusing on nineteenth century China. Her publications include *Shanghai: Crucible of Modern China* (1987) and *Old Shanghai* (1993). She has also written many journalist and scholarly articles in English and in Chinese. Her major scholarly effort, a biographical study of an eminent pre-Opium War Chinese scholar-official, Ruan Yuan, is forthcoming.

Elizabeth Li is a 'change agent' in the fields of Organization Development and Strategic Management. She worked for over ten years in industry, before becoming a management consultant in 1986. She is bicultural as she was born in Hong Kong, grew up in New York and has lived in London. Li returned to Hong Kong in 1980 where she devoted herself to education and explored the concept of cultural integration. Her vision is to have a community college in Hong Kong that reflects the integration of Western concepts in the Hong Kong society.

INDEX

Titles in the CULTURE**SHOCK**! series:

Argentina	Hong Kong	Paris
Australia	Hungary	Philippines
Austria	India	Portugal
Bahrain	Indonesia	San Francisco
Barcelona	Iran	Saudi Arabia
Beijing	Ireland	Scotland
Belgium	Israel	Sri Lanka
Bolivia	Italy	Shanghai
Borneo	Jakarta	Singapore
Brazil	Japan	South Africa
Britain	Korea	Spain
Cambodia	Laos	Sweden
Canada	London	Switzerland
Chicago	Malaysia	Syria
Chile	Mauritius	Taiwan
China	Mexico	Thailand
Costa Rica	Morocco	Tokyo
Cuba	Moscow	Turkey
Czech Republic	Munich	Ukraine
Denmark	Myanmar	United Arab
Ecuador	Nepal	Emirates
Egypt	Netherlands	USA
Finland	New York	Vancouver
France	New Zealand	Venezuela
Germany	Norway	Vietnam
Greece	Pakistan	

For more information about any of these titles, please contact any of our Marshall Cavendish offices around the world (listed on page ii) or visit our website at:

www.marshallcavendish.com/genref